P9-BIN-396

THE IRONY OF THEOLOGY AND
THE NATURE OF RELIGIOUS THOUGHT

In *The Irony of Theology and the Nature of Religious Thought,* Donald Wiebe argues that academic theology is not only not a religious exercise but is actually inimical to religion.

Lévy-Bruhl's dichotomy thesis is used to support the claim that Presocratic philosophers, in progressively abandoning the medium of myth, created a new mode of thought that transcended the essentially mythopoeic thinking of the pre-philosophic Greek world. Platonic thought, despite Plato's concern with the recovery of the wisdom of ancient Greece, is shown to have introduced a wholly foreign element of philosophic thinking into early Christianity. The "Platonization" of Christianity is then used to interpret developments in the eleventh and twelfth centuries in Europe, especially with respect to the emergence of theology as an academic discipline and the eventual undermining of the essentially catechetical character of early Christianity.

In questioning the pervasive assumption that theology is a religious mode of thought, Wiebe provides a new and more adequate understanding of the nature of religious thought. The perpetual conflict between science and religion in western culture and the failure of the varied compatability systems to reduce the tension between the scientific and religious communities become wholly explicable.

The Irony of Theology and the Nature of Religious Thought will be of special interest to philosophers and theologians. The argument draws on a wide range of resources, including history, anthropology, and sociology, and will be of interest to scholars in these disciplines as well.

Donald Wiebe is Professor of Divinity, Trinity College, and Associate Director, Centre for Religious Studies, University of Toronto.

McGill-Queen's Studies in the History of Ideas

THE IRONY OF THEOLOGY
AND THE NATURE
OF RELIGIOUS THOUGHT

Donald Wiebe

McGill-Queen's University Press
Montreal & Kingston • London • Buffalo

© McGill-Queen's University Press 1991
ISBN 0-7735-1015-X
Legal deposit first quarter 1991
Bibliothèque nationale du Québec

Printed in Canada on acid-free paper

This book has been published with the help of a grant from the
Canadian Federation for the Humanities, using funds provided by
the Social Sciences and Humanities Research Council of Canada

Canadian Cataloguing in Publication Data

Wiebe, Donald
The irony of theology and the nature of religious thought
(McGill-Queen's studies in the history of ideas ; 15)
Includes bibliographical references.
ISBN 0-7735-1015-X

1. Religion — Philosophy.   2. Theology.
I. Title.   II. Series.
BL51.W52 1991   200'.1   C90-090487-9
6638

This text was typeset 10/12 in Baskerville by Q Composition Inc.

To
Donald McCarthy, Thomas Settle,
Michael Ruse, Ninian Smart

Contents

Preface

This inquiry into the nature of religious thought is a by-product of attention devoted to quite a different problem. For several years now I have sought for a resolution to the "tug-of-war" between "insiders" and "outsiders" for methodological control of research on religion in our academic institutions. According to the "insiders" no proper understanding of religions is possible unless religio-theological categories are somehow incorporated into the methodological framework employed by the student of religion. The "outsider," on the other hand, sees such a methodological injunction as putting in jeopardy the very existence of an academic study of religion because it opens to debate whether the agenda for that study is finally to be determined by the academy or the "church." My work on the problem has been aimed at showing that the secularized scholarship of the sciences, broadly conceived, is the norm for *all* disciplines, Religious Studies included, seeking explanatory understanding of things and events in the world. And I have argued that such an approach to understanding the nature of the religious phenomenon has a transcultural perspective that cannot be matched by interpretive frameworks that employ religious or theological categories. The "insiders" in this debate do not deny that the academic study of religions must in some sense transcend the religious discourse of the devotees; they agree, that is, that such a study of religions must be more than merely an elaboration of the faith of those they study. They also argue, however, that properly critical theology is not partisan and that it can, therefore, provide a scientifically acceptable perspective from which to seek an understanding of the nature of religion, a perspective that is sympathetic to religion.

Reflecting on the arguments in support of the "insider" view of the nature of Religious Studies it seemed to me that a significant but unexamined assumption was being made, namely, that theology and religious thought are essentially indistinguishable enterprises. That assumption, even though not extraordinary, does not carry the force of a self-validating truth. But without that assumption the argument of the "insiders" carries little weight. It was evident, therefore, that a careful examination of the assumption and its implications might help yield a resolution of this dispute. And it is that task of clarification to which this book is committed.

The argument to be presented here is not merely speculative or philosophical. I will be concerned to provide a testable hypothesis about the nature of thought that will help determine the relation of theology to what might be more generally referred to as "religious thought." The essential structure of that theory derives from Lévy-Bruhl's dichotomy hypothesis that posits a radical difference between the mythopoeic thinking that predominantly characterizes the thought of "primitives" and the philosophic/scientific thought that predominantly characterizes "moderns." In tracing the development of philosophic and scientific thought in western civilization, refinements to that hypothesis become possible, I argue, that will allow us to make sense of the notions of theology and religious thought as quite distinct intellectual operations and so undermine that assumption which grounds the "insider" argument for a religio-theological approach to the study of religious phenomena. In structuring the argument presented here, I have had to draw upon a wide range of scholarship in fields in which I do not have specialist training. That, of course, involves risks but wholly unavoidable risks, I think, if general problems of the kind I raise are ever to find resolution. I have attempted, moreover, to minimize the problems that might emerge from covering unfamiliar terrain by means of a thorough and balanced assessment of the relevant expert analysis and argument. Time will determine whether I have been sufficiently judicious in that task.

It will not be possible to elaborate on the significance of this argument for the academic student of religion without significantly detracting attention from the primary aim of this book. It is therefore the history of the notions of theology and religious thought to which my attention will be confined in this book.

Acknowledgments

I would like to express my gratitude to a number of people who have assisted in one way or another in the writing of this book. The thesis of this essay had been a focus of attention for me for some time prior to writing. It was an invitation to present my views on the topic "Does the Emergence of Theology mean the Death of Religion?" to the Trinity College Colloquium, however, that finally drew me into this project. I am very grateful, therefore, to Larry Kerslake for the invitation and encouragement to fly that trial balloon. It is a pleasure as well to thank other Trinity colleagues for their advice and encouragement, sometimes despite a lack of sympathy for the thesis being argued here: Kenneth Schmitz, Graeme Nicholson, Bruce Alton, and Abrahim Khan. Other colleagues and friends have also given liberally of themselves in discussion and debate of various aspects of the argument developed in this book and I thank them for that: E. Thomas Lawson, L. H. Martin, Ivan Strenski, Hans Penner, Robert Thomas, David Reimer, Susan Story, and John Franklin. I alone, of course, must be held responsible for the thesis presented here. My special thanks also to Victoria Pinnington for her patience in dealing with the revisions to the manuscripts and for the long hours and hard work of getting the draft manuscript of this book into proper form for the publishers.

There are four teachers to whom I owe a great deal. Without their assistance and encouragement over the years I should never have found myself prepared to take up this thesis or any other problem for public discussion. Although I would not want them to be saddled with any responsibility for the substance and argument of this book, I do wish to acknowledge here their importance to me in the intellectual enterprise of which this book is to some degree symbolic, and I therefore dedicate this book to them.

I wish to thank the editors and publishers of the following journals for permission to use material I have previously published in article form: *The Dalhousie Review* for "Religion Transcending Science Transcending Religion . . ."; *Religion* for "The Prelogical Mentality Revisited," and *The Scottish Journal of Religious Studies* for "From the Open to the Closed Society? Michel Despland on the Philosophy of Religion."

I am grateful to the Provost and Executive Committee of Trinity College and the Centre for Religious Studies of the University of Toronto for a sabbatical leave during 1986–87 that provided me an extended period of time for the writing of the first draft of this book. And it is also a pleasure to thank the Master and Fellows of Corpus Christi College, Cambridge, for the invitation to spend a year as Senior Research Scholar there, which provided an ideal setting for that task. I also acknowledge with thanks the assistance of the Social Sciences and Humanities Research Council of Canada for providing me with a leave fellowship and research grant for that year.

THE IRONY OF THEOLOGY AND
THE NATURE OF RELIGIOUS THOUGHT

I

The Irony of Theology

PHILOSOPHERS OF RELIGION have in the past, and continue now, to give serious attention to religion, and in particular to those religious traditions that have developed explicit systems of doctrine and belief to complement their rites, myths, and moral-social structures of existence. And historians and phenomenologists of religion have concerned themselves with the development of taxonomies of religious systems of thought, while comparativists have constructed typologies of belief in an attempt to highlight the similarities and differences amongst them. Consequently, one finds in university departments concerned with the study of religious phenomena courses of instruction on, for example, Buddhist thought, Islamic thought, Jewish thought, Christian thought, and so on, as well as courses on how these diverse structures of thought compare to and contrast with one another. However, surprisingly little sustained attention has yet been given to determining the nature of religious thought *per se* – to the structure of religious thinking in general rather than to the religious thoughts of a particular tradition, community or individual.

The question as to whether or not religious thinking constitutes a separate and peculiar mode of thought either escapes the attention of this diverse collection of students of religion or it is assumed to be so complex and difficult as to be impossible to answer and therefore simply left unasked. I am quite aware, for example, that there may be grounds for thinking it virtually impossible to formulate a coherent research programme in this regard, given, say, Gilbert Ryle's lifelong but unsuccessful attempt to account for the nature of thinking *simplici-*

ter, let alone religious thinking, and the radically divergent and seemingly endless approach to understanding "what is called thinking" by
Martin Heidegger, to mention but two philosophical traditions.[1] The
widely held opinion amongst philosophers and other students of religion that no agreement even upon a definition of religion, let alone a
full-bodied understanding of its structures and functions, is likely soon
to be achieved, only further complicates the question.[2] Nevertheless,
until the question has been shown to be incapable of coherent formulation, it seems to me not at all inappropriate to proceed with its analysis.
Furthermore, the fact that the question of the existence of radically
different and mutually exclusive modes of thought has been a long-
standing and continuing debate in philosophical and anthropological
circles provides some positive justification for doing so. And this especially so, in that Lévy-Bruhl, with whom the debate originated, apparently thought his analysis of primitive thought was applicable to
religious modes of thought as well. In his attempt to account for the
obvious differences in structure and pattern of thought in primitive
cultures compared to modern western industrial societies he jettisoned
the widely held anthropological assumption of the rational unity of
humankind[3] and argued rather for a radical dichotomy of thought

1. For a review of Gilbert Ryle's work in this respect see Lyons, *Gilbert Ryle;* especially
chapter 13: "Ryle's Three Accounts of Thinking," and A. Goudge, "Ryle's Last Thoughts
on Thinking." On Heidegger see, for example, Fay, *Heidegger* or Halliburton, *Poetic
Thinking.*

2. I treat these matters in my *Religion and Truth.*

3. It should be noted that Lévy-Bruhl did not question the uniformitarian view of
the human species on the level of biology and brain physiology but only denied that
kind of view on the sociological level. With such an understanding it is obvious that on
the level of potentiality even Lévy-Bruhl accepts a full-blown uniformitarian assumption,
but the implications of that fact alter little, as can be seen in an analysis of Jarvie's critique
of Lévy-Bruhl in his *Rationality and Relativism.* Jarvie talks in a general fashion about the
anthropologists' belief in the unity of humankind's rationality as grounding a common
agenda for them, namely, the search "for universal principles or cultural laws that
govern social organization" (p. 17). Nevertheless, his criticism of the hypotheses of
Robin Horton and dependence upon the thought of Karl Popper and Ernest Gellner
leave him much less a critic of Lévy-Bruhl than might at first appear to be the case.
Indeed, he seems to recycle Lévy-Bruhl in that he also adopts a dichotomy framework
in his analysis of primitive cultures, as can be seen in the oppositions he himself perceives
between open and closed (static and changing) societies (p. 31), strong and weak rationality (p. 48), scientific and prescientific societies (p. 106), etc. It is obvious as well in the
kinds of questions he sets for himself to answer, for example: "how do savage societies
learn, *ever make the transition to open and changing ones?* How did it happen historically,
how does it happen now? *How is what Gellner calls the Big Ditch between the savage and the
modern mind crossed?*" (p. 62, emphasis added).

that implied an opposition between what I shall refer to here as the mythopoeic mind and the rational structures of thought of the modern scientific mind. Though his views about the nature of religious thought were never explicitly spelled out, there is no doubt but that for him it, too, stood opposed to and incommensurable[4] with modern western

---

Jarvie's talk of anthropological belief in the unity of humankind's rationality, more-over, seems contradicted in a later brief description of the anthropological task. He writes: "Most of the societies they study do not have science. A principal goal of anthro-pology is to give a rational reconstruction of such pre-scientific societies and their customs as being goal-directed and hence intelligible" (p. 95). The tension between this view and the one quoted above is obvious. It is overcome by Jarvie, however, by his taking the so-called assumption of the rational unity of humankind not as an article of belief but as a social programme (p. 63). This supplants the cognitive focus with a practical one, namely, requiring one to respond to human beings in a distinctly different way from the way we respond to the rest of the animal world. (I have no doubt, however, that Jarvie wants more than this, but need not press the matter here.) On this account of the assumption, Jarvie's position is to all intents and purposes indistinguishable from the broad reading of Lévy-Bruhl's position described above. The following statement by Jarvie, for example, is wholly compatible with a Lévy-Bruhlian stance: "If . . . the rationality of science consists not so much of thought processes of a special and exclusive kind, but of a means of organizing thought, of a set of social institutions, then we need deny no society some rationality and potential for more" (pp. 95–96, emphasis added).

In the following chapter I shall take up the justification of Lévy-Bruhl's position and in chapter 3 answer Jarvie's question as to how the historical transition was made from the savage to the modern mind.

4. Without incommensurability the dichotomy thesis does not exist. It refuses to understand or explain primitive/archaic thought in terms of the assumption that modern western scientific thought provides a kind of benchmark for all intellectual achievements (though it may not object to accepting it as the benchmark of achievement in coming to know the world around us).

Jarvie (*Rationality and Relativism*), with whom I have much in common, argues (along intellectualist lines laid out by Tylor and Frazer) against those "who try to make a case for some qualitative difference between systems of superstitious thought and science" (p. 34), since magic and religion as examples of superstitious thought are, like science, attempts at cognition. His understanding of the notion of "attempts at cognition," however, is seriously and misleadingly ambiguous. Jarvie adopts his position on the basis of the fact that magic and religion are cognitive or scientific, even if there is no conscious intent to be so. Though I would not deny that in a very important sense primitive persons know the world that they inhabit (and by that I mean the objectively existing world in which they exist subjectively), and therefore find myself in agreement with Jarvie on the truth of this claim, nevertheless, I disagree as to the significance of its implications. As I will show in chapter 3, the cognitive intention that first emerges with the Greek (Presocratic) philosophers requires a new and radically different set of intellectual techniques that distinguishes Presocratic thought from the intellectual activities engaged in in that undifferentiated thinking that embodies both an apprehension of the world and the projection of meaning upon it – that indissoluble amalgam of cognition and fabrication that constitutes meaning. Nonhuman animals, as Jarvie knows,

scientific thought. "For him," writes E. E. Evans-Pritchard, "Christianity and Judaism were also superstitions, indicative of prelogical and mystical mentality, and on his definitions necessarily so."[5]

It is my intention in this book to establish the essential soundness of Lévy-Bruhl's understanding of the nature of religious thought and to show that it is a hypothesis[6] that can better account for much, not only

---

also learn from their experience in the world. Animal behaviours, that is, also constitute "attempts at cognition." That, however, does not prevent us from distinguishing the peculiar character of consciousness in human knowing as significantly different from, even if not wholly discontinuous with, those behaviours. Similarly the explicit and conscious intent to know the world rather than to interpret its significance or discern its meaning for us (which is what mythopoeic knowing is all about) introduces a radical distinction. (The difference here, of course, is a social one and not a biological or racial difference.)

Insofar as I agree with Jarvie that primitive persons know the world in which they live, I also find myself in agreement with his claim that science "deserves credit for being nearer the truth than the world-view systems that preceded it" (p. 105). That, of course, appears to put me into some difficulty, for in agreeing that science and magic (or myth, or religion, etc.) are incompatible, they cannot be incommensurable, for the former requires the two modes of thought to be comparable. But the difficulty is only apparent, for surely we can – etically, that is, as outsiders to the archaic/primitive world-view – compare its unintentional cognitive component, isolated by us from its richer matrix of fabrication and meaning-construction, with the achievements of science, all the while recognizing that this constitutes a kind of distortion of the primitive/archaic world-view as a whole. Their distilled world-view constitutes the only knowledge (for us) of which they were capable, but which now is a knowledge that stands in conflict with the explicit, scientific knowledge succeeding it. As distilled, it is not their knowledge – it is their knowledge only insofar as it is seen in terms of the matrix from which we have abstracted it. Consequently, if one recognizes that the two modes of thought are incommensurable with respect to intention but commensurable with respect to function, the apparent contradiction referred to above is resolved.

The exact opposite of this view has been proposed by Neville in his *Reconstruction of Thinking*, in which he argues that the role of valuation in thinking has been obscured, and especially so in the scientific thinking of the West (pp. 54–56). His view is in many respects Platonic and since I provide an extensive critique of that view in chapter 4 I shall forego discussion of Neville here. Similar objections are raised by Habermas. A critique if his work, however, would require separate treatment.

5. Evans-Pritchard, *A History of Anthropological Thought*, p. 130. According to Evans-Pritchard, Lévy-Bruhl left this aspect of his general theory implicit in order not to cause offence.

6. On this score I diverge from Jarvie (*Rationality and Relativism*, p. 63), because the problem raised here is a cognitive/epistemological one. I do not mean that his proposal to accept the uniformitarian principle as a social programme is without merit; indeed, I should join with him in the project which he describes as an "attempt to construct a

in our own culture, but in the growth and development of culture more generally. Defence of that view will obviously depend upon a successful defence of his much maligned thesis on "how natives think."[7] But that by itself, I admit, is unlikely to be sufficient, since it could well be argued that religious thinking, even though it may involve elements of what I have referred to as mythopoeic thought, is essentially rational. It could be argued, that is, that the religious thought of the great world religions is a complex and multifaceted intellectual activity, comprised not only of myth and story but also of very sophisticated rational structures called theology. Nevertheless, even though not denying such claims, I do not think the status and significance of theology as an aspect of such traditions to be wholly unambiguous. And I shall try to show that the ambiguity that surrounds it, arises because there is something deeply ironical about theology understood as rational religion or as a process of rationalizing religion. I use "irony" here in its most general sense of involving an awareness of a discrepancy between appearance and reality, whether that be an incongruity between words and their meanings or between actions and their results, because I think it can be shown that, even though theology's object of interest is "the gods," it is not itself an essentially religious undertaking. To put it bluntly, it can be shown that, even though theology appears to emerge from within the matrix of religion and in aid and support of religion, it is in fact detrimental to religion and the religious form of life because its primary intention is at odds with fundamental religious aspirations. That irony, I suggest, is already apparent in theology's first emergence with the Presocratics.[8] Gregory Vlastos has argued that their theology made "a unique contribution to religion" because they, "among all the people of the Mediterranean

---

certain sort of community of men [and women] in which we face openly and unsparingly the necessity and value of learning from experience, articulating our problems and assessing our solutions and hoping that in the process we make some modest progress in alleviating the worst features of our environment and our lives together" (p. 63).

7. This phrase is the title of the English translation (by Lilian A. Clare) of Lévy-Bruhl's first major work expounding the dichotomy thesis – *Les fonctions mentales dans les sociétés inférieures*. A recent edition of this translation was issued by Princeton University Press (1985) with a lengthy new introduction by C. Scott Littleton. I shall take up a defence of this thesis in chapter 2.

8. I am following Aristotle's judgment although, as I shall note, he also referred to Homer and Hesiod as theologians. See n. 21.

world," as he puts it, "dared transpose the name and function of divinity into a realm conceived as a rigorously natural order and, therefore, completely purged of miracle and magic."[9] The irony of the reduction of the gods to something wholly immanent in the order of nature and therefore wholly explicable in the same fashion as all other natural phenomena, however, seems to have eluded Vlastos. A brief comment on the problem involved here may help to clarify the nature of the thesis to be defended.

The reason for the difference of perception as to the meaning and significance of this "transposition of the name and function of divinity," as Vlastos describes the Presocratic theological achievement, will become clear in my reading of the history of the emergence of philosophy in ancient Greece in light of Lévy-Bruhl's analysis of the nature of primitive thought. I shall argue later that a Lévy-Bruhlian dichotomy is very much an element of our western tradition of thought established, to put it somewhat dramatically, in a revolutionary shift in the thinking of the early Greek philosophers that transcended the quasi-mythopoeic patterns of thought still dominant in Homeric Greece.[10] Philosophy, that is, will be shown to emerge from within, and over against, a nonphilosophic mode of thought that has much in common with the mythopoeic structure of thought of Lévy-Bruhl's primitives. Indeed, that early philosophy in some sense constitutes the creation of a scientific world-view that amounts to a disenchantment of the mythopoeic, or at least quasi-mythopoeic, world it succeeds. On this I am in agreement with Vlastos, though he makes the point less forcefully than he might. The Presocratics, he is convinced, created the basic conceptual framework of modern science – precisely that "mode of thought" Lévy-Bruhl saw as the "opposite" of the mythopoeic world-view. "This was," he writes, "their great bequest to the intellectual heritage of mankind and this they did not derive from religious sources."[11] The early philosophers had as their primary aim an understanding of nature and not the reform of religion. Their thought, that is, was undertaken independently of the public cult and was, in a sense, therefore, incommensurable with the mode of thought that underlay it. However, even

9. Vlastos, "Theology," p. 119.

10. I use the word quasi-mythopoeic to indicate that I do not believe the thought of the poets such as Homer and Hesiod to represent a primitive stage of Greek religious thought. On this point see, e.g., Kirk, *Myth: Its Meaning and Function* as well as his *The Nature of Greek Myths*. I shall take this matter up again briefly in chapter 3.

11. Vlastos, "Theology," p. 55.

though their thought was neither derived from the cult nor directed towards its reform, this does not mean that it had no influence or effect upon it. Indeed, it is not an overstatement to say that the eventual demise of Olympian religion is directly attributable to this wholly different though apparently complementary mode of thought.

With the emergence of Greek philosophy displayed in such a light I shall then be in a position to show that the theology of the Presocratics is all of a piece with their new philosophic/scientific mode of thought and that it too, therefore, is not only not mythopoeic but necessarily destructive of mythopoeic patterns of thinking, although not necessarily intentionally so. Consequently, though agreeing with Vlastos as to the theological nature of much of Presocratic thought, I hold a radically divergent view of its religious significance. Vlastos assumes that their theology, simply by virtue of the fact that its subject-matter is the gods, is but another mode of religious thinking. But this can hardly in itself constitute justification for the assumption, unless he is also willing to count atheistic thought as a mode of religious rather than irreligious thinking. Examination of the patterns of religious thinking, and especially of western biblical modes of thinking, moreover, place an even greater strain on Vlastos's understanding of the nature of theology. The major occidental religious traditions reveal an essentially mythopoeic structure that stands opposed to both ancient Greek philosophy and theology, and their subsequent developments.

Vlastos, it might be suggested, could find some support for his assumption in recent religio-philosophic discussions in which it has been argued that thought concerning the gods is religious thought precisely because of the nature of its object. The support, however, is illusory, for such claims are but part of a wider argument with quite contrary implications. Nevertheless, an understanding of the implications of that argument can introduce a helpful distinction for use in my discussion of the nature of religious thought.

The philosophies to which I refer[12] maintain that there are certain objects, or subject-matters (it is difficult to know whether any terminology in these discussions can ever be wholly nonobjectifying), that are

---

12. Perhaps the best known of such arguments are to be found in Buber's *I and Thou*, and in Bultmann, particularly in his essay, "What Does It Mean to Speak of God?" in his *Faith and Understanding*. Similar arguments can be found in the work of the analytical philosophers of religion, especially those influenced by Wittgenstein. A good example of this kind of argument, emerging from the later ordinary language interest in philosophy is Donald Evans', *The Logic of Self-Involvement*.

so extraordinary that they require a peculiar kind of response to their presence, if they are ever to be properly understood (experienced, engaged, etc.), and religious objects, namely the gods, number among them. If the response to the gods referred to here is in no way cognitive, one certainly evades espousal of a Lévy-Bruhlian dichotomy. However, if the expressions which flow from the special kind of response required in the presence of this extraordinary object of experience have either an explicitly or implicitly cognitive significance, then, quite obviously, one has adopted a Lévy-Bruhlian dichotomy that opposes religious thought, as mythopoeic, to ordinary commonsense and scientific modes of thought. The knowledge gained in that experience would be virtually indistinguishable from the religious experience and ought, therefore, to be referred to as "religious knowledge," for it is the product of a mode of thinking quite different from the ordinary cognitive/rational activity employed in the gaining of a knowledge of the world in commonsense and science. Therefore, theology, in the way Vlastos sees it being practised by the Presocratics at least, does not provide religious knowledge but rather something that would better be referred to as knowledge about the gods, since it is like the knowledge the other sciences provide us about different aspects of the universe.

If this distinction between religious knowledge and "thinking *about* 'the gods' " is sound, it must then be conceded, that theologians, using a Wittgensteinian metaphor, are really playing a metareligious rather than a religious language-game. Thinking about the gods implies explaining and accounting for what can be known about them, but without any *a priori* assumption as to whether they have an ontological or a merely socially constructed reality. Given the nature of religious aspirations, then, "thinking religiously" and "thinking theologically" are obviously incommensurate modes of thought. (And if religious thinking is also understood to be cognitively significant rather than merely poetically[13] so, the two modes of thought will also be incompatible, at least on the methodological level.)

Given the argument sketched out briefly in the foregoing discussion, an attempt to determine and delineate the nature of religious thought does not appear to present any insuperable problems. In Lévy-Bruhl, I have suggested, we have a tentative hypothesis that, slightly

13. My use of "poetic" to designate a noncognitive kind of thinking is based on Max Rieser's analysis of poetic thinking that will be discussed below.

amended, can be tested against the empirical data – against the facts. The steps involved in establishing the value of that hypothesis, to summarize, are three. The first involves the clarification of the precise nature of Lévy-Bruhl's hypothesis and a demonstration of the cogency of its formulation. And that will require, of course, justification of his more general theoretical account of the apparent disparity between primitive and modern structures and processes of thought. Having provided that, it will be necessary to show that the pattern of thought typical of "autonomous religious communities"[14] is more like that of Lévy-Bruhl's primitives than like modern scientific thought. In turn, finally, it will be necessary to be able to show that theology, which it is generally agreed is a rational/scientific enterprise, is not an essentially religious activity but rather, quite to the contrary, one ultimately detrimental to the religious life. If theology were an essentially religious undertaking, of course, at least some systems of religious thought or some religious traditions at a particular stage of their development, it would have to be argued, are not, or at least are no longer, simply to be identified as mythopoeic structures.

Before proceeding to the task of providing argument and evidence in support of such claims, however, it seems to me that some clarification of the categories employed in this project is required. That perhaps especially so with respect to the notion which, it will no doubt be objected, has a much broader and more complex range of meanings and implications than I seem willing to acknowledge and which, if acknowledged, would have a considerable effect on the outcome of the project adumbrated here.

CATEGORIAL CLARIFICATION: THEOLOGY

Given common contemporary usage of the word theology it must be admitted, though it may appear contradictory to do so, that theology is a religious undertaking or, at the very least, can be a religious undertaking. Not all forms of theology, that is, are structurally incompatible with religion and religious thought. Nor shall I insist here that they are, although I shall argue that neither are such theologies indicative of the existence of a rational form of religious thought. The

---

14. I use this phrase to refer to religious traditions that, even though they may in many respects pervade their society, are distinct from the society at large of which they are a part.

only theology that provides possible academic grounds for viewing the religion of which it is a part as rational is that which I shall here refer to as academic theology, by which I mean theology as a scientific discipline of the same order as the other disciplines to be found in the university curriculum. Without it, or something very like it, no nonmythopoeic conception of the nature of religious thought can be constructed. Consequently it is that understanding of theology with which I shall operate here. Since, moreover, independent argument exists to account for the emergence of just such a discipline, little objection can be raised for my doing so; the notion is neither incoherent in itself nor is it selected arbitrarily.

Theology as an academic discipline, as G. R. Evans has clearly established, emerged "hand in hand with the slow development of the twelfth-century Schools into the first universities."[15] It was the offspring, using her metaphors, of the marriage of secular and Christian learning, in which the substance of the Christian faith (its beliefs and doctrines) were subjected to the same intellectual attention and treatment that other subjects received in the liberal arts. Scripture and doctrine were now examined and adjudicated, so to speak, by means of the same intellectual instruments applied to the subjects of the *trivium* and *quadrivium*. Of prime importance, therefore, were the rules of argument, laws of evidence, and the procedures for organization of their material, while piety and devotion were relegated, at best, to second place. The marriage therefore appears to have introduced into the Christian community a new intentionality that had not characterized it or its theology until then. The new theologians appeared to have shifted from wanting "to know in order to believe" to wanting "to know for the sake of knowing." And this, I maintain, constitutes a substantial, even revolutionary, innovation. According to Evans, such a theology "offered a method of making some progress in the knowledge of God by procedures open to any educated man, even if he had no exceptional spiritual gifts."[16] The new theologians, given this account, had created a subject-matter that was capable of being reduced to order and form, allowing knowledge of it to be conveniently packaged so as to be teachable within a classroom rather than being something that could only be acquired through slow absorption, so to speak, by the spiritually sensitive person. The new theology, therefore,

15. G. R. Evans, *Old Arts and New Theology*, p. 11.
16. Ibid., p. 105.

as "an activity of the mind in which religious emotion had little or no place, and . . . could be taught and discussed in the classroom,"[17] stood in direct opposition to that earlier patristic and monastic form of theology that had relied so heavily upon contemplation and devotion.

It must be noted here that Evans, amongst others, does not consider this shift of attention in the twelfth-century theologians to have the radical quality I have attributed to it here. A careful examination of the arguments to this effect, as I shall show later, however, can leave little doubt but that it created a profound tension, if not outright hostility, between "the love of learning and the desire for God."[18] It has been rightly referred to, therefore, as an "axial shift,"[19] the product of which is discontinuous with that which precedes it, in the same way that the philosophic thought of the Ionian philosophers already referred to, is discontinuous with that which antedates it. This is not to say that the desire of "knowledge for the sake of knowledge" was indicative of doubt in the truth of the Faith but rather that it introduced a spirit of critical reflectiveness that refuses to recognize extracritical attempts to contain it and so, implicitly, transcends the tradition that espouses it. In this, academic theology captures the essentially etymological meaning of "theology" as a science, which, like geology, or biology, or psychology, etc., attempts to provide an understanding of a particular aspect of the universe of which the gods (i.e., the everlasting or unchanging in the world) are a part. And this is the meaning it often has in the theology of many Greek philosophers, and especially of the Presocratics, as I have already noted, although that is not easily established, given that they were not consciously in possession of a theology and the word was consequently not much used by them. Indeed, it is not until Plato that the term is coined, although its late appearance with him means neither that the concept did not exist nor that it is inapplicable to earlier forms of thought from which it is absent. There seems to be some hint of the etymological meaning in Plato's use of the word and yet the autonomy of the *logos* in *theologia* is subordinated to a prior commitment to the ontological reality of the gods.

17. Ibid., p. 93.

18. The phrase is taken from the title of Jean Leclerq's study of monastic culture. Both Evans' and Leclerq's interpretations of the twelfth century will be submitted to a more detailed analysis in chapter 5.

19. By Nelson in his "Civilizational Complexes and Inter-civilizational Encounters." Further attention will be paid in chapter 5 to his understanding of the significance of the twelfth century.

What is most obvious about the use of the word theology in Plato, and ever since, is its ambiguity, the result either of its use in an ideological sense or of its inconsistent application to vastly different structures of thought. Implicit in the ambiguity lie contrastive understandings of the term that parallel the academic/nonacademic polarity to which I have drawn attention. Although for Plato, for example, the word is used to designate a body of doctrines about the gods which he considered, in some senses, absolutely unquestionable, it is not quite so obvious that it designates a methodological procedure for demonstrating those claims. Plato's theological claims appear to be grounded by tradition and authority rather than argument; his philosophical theology is incomplete without a political philosophy that allows for the use of physical force to coerce belief where argument has failed.[20] Whatever the nature of his theology, therefore, it is not academic in the sense that has been discussed here, even though it attempts to pass itself off as such.

The use of the term in Aristotle is also ambiguous but for different reasons. It is not that Aristotle attempts to use the word to designate what might be referred to as a hybrid mode of thought that somehow combines both reliance on authority and critical reason, but rather that he uses the same term to apply to two quite different intellectual undertakings. Not only does he use "theology" to refer, for example, to the substance of Hesiod's *Theogony*, whose thought, he claims, is best characterized as mythological speculation, but he also uses it to designate his own metaphysics or "first philosophy," of which he has no doubt but that it is an advance upon and superior to Hesiod.[21] The term is therefore used to designate not only rational discourse about the gods, but also a form of symbolization that lies between mythic and philosophic modes of thought or, rather, constitutes a mode of thought that involves both mythic and rational elements. The hybrid form of thought, however, does not differ radically from that of Plato as will eventually become apparent.[22]

20. See here especially Plato's *Laws*, Book x.
21. See his *Metaphysics*, books iii, v and xi.
22. Although I refer to hybrid modes of thought, it must be emphasized that I do not regard them as genuine or distinct forms or structures. They are but mixtures of mythic and rational thought, where the latter seldom has more than a subsidiary role. Hybrid thought structures are therefore only rationalized forms of myth and consequently still essentially mythopoeic. This point is well illustrated in Gilson's comments, for example, on the relation of philosophy to the Christian faith (myth?): "Can it [i.e., philosophy] be

A full historical review of the variety of meanings of "theology" is not possible here, but I do not think much will be lost by that.[23] Both descriptively and ideologically, so to speak, it seems that the term has, from its earliest use, applied to two radically different and mutually exclusive types of thought which, if they are not clearly distinguished, can create considerable confusion. On the one hand there is theology as "God-talk" (henceforth, "theology"), and on the other, theology as "talk about God" (henceforth, theology).[24] They may in some senses overlap, but they are neither identical nor, in at least one essential particular, complementary. Consequently, though both uses of the term may have a kind of legitimacy, they cannot be used interchangeably. And, as I have already indicated, I shall use the concept here in the sense of an enterprise concerned with "talk about God," since only a theology of that variety can possibly characterize the religion of which it is an element as nonmythopoeic.

I am aware that this latter claim is open to challenge and acknowledge that forceful arguments have been raised against it. I recognize, that is, that recent formulations of "nonacademic" theologies have appeared that refuse to accept the assumptions made by the twelfth-

---

thus used by theology towards ends that are not its own without losing its essence in the process? In a way it does lose its essence, and it profits by the change" (*The Philosopher and Theology*, p. 100). The radicalness of that subordination of reason in the new mixture of "theology" is brought out even more strongly when he goes on to claim: "theology is not a compromise, it is not composed of heterogeneous elements of which some would be philosophy and the rest Scripture; all in it is homogeneous despite the diversity of origin. 'Those who resort to philosophical arguments in Holy Scripture and put them in the service of faith, do not mix water with wine, they change it to wine.' Translate: they change philosophy into theology, just as Jesus changed water to wine at the marriage feast in Cana. Thus can theological wisdom, imprinted in the mind of the theologian as the seal of God's knowing, include the totality of human knowledge in its transcendent unity" (p. 101). In chapters 4 and 5 I will show that Gilson's assessment here is on the mark and that such hybrid modes of thought are inherently unstable, as well as why they are so. It is ironic, however, that Gilson has been seen as one who is guilty of changing theology into philosophy, as is shown in chapter 5.

23. As Gilson (*The Philosopher and Theology*, pp. 194–95) points out, the word theology appears in very few Christian works from Justyn Martyr to Thomas Aquinas, and even in Aquinas, he suggests, the word is used sparingly. I shall, however, pay some attention to more recent uses of the concept below.

24. "Theology" (i.e., with double scare quotes), then, is used to refer to that intellectual response within religion that rationalizes the Faith, so to speak, but only "within limits." Using the term without scare quotes will be reserved for academic theology which, in the final analysis, is indistinguishable from its etymological meaning as discussed above.

century academic theologians about the nature of what constitutes
being scientific and rational and that lay claim to being the only theologies that are truly scientific, because they alone are true to their ultimately mysterious subject-matter.[25] And the challenge such theologies
present cannot, or ought not, simply to be ignored, especially given
the fact that they are now the more numerous and seem to represent
the dominant mindset in contemporary theology. Before proceeding I
shall therefore critically examine several such alternative "theological"
proposals in order to lay bare precisely what their claims amount to.
It will become obvious that though they may be religiously more
sound, their claim to being more scientifically sound than the academic
theology discussed here is unpersuasive.[26]

VARIETIES OF "THEOLOGY": ALLEGORICAL, METAPHORICAL AND POETIC

Examination of the "allegorical theology" of Andrew Louth, the "metaphorical theology" of Sallie McFague, and the "theopoetic theology"
of Amos Wilder will provide fair and representative treatment of the
argument that theology ought to be perceived less restrictedly than I
intend to take it here.[27]

---

25. The notion of mystery plays a large role in "theology" as the discussions to follow
will show. Essential to the notion is that it would be absurd, indeed illogical, to attempt
to analyse mysteries philosophically or to discuss them in ordinary or scientific language.
Mystery, therefore, is for ever beyond an academic theology, though not, it would
appear, beyond "theology." Although it possesses a different focus, it seems to me of
some benefit here to refer to the introduction – "The Language of Mysteries" – in
Wind's *Pagan Mysteries in the Renaissance*. There may be some structural similarities
between Gilson's reduction of philosophy to "theology" and the Christian response to
non-Christian mysteries discussed by Wind. Theology with respect to the mysteries,
claims Wind, is a poetic theology which follows a basis of "mystical reduction." Such a
method operates on the basis of the "assumption of concordance" that allows for the
discovery of a sacred truth in pagan beauty which is taken as but a poetic medium of its
expression. This permits a reconciliation of pagan, Hebrew and Christian beliefs and
ideas even where, in respect of outward, dogmatic expression, reconciliation would not
be possible. Further exploration of those parallels is not, however, possible here.

26. For much of this discussion I have drawn upon the work of Evans (*Old Arts and
New Theology*), to whom I shall return for a more detailed discussion of academic theology
in chapter 5.

27. I have chosen these theologians because they seem to me to represent most
clearly, but fairly, the general position that is under criticism here.

Allegorical Theology

In *Discerning the Mystery: An Essay on the Nature of Theology*, Andrew Louth argues that to conceive of theology as an essentially academic/ intellectual exercise is to fail to see that it really involves a unified spiritual/intellectual apprehension of God. "Thought about God" *and* "movement of the heart towards God" constitute theology as it was understood by the Church Fathers. In patristic texts *theologia* is used for both "theology" and "spirituality." "There is here," writes Louth "no division between theology and spirituality, no dissociation between the mind which knows God and the heart which loves him. It is not just that theology and spirituality, though different, are held together; rather *theologia* is the apprehension of God by a man restored to the image and likeness of God, and within this apprehension there can be distinguished two sides (though there is something artificial about such discrimination); what we call the intellectual and the affective."[28] *Thought about God*, therefore, cannot be separated from *commitment to God*. Nevertheless, theology understood as an academic discipline (i.e., as a purely intellectual undertaking), does precisely that and therefore cannot truly be theology.

The division between "the intellectual" and "the affective," according to Louth, has entered theology under the pressure of the Enlightenment and the rise of modern science, which gave birth to the idea that there exists only one method of intellection whereby all truth can be known. (Louth denies, it should be noted, that the divergences between the academic theology of the cathedral schools and the "theology" of the monastic communities is indicative of that division, although I shall not argue the matter here.)[29] With the success of the natural (physical) sciences, it was soon taken for granted that only those branches of learning that could successfully adapt their methods could provide us with knowledge and truth. And the unwise choice of some theologians to follow that path laid down by the sciences by restricting theological knowledge to the boundaries of the historical-critical method gave birth to that pseudoscience of academic theology that fails to reflect the full significance/meaning of Christian existence.

Louth, obviously, sees the Enlightenment claims for science as inflated if not simply wholly mistaken. The choice by theologians to

---

28. Louth, *Discerning the Mystery*, p. 4
29. I do, however, treat this question at length in chapter 5.

follow the Enlightenment lead is particularly unwise, however, because, claims Louth, sound argument had already been provided to legitimate a knowledge from experience that transcends the boundaries set by the (natural) scientific method. Although that argument cannot be rehearsed here, it must be noted that it depends heavily upon Gadamer's hermeneutical theory, which itself rests on earlier (eighteenth-century) resistance to similar Enlightenment claims. Gadamer's hermeneutical theory, Louth maintains, constitutes a method that more adequately suits a study of human phenomena, for hermeneutics *initiates* one into the tradition which constitutes the perspective from which one can know anything at all in the moral/ spiritual world. Such *Bildung*, (i.e., initiation), as Louth puts Gadamer's claims, "fashions the individual so that he can benefit as fully as possible from his historical situation whereas method attempts to transcend the situation of the observer so that he can record reality objectively."[30] In the cultural/spiritual realm, that is, accurate knowledge is to be obtained from the engaged insider's critical reflections.

Although Louth then urges that theologians should look upon the humanities rather than the (physical) sciences as a possible analogy for their own work, he does not claim that the natural sciences are altogether without relevance to theology. Insofar as the natural scientist reveals truth about the world, he maintains, it will have a bearing "on the theologian's articulation of his vision."[31] He does not, however, raise the spectre of possible differences between such knowledge and the theologian's vision. Instead, he attempts to undermine the distinction assumed here between the two, arguing, via Gadamer and Polanyi, that science really proceeds much more like the humanities than is generally assumed to be the case. As he puts it, "to look to the sciences to find some light for the theological task is needless. For what we have now found is that the way of understanding in the sciences is fundamentally the same as the way of understanding in the humanities. It is a popular misconception that the sciences have discovered some key to knowledge denied to the humanities (and to divinity or theology); the ultimate pattern of knowing is one."[32] The humanities, he then argues, provide knowledge in a process of "understanding by engagement" that goes beyond the simple use of historical-critical

30. Louth, *Discerning the Mystery*, p. 43.
31. Ibid., p. 58.
32. Ibid., p. 64.

techniques, even though they may also make use of such techniques. And through such a procedure the humanities, he suggests, come to grips with the mysteries of human life rather than simply with problems in, and about, the course of human history. Since therefore, theology is concerned with mystery as well, it is this deeper dimension of reason as contemplation that must characterize theology. And in going beyond mere problem-solving it becomes immediately obvious, Louth claims, that theology is something more than the academic exercise I have described above.

Theology, like human culture generally, is not, therefore, simply a bundle of messages available in propositional form for purely intellectual manipulation. Both are practices that involve the whole person – their explicit messages being enveloped within a framework of tacit understanding that makes them mysterious. (The propositional message, one might say, is the framework that houses the mystery.) That which is able to be conceptualized is never the whole truth, for its full meaning is *determined* in subtle but ultimately significant ways by the tacit meanings available *only* through "living the practice." And that requires, of course, participation in and passive reception of the tradition rather than an active interrogation of the tradition from without. As Louth puts it with respect to theology, "the mystery of the faith is not ultimately something that invites our questioning, but something that questions us."[33]

Submission in the tacit knowledge of the tradition in theology, Louth then argues, can be achieved by means of a return to allegory; a move that, quite obviously, transcends and therefore abrogates the hold of the historical-critical method on the truly theological mind. Allegory is not simply obfuscation, he insists, because it is not trying to resolve mere *problems* – to which historical-critical techniques are quite appropriately applied, according to Louth – but to introduce the reader to mystery, of which the historical-critical techniques can have no knowledge. As Louth puts it, "we [theologians] are not concerned with a technique for solving problems but with an art for discerning mystery."[34] Allegory, according to Louth, does not require a rejection of science and scientific thinking, but rather presents itself as something more than a mere intellectual activity. "It is," he writes, "a matter of realizing [i.e., achieving], our participation in the mystery of

33. Ibid., p. 95.
34. Ibid., p. 113.

Christ."[35] In the words of the title of the final chapter of the book, it is "living the mystery." Allegory, therefore, is "an older form of attaining knowledge" "that betrays itself if it seeks to become 'scientific' by any attempt to fashion an objective scientific method."[36]

In such an analysis it is quite clear that the academic theology that I have invoked above is not a possibility, even though, as I have argued, it can be shown to have come into being with the university theologians in the twelfth century. And yet, even though Louth disagrees with my reading of the twelfth century, he seems to agree that such a theology, paradoxically, did in fact emerge, although only later with the Enlightenment. Indeed, his whole argument is directed to the end of understanding the influence such a theology continues to have on the modern mind. Louth manages to avoid outright contradiction in his discussion of the problem, however, by denying that such a scientific or academic theology is real theology. But that he is successful or persuasive in making this move is open to question. His argument, for example, appears at times to involve both the affirmation and rejection of historical-critical (theological) knowledge. Nevertheless, even in its affirmation he ultimately denies it any validity or authority, for its true significance can only be determined within the broader understanding of "the mystery" which envelops it and that is delivered in allegorical interpretation. It seems, therefore, that Louth wishes to eat his cake and have it too; he desires, that is, the benefits of historical-critical thought but only within the boundaries of a predetermined religious truth understood from within a practice of that truth. And that, of course, is to destroy what historical-critical knowledge is all about. It is to distort its nature entirely and to make of it what it is not, thereby denying the claim that any such knowledge is at all possible.

It can be shown, I think, that Louth's argument with respect to historical-critical method in theology involves a more general, but obviously less persuasive, claim that scientific knowledge (even in the natural sciences and not only in the cultural sciences), is not real knowledge. The argument is not explicitly formulated, yet is tacitly assumed, for without it Louth would still be stuck with an epistemological dualism that contrasts the knowledge of physical reality with knowledge of cultural/spiritual realities, a dualism which would harbour the very conditions that gave birth to the problematic he has set out

35. Ibid., p. 120.
36. Ibid., p. 132.

to resolve. And yet it is impossible, even for him, not to recognize the success of such a method and therefore its validity – with respect to some aspects of reality. Louth attempts to evade the worst implications of the admission of the value of science and the scientific method by means of a reductionistic argument that claims to reveal science and its techniques as resting upon a deeper and more fundamental cognitive activity. Science's validity, he insists, comes not from the methodic use of techniques as it appears to do, but rather from a nontechnical kind of knowledge and perception on which use of those techniques is based. He invokes the work of Gadamer and Polanyi, then, to reduce *all* knowledge to "*Bildung* knowledge" which implies that our so-called scientific knowledge, even in the physical sciences, is not really scientific. Strangely, then, Louth's argument in this essay appears to be directed to the end of denying the very assumption on which it is based.

There is much in Louth's essay about our knowledge of the nature of human life in general and of Christian existence in particular with which I fully concur, and his intuitive perception of the inadequacy of academic theology to Christian experience also seems to me to be on target. But his argument that theology must be other than scientific is too problematic to be persuasive. However, that is not, it seems to me, required to establish his point.

The essential point of his argument is not that theology cannot be scientific, but rather that theology as a scientific enterprise is incompatible with the religious life that involves a wholly different mode of thought. And in some sense this is precisely what Louth does argue, however much he has obscured it. For Louth, theology is what Christians *qua* Christians do, not what Christians *qua* scientists do. So theology is not an intellectual activity but rather a faith-event, where faith is understood as "thinking with assent" as opposed to "critical thinking."[37] Consequently, theology is a matter of *living* Christianity – it is "a matter of realizing our participation in the mystery of Christ,"[38] and is therefore indistinguishable from faith.

If faith finds deeper reasons for such participation in the life of Christ, reasons that go beyond reasoning and arguments, scientific methods and techniques, as he maintains it does, his argument would have been more to the point had it been on behalf of "a religious mode

37. Ibid., p. 3.
38. Ibid., p. 120.

of thought." In fact, he refers to that theology which is his concern as a kind of "faith-thinking" which differs from the *ordinary* exercise of reason that argues from facts to conclusions. Regardless of the names we attach to these two modes of thought, therefore, they are different and, judged by their differing effects on the state of the religious life, are logically incompatible.

Metaphorical Theology

Sallie McFague's "metaphorical theology" is, like Louth's "allegorical theology," based on a post-Enlightenment form of thought. The first and more radical statement of her position is to be found in her *Speaking in Parables: A Study in Metaphor and Theology* which seems to be a complete rejection of academic theology, whereas her elaboration of that thesis in her later work, *Metaphorical Theology: Models of God in Religious Language*, seems more an attempt to tame it – that is, to bring it into subjection, so to speak, to a mode of knowing which is ignored by the abstract theorizing of academic theology. Her intention throughout the two-volume essay, however, is to show the absolute importance of imaginative/metaphorical language as the permanent source of what she refers to as a more ordinary conceptual theological language. The metaphors of a parabolic theology keep "in solution," as she puts it, "the language, belief, and life we are called to, and hence they address people totally."[39] By implication, of course, the abstractions of academic theology are different because they do not address people totally.

In *Speaking in Parables* McFague insists that a metaphorical theology is not simply a more powerful way of communicating the contents of the Gospel that are cognitively available to the intellect alone. It is rather a separate and distinct way of knowing[40] which, as she tries to show in the later volume, constitutes a kind of critical realism,[41] although not of the positivistic variety to be found in abstract scientific knowing. Indeed, within the framework of a metaphoric/parabolic theology, she argues, we have a primal language which alone can grasp strange truths beyond the pale of ordinary abstractive reason and

39. McFague, *Speaking in Parables*, p. 1.
40. Ibid., p. 44.
41. McFague, *Metaphorical Theology*, pp. 101, 132.

within whose light old doctrines of abstractive academic theology take on new meanings.

McFague's metaphorical theology has very much the character of Louth's allegorical theology. The knowledge it provides is of the character of insight[42] or revelation[43] which is generated by metaphor's capacity to unite life and thought. In it is reflected our original unity with all that there is, and it therefore overcomes the abstract distinctions between body and mind, reason and feeling, the object and the subject, and so on, by the creation of inclusive meanings.[44] As embodied language, or participatory thinking – since "metaphor is the language of 'a body that thinks' "[45] – metaphor simply delivers more than can abstract thought and talk. The cognitive nature of that "more," however, is in some doubt, in that she sees such participatory thinking to be more like sexual union than like ordinary thinking, even though she adamantly insists that only such knowing is real knowing.[46] Indeed, in contrast to it, she tells us, post-Cartesian epistemologies are subhuman. McFague therefore counsels theologians not to approach an understanding of the Faith/Gospel in an abstract/conceptual fashion but rather to transcend the shortcomings of such a scientific approach in a return to metaphor, parable, and story. "What cannot be conceptualized – the mysteriousness of God's love," she insists, "can perhaps be made manifest through the story of one's own life."[47] A rejection of the spectator knowledge of academic theology, it is suggested then, is the only true way of being really scientific, because it alone is true to its subject-matter. In the Gospel "what is being offered is not information one can store but an experience."[48] For the Gospel is successful in communicating its message (knowledge) not by passing on a packet of verifiable information, but rather by creating an encounter with God. Proper theology therefore requires metaphorical thinking and must be a metaphorical theology.

McFague's proposal for the establishment of a metaphorical theology runs into as much difficulty, if not more, than does Louth's proposal for theology as allegory. She wants a theology that provides us with

42. McFague, *Speaking in Parables*, p. 7.
43. Ibid., p. 15.
44. Ibid., pp. 32–33.
45. Ibid., p. 60.
46. Ibid., p. 58.
47. Ibid., p. 37.
48. Ibid., p. 78.

knowledge, but with a knowledge that is far richer and transcends the kinds of knowledge we ordinarily – that is, scientifically – have access to. She recognizes that such different kinds of knowledge will be radically unlike scientific knowledge, and that such nonscientific knowledge will be tentative and relativistic in character. Indeed, she claims that it must be so because it is not translatable into concepts, and if it were, it could not be distinguished from them.[49] Nevertheless, she feels it important to emphasize that the resultant metaphorical theological language is not an exercise in fuzzy or sentimental thinking, although, strangely, she says it does not abjure ambiguity.[50] It has a precision, although this is best described by her in a rather circular manner as "metaphorical precision"[51] which "is not of the logical sort."[52] And yet she seems to shy away from that conclusion, for she also maintains, and contradictorily so it seems, that without the logical/conceptual thought of some more traditional (i.e., conceptual) systematic theology, metaphorical theology is liable to sink into obscurity and aberration. It is necessary, therefore, for metaphor to develop into a model which is "a movement from revelatory insight to the possibility of conceptual and systematic elaborations,"[53] despite her hope, expressed earlier on, for a new genre of theology that would attempt to stay close to the parables.[54]

Similar ambiguities and mixed messages are presented in her *Metaphorical Theology*, in which she elaborates on her just noted suggestion that a new kind of theology can emerge if only we are able to recognize the nature of metaphors as knowledge. Her concern here, it seems, is to articulate a theological structure that can provide her with a justification for a religious knowledge she already possesses but which is outside the pale of normal cognitive justification. Models, she maintains, are dominant metaphors that have a comprehensive organizational potential and so can be used to provide a more abstract kind of knowledge than is available in simple metaphor. Since metaphor is never fully translatable into concepts, concepts must be latently imagistic.[55] So, models constitute a mixed type of language that, in standing between metaphor and concept, combines them, subordinating each

49. Ibid., p. 67.
50. Ibid., p. 114.
51. Ibid., p. 87.
52. Ibid., p. 39.
53. Ibid., p. 84.
54. Ibid., p. 3.
55. McFague, *Metaphorical Theology*, pp. 2, 22, 124.

to the other. This allows McFague's theologian to be both metaphorical and conceptual at one and the same time; and in achieving this end McFague, like Louth, makes use of the work of Gadamer and others fond of hermeneutics. Although not all language is metaphor, all thought is based on metaphor – in the final analysis, that is – which puts all language in need of interpretation. Thus again, like Louth, McFague maintains that all human thought "is of a piece"[56] and neither conceptual thought in general nor abstract theology in particular is a new and more successful way of knowing the world. In showing that the so-called scientific achievements are really essentially metaphorical, she maintains that nothing substantial is gained by theology in the attempt to ape the sciences, that is, in the attempt to gain cognitive acceptability in a wider community than that of the devotees.[57]

McFague's work is bewildering in the ambiguity created by its repeated affirmations and rejections, submissions to and transcendings of both metaphorical and conceptual thought. She seems to want a theology which attempts to stay close to parables but which is also a conceptual structure characterizable as a critical realism. And though espousing a critical realism, she yet insists that true theology is essentially a matter of telling stories. In it all, her anxieties to be intellectually respectable and to retain the scientifically suspect truths of the Gospel are unmistakable.

Poetic Theology

Amos Wilder in his *Theopoetic: Theology and the Religious Imagination* also laments theology's "long addiction to the discursive, the rational and the prosaic."[58] "The kind of truth and reason that theology is concerned to clarify," he continues, "does not permit of merely abstract,

---

56. Ibid., pp. 2, 17, 28.

57. This is essentially the substance of much post-Kuhnian apologetics. Whereas apologists used to strive to show that religious (Christian) beliefs were as sound, rational, or justifiable as scientific beliefs, they now tend to argue, rather, that scientific beliefs are no more rational (or no less irrational) than religious beliefs. Such was the line I followed in my doctoral research, "Science, Religion and Rationality: Problems of Method in Science and Religion," and in my early essays, beginning with " 'Comprehensively Critical Rationalism' and Commitment." I no longer see such an apologetic as feasible for reasons I have set out in my "Religion Transcending Science Transcending Religion . . . ," "Is Science Really an Implicit Religion?" and elsewhere.

58. Wilder, *Theopoetic: Theology and the Religious Imagination*, p. 1.

wooden or pedantic treatments."[59] He denies that he wishes to disallow rigorous thinking in theology, or the critical study of the origins of the Faith, but claims that there is, and must be, "a revolt against the academy," because our present theological tradition in that context has lost its cogency. And this, he further maintains, is not just a matter of the communication of truth but also of its discovery. Traditional theology requires transformation, for it fails to comprehend the full content of the truth of the Gospel because it does not come to terms with its ruling metaphors. To be able to do so, however, it will have to complement its present conceptual and scientific approach to the Faith with a visionary capacity able to capture the knowledge explicit in our somatic and affectional perceptions. "Certainly man's deepest apprehensions of the world and the gods, or of God himself," he writes, "have always been poetic in the sense of symbolic and metaphorical. All the great ways of mankind and of particular tribes have been based on decisive hierarchies or disclosures of the sacred through which the transcendent related itself to creaturely circumstances and language."[60] Theology therefore needs a transformation of consciousness that will erode the present objective consciousness of the academy that has dominated its activity. He writes: "If imagination plays such a necessary part in religion a touchstone for the vitality of theology will be its attitude to the symbolic order and to the creative impulses, images and dreams of men."[61] Ecstasy, imagination, and insight must replace abstraction, rationalism, and stereotype. A new naiveté must emerge that permits of extranormal perception through a heightening, or even derangement, of the senses.[62] It is not that the ecstasy involved itself bears cognitive significance, but rather that it can function to awaken the mind to a knowledge of a more extensive order of existence. Theology must therefore always break away from and go beyond (i.e., transcend) the boundaries of logical and scientific appraisal. "Another name for theology," Wilder insists, "is divinity, and divine wisdom has always been thought of as imparted by the Spirit to those 'in the Spirit'."[63]

Such theologizing Wilder calls "theopoetic" and it cannot, he argues,

59. Ibid., p. 3.
60. Ibid., pp. 41–42.
61. Ibid., p. 42.
62. Ibid., p. 58.
63. Ibid., p. 57.

function without "mythical thinking." Mythical thinking, he admits, is an imaginative world-making kind of thought which is pliable and plastic and so alien to logic. And yet he also maintains that through its imaginative dramatizations and narratives – its use of metaphor, fable, and myth – it reveals a "reality-sense" that shows it to possess a noetic or cognitive component and, consequently, to be a kind of preliminary science: "Our visions, stories and utopias are not only aesthetic: they engage us. They also present some kind of knowing as well as fancying."[64] Though he cannot further specify what kind of knowing is involved, he nevertheless insists that whatever cognitive orientation such mythic thinking communicates it must be grasped "by the same kind of imaginative apprehension that first shaped it," although it can, subsequently, although only provisionally, be transposed into conceptual statement.[65]

Wilder's argument for a theopoetic theology reveals what is by now a familiar structure: real theology must be more than the academic theology with which we are all so familiar. And his argument shows a similar ambivalence towards the conceptual and scientific – it is something to be overcome, and yet not wholly discarded. Finally, that

64. Ibid., p. 79; "The some kind of knowing" is, of course, left ambiguous, but it does not, it is clear, refer to revealed propositional truths (dogmas, doctrines), for that would make it a scientific kind of knowing. Daiches in his recent Gifford lectures, *God and the Poets*, makes a similar claim for poetry as involving belief (knowledge) and going beyond belief at the same time. Poetry can be a "unique revelatory insight into some aspect of experience" (p. 218), but it must not be formulated in such a manner that it, like Christianity, demands too much (p. 213). The simultaneously noetic and fictive character of poetry that Wilder is here pointing to is clearly captured in the following passage: "The truth of poetry, as distinct from that of philosophy or theology, is self-authenticating. Other truths or alleged truths can be argued about, there can be proofs and disproofs, believers and unbelievers, demonstrations that this theory or that is the reflection of social and economic structure or in some way a projection of self-interest; but poetry operates differently. As it weaves its cumulative meaning through the use of all the resources of language, with image, symbol, cadence, rhythm, pattern, structure, as well as propositional meaning all playing their part in building up the reverberating whole, it gets beyond belief to the human dilemmas that belief arose to cope with, even though it may be ostensibly basing itself on a given belief' (p. 214). As my discussion of Rieser below will show, this kind of understanding of poetry is incoherent, in that it tries to make noetic claims and yet transcend them at one and the same time, or at least to avoid the procedures for assessing those implied noetic claims. A more coherent statement respecting the relations of the poetic to belief and knowledge, and especially so in the religious sphere, is to be found in the work of Northrop Frye to which I have given some attention in my essay, "The Centripetal Theology of *The Great Code*.
65. Wilder, *Theopoetic: Theology and the Religious Imagination*, p. 84.

ambivalence is the source of paradox and ambiguity, even if not in the massive doses we find in McFague. With the subjection of conceptual theology to theopoetic theology we have also the ascendance of mythopoeic thinking that parallels Louth's and McFague's allegorical and metaphorical thinking – all three characterized as essentially other than logic and science, and as "more than" logic and science, the latter characterization making it, paradoxically, more truly scientific.

Theology and "Theologies"

It is important here, despite differences of labels and styles of expression, to take special note of the fundamental similarity in the thought of Louth, McFague, and Wilder. There is a pattern of assumptions and presuppositions that is common to all. Each reacts in an almost instinctively defensive manner to the existence of a conceptual mode of thought applied to religion and the religious life, and this involves them in a peculiar paradox. In vigorously denying that conceptual theology is proper theology, each also implicitly acknowledges not only that theology as a conceptual and scientific affair exists, but also that it possesses, in being deemed scientific and rational, an intellectual respectability that their own modes of thought do not appear to possess. Through such procedures, it is admitted, Christianity's cognitive claims were provided with intellectual respectability, but at a price each thinks too dear to pay. Intellectual respectability was gained by such academic theologians, they insist, only by restricting themselves to talking about those aspects of God, and life in God, which lend themselves to technical and logical manipulation. But since more than just that can be shown of God in and through the religious life, such theology is not only deficient but also distorts its subject-matter and therefore cannot truly be theology; cannot truly be scientific with respect to Ultimate Reality. However, they do not seem to reject either the notion of theology or the notion of gaining intellectual respectability. Consequently, they seek to construct a new kind of science that provides cognitive justification for the broader set of claims about God and the religious life, which they wish to affirm on the basis of their own religious experience. They appear to want, that is, a science that *reproduces* life rather than describing and explaining (accounting for) it.[66]

66. For a critique of that expectation see my "Theory in the Study of Religion.

There are superficial differences in the approaches to the constructive (or reconstructive) scientific work which each of these theologians
undertakes, although here again each eventually comes to terms with
conceptual theology in fundamentally the same way. Though one or
the other may be more or less vehemently anticonceptual, none rejects
conceptual thought in an absolute fashion. However, whether invoking
allegory, metaphor, or the poetic, each attempts to appropriate the
fruits of the much feared academic theology by insisting on its limited
significance. The full meaning of the results of such abstract/conceptual
thought they insist can only be determined within a broader context
of meaning. But this, of course, involves compromising the essentially
conceptual nature of academic theology, for it involves *subjecting* it to
a set of nonconceptual and nonscientific parameters of assessment
which are "known," on religious grounds, to take precedence. That
compromise, they insist, however, does not jeopardize the intellectual
respectability once accorded the purely conceptual thought of academic theology, because the compromise of its logical/conceptual
nature actually increases its scientific respectability in that it makes
their theologies more adequate, so to speak, to the peculiar subject
matter, than it was in its strictly academic form. As one theologian has
put it, for theology to provide a true understanding of its subject-
matter, it must "stand under" its subject and allow itself to be shaped
accordingly.[67] And even though one theologian chooses allegory rather
than metaphor, or another a more general form of the poetic as
the non-Procrustean frame within which to make sense of God, their
differences here are negligible, for they all propose an essentially
narrative/linear mode of thought for theology as opposed to the hierar-
chical/logical mode characteristic of the natural (physical) sciences and
academic theology.[68] Strangely, however, none adopts such a mode of
thought to present the case. We do not have, that is, allegory, metaphor, or poetry but rather argument – a discursive, logical structure
(although it appears in each instance to involve itself in contradiction
or inextricable ambiguity). They seem, therefore, to espouse precisely
that which they have set out to transcend, for the only way to transcend

67. Namely, Torrance in his *Theological Science*; a view which I gave ground for
rejecting in my "Science, Religion and Rationality" referred to in n. 57.

68. It is for this reason that the notion of story has had such vogue in recent theology.
A good example of the theological use of that notion can be found in Slater's *The Dynamics
of Religion*.

it, it appears (and so I shall later argue), is to reject it *in toto;* to move from discursive thought to mythopoeic thought rather than to argue for it. But that would involve surrendering their intellectual respectability in the wider academic/intellectual community which, seemingly, they are not yet quite ready to do, even though they obviously want what only a fully nondiscursive, narrative thought can supply.[69]

What Louth, McFague, and Wilder argue for but do not quite achieve, is a mode of thought structurally and functionally distinct from rational scientific thought. Such thought in fact, in its opposition to scientific thought, would not concern itself with a search for intellectual acceptability by attempting somehow to incorporate it. Whether one calls their ideal thinking or the conceptual academic enterprise against which they write "theological," is neither here nor there. What is of importance is the recognition that, given the mutually exclusive nature of the two types of thinking, they cannot both be theology. Therefore, given the etymology of the word and its technical usage since at least the twelfth century (recognized even by those who oppose it), I shall use the word theology to designate that conceptual, scientific approach to understanding the Faith established in the medieval university setting, and I shall refer to the other "unitary head/heart thinking" that antedates it in the Christian tradition as religious (thinking) thought or, if we must use the word theology in that more Patristic or monastic sense, enclose it in scare quotes – "theology" – to make clear its distinctly different nature. The suggestion that "theology" is religious thought, it must also be noted, comes not simply from distinguishing it from academic theology, but rather from the poetic and mythopoeic qualities usually attributed to it. Their mutually exclusive characters can be established beyond question by here adding to the understanding of the notion of scientific thinking, already provided in the discussion above, clarification of the meaning of "poetic

69. That would, in a sense, be to proceed deconstructively, although I shall not press the matter in those terms here. This does, however, create some serious difficulties for those who wish so to proceed. To assume rational argument to destroy it, one must originally be bound by the accepted criteria of reasoning. But to assume the criteria to undermine the criteria is not itself a coherent project and so seems to preclude adopting that original assumption. Yet not to adopt it, to proceed on a wholly different footing, is to read oneself out of that community which confers the sought-for intellectual respectability. For some self-consciously deconstructive work in theology see Taylor's *Deconstructing Theology*, and the volume of essays edited by Altizer (and others), *Deconstruction and Theology*.

thinking." At the risk of belabouring the issue, I shall provide a brief account of the notion as it is to be found in Max Rieser's *An Analysis of Poetic Thinking*.

According to Rieser "poetic thinking" is distinctly other than scientific, conceptual, and abstract. It is on the contrary the result of a higher degree of excitement of the poetic mind which, he says, is differently affected by the welter of sense impressions (experiences) that impinge upon the human mind. The human mind seeks to bring some order to this chaos of experience for, unless it is somehow assimilated, the individual remains in a state of tension. Instead of using words to mirror the world in a realistic-scientific manner, however, the ordering factor is relegated to the subjective realm – to the affective ingredients of the objects and situations encountered. Thus, whereas analytical thinking involves concept-building directed towards a cognition that brings intellectual mastery over the objects of experience, the poet "achieves solely a liberation from the painful burden of a mood of feeling through visionary (symbol-laden), emotionally saturated description in musical, rhythmical dress."[70] In this the poet mimics an archaic mode of thought, although the "archaic mind" is less sophisticated and therefore more "subservient to the needs for expression because most objects transform themselves to his inexperienced mind into causes of passions, (fear, hate, love) and as a consequence become carriers of symbolic functions."[71] Archaic poetic thought, Rieser admits, however, constitutes a more purely verbal and tonal creative phase than its contemporary forms, but elaboration of that distinction is not necessary here.

Rieser's comparison of poetic with archaic thought is important, for the similarities and differences between the two highlight the contrast between academic and poetic theology, between theology and "theology." The order which the human mind seeks in its experience, Rieser points out, is twofold in nature: it involves the integration of experience into a realistic-analytical system through explanation and theory (i.e., cognition) and an integration of that experience within the world of feelings through expression. In the archaic mind, poetry filled both these functions – the cognitive and the psychic; the need to understand the world and solve problems within it and the need to become aware

70. Rieser, *An Analysis of Poetic Thinking*, pp. 44–45.
71. Ibid., p. 8.

of oneself within that world – but in an undifferentiated manner.[72] Originally all human knowing was poetic and psychologizing, with only the commonest elements of experience being subject to realistic treatment. But the symbolic-explanation provided in such knowing, he insists, is but an expression of the need for scientific explanation that could only emerge by "supplanting affects from the cosmos" and substituting "logical analysis and objective investigation for symbolism."[73] Words needed to be given a designative function to dissociate them from their function as tools of expression.[74] With that dissociation we have the emergence of science with its "purely cognitive" intention[75] that dissolves (at least in part) ignorance about the world of objects and contributes to a practical and realistic aim rather than to an expressive one. The expressive use of language – both the musical (rhythm and rhyme) and the plastic (symbolism) – inherent in the primitive context is now restored by the poet "because of that ecstasy which carried him back into the original status of the sensuous word-creative mode of thinking."[76] And it involves, he insists, the destruction of the realistic-scientific mode of thinking that has been acquired by human beings in intellectual development beyond the archaic mind – "subtler intellectual capacities for thought" that allowed for "critical discernment" and "subjective disinterestedness" that made possible a clear distinction between subject and object.[77]

What Rieser sees as true of the symbolizing activity of the poetic mind also characterizes, I suggest, the thought of the poetic theologians. In his words: "the outcome of symbolizing, objectively speaking, is nothing but an enrichment of language, which nonetheless does not bring with itself any emendation of our knowledge about things. It is merely

72. Ibid., p. 57. It provided knowledge, but only as an aspect of a broader world-view that, so to speak, created "a house of meaning" within which existence is lived. To compare mythopoeic thought in general with the knowledge intentionally gained by modern science, is therefore quite inappropriate, although one is entirely justified in comparing its cognitive or noetic component (aspect) to the achievements of the sciences, provided one recognizes that isolating that component/aspect and taking it as a unit is a distortion of the mythopoeic structure which it still, nevertheless, represents. For further explanation of this matter see n. 4.

73. Ibid., p. 68.

74. Ibid., p. 85.

75. Ibid., p. 85. See also n. 72.

76. Ibid., p. 29.

77. Ibid., pp. 49–50. Showing that to be the case is in part the task of chapters 2 and 3.

an enrichment of our expressive capacity for mental phenomena. The presupposition for this mode of thought is a lowered ability for the examination of reality, as it were a blurred, almost enchanted form of vision. Today the poet fails in this examination of reality because of the ecstasy into which an emotional disturbance transports him. The primitive neglected it out of naiveté and actual poverty of experience, and beyond this, surely also out of inner excitement, because only the latter could release the need for expression and thus stimulate the invention of new words and symbols."[78] Although the truth of this contentious suggestion will not be argued directly in this chapter it will – or at least something very nearly like it will – be borne out by the argument in the chapters to follow.

FURTHER CATEGORIAL CLARIFICATIONS: RELIGION, THOUGHT, AND MYTHOPOESIS

The Nature of Religion

Having determined the meaning of "theology" I pass now to discussion of that other key category, "religion." Although defining the notion of religion seems generally to have been no less contentious than discussions about the nature of theology, in this context its meaning is much less ambiguous than one might expect.

I shall use the term religion here to refer to those structures of meaning that make sense of human existence in face of an overwhelming and engulfing environment that so clearly reveals the limitations of human beings; of individual and society. Religion, that is, will be taken to consist of the stories of transcendence; of another realm of reality; of superhuman/supernatural being(s) that have the power to help (or to harm), humankind. The recognition of human limitation – of finitude – in face of the inexorable processes of nature that eventuate in death, and the transcending of those limitations by postulating (recognizing/assuming) the existence of a superhuman source of power on which humans can draw, is what religion is essentially all about. In such an extension of the universe, peopled by supernatural agents, the meaning of an otherwise meaningless existence is created; only such a world provides a comprehensive framework of existence that overcomes death. Such a framework redeems the fleeting quality of

78. Ibid., pp. 103–104.

human life by providing it an ultimacy that, in its natural setting, it does not and cannot have. The otherness of that world and of the god(s) that populate it is essential; though modelled upon the human/cultural world which it redeems, it differs in its ultimacy or infinitude which is symbolized in the supernatural power of the gods.[79]

On such an understanding, then, religion is "a kind of cognition," for it involves beliefs, even though such beliefs may not be consciously set out in explicit "theologies." They are often contained implicitly in rites and rituals and in structures of behaviour that are never explicitly analysed or conceptualized, although they are usually clothed in myths and stories that "surround" or accompany those behaviours. It is precisely in this respect that an – obvious, some would say – affinity between religious thought and theology resides. And yet, I shall maintain that the two are *incommensurables*, for I shall show that, in one very important sense at least, religious belief is not knowledge. In another respect, however, I shall maintain that religious belief is "knowledge," but that in that respect it is *incompatible* with our critical scientific knowledge and consequently incompatible with theology, odd as that may sound.[80]

To understand "religion" in this way finds warrant in the fact that, negatively speaking, it is not obviously counterintuitive; it fits quite well the historical use to which the term has been put. Moreover, and more positively, it is cross-culturally applicable, if not in fact universal. In concert with M. Spiro, therefore, I would conclude "that the belief in superhuman beings and their power to assist or to harm man approaches universal distribution, and this belief . . . is the core variable which ought to be designated by any definition [understanding] of religion."[81]

Although I do not wish to argue this matter at length or to become embroiled in the complex "definition of religion" debate, it must be noted that some scholars have proposed a functionalist definition of religion that, if found acceptable, would have considerable impact on the argument of this work. I think the proposal fundamentally wrongheaded and unacceptable, but it has often been very persuasively argued and requires some response. Thomas Luckmann's argument

79. I have treated the question of the definition and nature of religion at greater length in my *Religion and Truth*.
80. On the reasonableness of this rather paradoxical claim see notes 4 and 72.
81. Spiro, "Religion: Problems of Definition and Explanation," p. 94.

to that effect in his *The Invisible Religion* provides a suitable focus for such comment.

According to Luckmann, it is wholly inappropriate to identify, as so many do, the church with religion, for in modern industrial society the values institutionalized in church religion are no longer of any relevance for the integration and legitimation of everyday life in that society. The secularization involved in such societies, he suggests, contributes to the development of another socially objectivated cosmos of meaning that may well be a new religion in the making and not the emergence of a society characterized by the absence of religion.[82] This can be seen only if narrow, substantive definitions of religion, of the kind I have just proposed above, are rejected. He himself seeks a definition (understanding) in terms of the anthropological conditions of religion, and, therefore, virtually equates religion with humankind's "transcendence" of its biological (animal) nature, thus making religion *radically* universal.

The transcendence of which Luckmann speaks comes first in face-to-face relationships and is established, so to speak, in an official world-view. He writes: "We may conclude, therefore, that the world-view, as an 'objective' and historical social reality, performs an essentially religious function and defines it as an *elementary form of religion*. This social form is universal in human society. . . . [T]he world view as a whole, as a unitary matrix of meaning . . . provides the historical context within which human organisms form identities, thereby transcending biological nature."[83] Luckmann refers to this world-view, then, as a universal but nonspecific social form of religion but admits, reluctantly it seems, that there are no societies as yet that have religion only in this nonspecific form. He also admits, moreover, that within this world-view there is a domain of meaning that can be called religious in a peculiar sense. He writes: "Although we have just said that the world view as a whole performs a religious function and that no single element of the world view is to be designated as religious, we must presently qualify that statement. Within the world view a domain of meaning can become articulated that deserves to be called religious."[84]

---

82. A similar claim is made by Stark and Bainbridge in their *A Theory of Religion*. They, like Luckmann, do not see the possibility of a society without religion, but for them religion is not the vague, all-pervasive force that it is for Luckmann but involves, rather, particular institutional structures.

83. Luckmann, *Invisible Religion*, p. 61.

84. Ibid., p. 56.

He insists, however, that it is only because this domain stands for the religious function of the world-view as a whole that one is justified in calling it religious, but this seems, in the light of the fact that no society yet studied reveals a "world-view only," somewhat odd. Nevertheless, it is in terms of this model that he suggests that the "inner seculariza-tion" of Christianity in the West is really the replacement of institu-tional specialization of religion with a new social form of religion. He then argues that the end of the institutional specialization of religion is not the end of religion *simpliciter*.

As I have already intimated, there is a great deal of persuasive force in Luckmann's argument and it cannot lightly be rejected. The definition, however, does have an aura of counterintuitiveness about it that ought to raise one's suspicions. If true, everyone, willy-nilly, is religious. Moreover, those who believe in the reality of a transcendent world of powers and beings, obviously handle their problems with the ultimate meaning of human existence in so radically different a way from those simply implicated in "the (universal, nonspecific) invisible religion," as to call for special explanation.

Furthermore, as Peter Berger points out, Luckmann's definition of religion is heavily biased and constitutes "assassination through definition" since it "serves to provide quasi-scientific legitimations of a secularized world-view."[85] A secularized world-view is assumed (true) without question by means of, as Berger puts it, a simple cognitive procedure: "The specificity of the religious phenomenon is 'flattened out'."[86] Berger, of course, sees this as the legitimation of the avoidance of transcendence that is in full accord with the present secularized *Zeitgeist*, but that is a matter that need not be broached here. It needs only to be noted that, as Berger makes clear, it threatens to lose sight of the very phenomenon of religion itself.

To face the question of finitude, knowing of (i.e., having faith in) life's redemption (salvation) through commerce with another more powerful world, and to face our existence by accepting it for what life is in this world and enjoying the limited meanings/pleasures it provides (i.e., unredeemed in its essential finitude), are so radically different that it hardly makes sense to call them both religious. That world-views embodying the latter attitude (belief) fulfill *some* of the functions

---

85. Berger, "Some Second Thoughts on Substantive Versus Functional Definitions of Religion," p. 128.
86. Ibid., p. 129.

once filled in the past by institutionally specialized religion, hardly makes it the equivalent of those specialized forms of religion. Using a shoe for a hammer hardly makes the shoe a hammer, even if it is for the moment a hammer. The belief, implicit or explicit, in a transcendent world of supernatural powers and beings is that which makes religion what it is. And it is that understanding of "religion" that I assume here.

The Meaning of "Thinking"

Although not all one's concepts and categories require the kind of attention I have given to that of theology and religion, some comment on the basic notions involved in the argument to follow may help to avoid serious distortions and permit a more cogent testing of the hypothesis set out here.

A brief comment first upon "thinking" itself. I use the concept here primarily in the sense of conceptual cognition and therefore in connection with the concept of belief. I take thinking to be primarily an activity of mind or intellect that stands over against or goes beyond experience – that is, that transcends experience. In this I follow H. H. Price in his assessment that such transcendence constitutes "an enormous step forward in our mental development."[87] He traces that development through two primitive stages of experience that he refers to as primary and secondary recognition. Recognition is understood as that fundamental intellectual process upon which both intelligent action and thinking depend. Primary recognition is simply a primitive awareness of identities and differences in our interaction with the world. It is preverbal and preconceptual and, though not pure experience or immediate experience, it is not a great distance removed from it. Secondary recognition, however, is more than the simple intuition of the primary act. It is a complex act that involves an atemporal inferential movement that consists in attributing characteristics to objects beyond those perceived. As Price puts it, "the noticed characteristics are taken as signs of others which are not at the moment noticed."[88]

There is no need here to go into further detail in elaborating Price's notion of thinking. It is obvious that recognition, the foundation of all

87. Price, *Thinking and Experience*, pp. 94–95.
88. Ibid., p. 46.

thinking, is subject to error, unlike pure experience. As Price sees it, "a purely sensitive being cannot err. Only *thinkers* are capable of so distinguished an achievement as making a mistake."[89]

When such thinking becomes critical in recognizing its capacity to err – of believing mistakenly that something is the case – and responding appropriately to such recognition, we have the origins of what I refer to in this book as rational/scientific thought. An appropriate response is simply one that permits learning from mistakes made, which means that one is *not* under an obligation to protect the belief(s) in question. The rationality that characterizes scientific thought as used here, therefore, is not simply a matter of logic or of any other characteristic that inheres in sets of beliefs, as is so often assumed, but rather a matter of the nature of the attitude taken up with respect to the holding of beliefs and world-views. By consciously remembering the essentially corrigible nature of all belief, one is encouraged not simply to submit to one's beliefs but to search amongst them for errors, inconsistencies, and contradictions. In so doing, beliefs and world-views are open to modification and development, and the person holding them therefore open to learning. Learning consequently involves transcending simple attachment and commitment to one's world-view and beliefs.[90]

Critical thinking – rational/scientific thought – therefore characterizes neither sets of beliefs nor individuals' intellectual capacities, but rather attitudes of mind and social structures that allow persons to learn from experience. And science, as Popper has clearly shown, is thus far humankind's highest achievement in learning from experience.[91] It is characteristic of particular types of social/intellectual structures which, as I shall show, have only recently emerged. Science is of course not the only possible mode of thinking, and neither is it the only institution to facilitate learning from experience although, as I shall show, it is the only institution consciously to make that its primary intention and aim.[92]

89. Ibid., p. 95.

90. This characterization, of course, is essentially Popperian, and I have relied on Jarvie's (*Rationality and Relativism*) redescription of it in terms of learning for this account.

91. See, e.g., his two volumes, *The Open Society and Its Enemies*, or the essays in *Conjectures and Refutations*, amongst other works.

92. Hence Jarvie's (*Rationality and Relativism*) summary: "A characteristic aim of the scientific world-view is to hold all questions open, allow all existing ideas to be challenged, to forbid entrenched clauses in the cognitive reconstruction" (p. 106).

The Structure of Mythopoesis

"Mythopoesis," already much used in this introductory chapter, will also play a primary role in the discussion to follow. Since it is not always used in the manner in which I shall employ it here, it too requires some clarification.

Myths are stories – normative stories that concern humankind in the world rather than merely providing objective data about the world – and they provide a person with some orientation *in life*. The mind, governed in its existence by acquiescence to such a story (myth), operates mythopoeically in the sense that its use of (i.e., commitment to or submission to) the myth is itself the creation of the reality the myth narrates. It is not, however, that myths are consciously created and then naively believed to be true; rather, myths are the expression of the emotions, feelings, hopes, and fears of a people that are then used as *a kind of* pictorial hypothesis[93] about the nature and meaning of human existence, although unlike ordinary hypotheses they are not open for testing but rather permeate society as a model for thought-and-action. Indeed, the very telling (recitation) of the myth is already an act of creation – of making (*poiesis*) – for it is a participation in the activity whereof it speaks.[94]

Another meaning of "mythopoesis" concerns a modern rather than an ancient enterprise. In this sense mythopoesis refers to the recovering of the value of the ancient stories (myths) for a culture that can no longer believe that what the stories narrate actually took place. (In their inability to believe, such modern minds were also unable to tell, rather than simply to repeat, the stories and hence were impotent in recreating the reality narrated.) The values the stories contain are transposed into symbolic meaning. As H. Slochower puts it, mythopoesis then is the redemption of "the values of the past and present in their *symbolic* form, transposing their historic transitoriness into permanent promises. . . . In the primitive myth and Oriental

93. The phrase is borrowed from Slochower's *Mythopoesis*.

94. I have in mind here the notion of myth as used by Lévy-Bruhl as will become clear in chapter 2. The recitation of the myth is not simply the telling of a story; it requires a proper setting of place and time and is closely tied to rites and ritual performance because its telling is a kind of replication of its substance – a recreating or sustaining of the action whereof it speaks. On this matter see also Frankfort, *Before Philosophy*, and Eliade, *Myth and Reality*.

mythologies, the elements are divine powers; in mythopoesis, they become *verbalized symbols* of these powers."[95]

Whereas Slochower's "mythopoesis" is meant to rescue what he refers to as "the living relevance" in myths from the romantic view of mythology as "an ineffable universal," John L. Greenway's notion of "mythopoesis" seems an apologetic for just such a romantic interpretation of myth. The "ineffable something" is for Greenway that which makes heroism possible. Mythic narrative, that is, reveals a sacred why for existence, and mythopoesis is the means by which modern humankind can also apprehend that "ineffable something" as a mythic fact despite the demythologization of modern consciousness in the Enlightenment and its aftermath. Greenway, therefore, unlike Slochower, claims no interest in the conscious use of mythology in literature. "Rather," he writes, "our concern is with the spontaneous reconstruction of the past to support the factual nature of the values of the present. In a sense this creative act of the mythic imagination is mythopoesis, but the expression of the mythic imagination is not limited to literature, nor is it an act of conscious creation. We must distinguish, then, between the ironic use of mythology and unconscious mythic constructs, for the power of the mythic symbol in both primitive and modern cultures stems from the intensity with which it is believed."[96]

A TENTATIVE THESIS PROPOSED

In raising the question as to the nature of religious thought and in attempting to fashion something of a categorial framework for its answering, I have also put forward a proposal or thesis about its character or nature. Religious thinking, I have suggested, is mythopoeic in nature – that is, it is a mode of thought that is not rational or cognitive in the sense that modern western science is rational and cognitive. It now remains for me to show the cogency of the hypothesis and the evidence that might warrant its acceptance.

The first step in that task will be to ground the assumption on which it is predicated, namely, that a mythopoeic mode of thought that is sufficiently different from modern scientific thought so as to be incommensurable with it exists. I shall do so in a twofold fashion. I

95. Slochower, *Mythopoesis*, p. 15; see also p. 35.
96. Greenway, *The Golden Horns*, p. 20.

shall first argue that the thesis to that effect put forward by Lévy-Bruhl, when properly understood, is both sound and persuasive; that is, that Lévy-Bruhl's dichotomy thesis, as it has come to be referred to, better accounts for a significant set of anthropological problems than the evolutionist theories of his English counterparts (chapter 2). An understanding of the nature of philosophy in ancient Greece and the conditions of its emergence, I shall then argue, provides overwhelming support for Lévy-Bruhl's analysis of archaic/primitive thought (chapter 3). It can be shown that the philosophical mode of thought stands in conflict with the mode of thought that precedes it, both structurally and substantively, and that it therefore constitutes the very birth of a new mode of thought that had nowhere existed until then.[97] Not only

97. This is the task of chapter 3, where I show that it emerges in ancient Greece. I do not, however, show that it hasn't emerged elsewhere, although it is universally agreed that modern science, at least since the seventeenth century, is the product exclusively of the West. This is not to suggest that the great Eastern civilizations in India and China remained bound, so to speak, within a primitive mode of thought. (See, for example, the essays by Gernet and Vernant, "Social History and the Evolution of Ideas in China and Greece.") To what extent "the East" extricated itself from a mythopoeic form of thought and what effects that emancipation, or partial emancipation, had on society more generally, and especially so with respect to religion, is very much relevant to the thesis of this book. Determining these matters, however, is too vast a task to be taken up here. Some interesting suggestions in that regard can be found in Haas's *The Destiny of the Mind, East and West*. Haas has no doubt that both East and West transcended a primitive mythopoeic pattern of thought (p. 123) but maintains that they did so in opposite ways (p. 37; see also p. 133); indeed, for him, the West severed its ties with the magic world whereas "Eastern knowledge" "clearly points back to its magic origin" (p. 159). Whether that claim applies to China in the way Haas thinks it does, is in doubt in light of Joseph Needham's work on Chinese science to which I shall refer below. It does seem to apply to Indian thought, even though they made startling discoveries in logic and mathematics and have given birth to various materialistic/empiricist schools of philosophy such as that of the Carvaka and Lokayata. I have in mind here comments by Zimmer in his *Philosophies of India*. Zimmer maintained that the West's critical candour did not surface in India where there was, rather, a readiness to submit to the authority of tradition. He writes: "There was never in India any such close affinity between natural science and philosophy as to bring about a significant cross-fertilization" (p. 31). The person of learning in that culture, he even suggests, is more like "a primitive medicine man" than like the intellectual in the West (p. 67). Shils in "Some Observations on the Place of Intellectuals in Max Weber's Sociology," makes a similar claim: "The extraordinary rationalizing powers of the Brahmanical intellectuals did not entail, as similar powers among Western Intellectuals have done, the eradication of magic" (p. 435). Tambiah's "The Reflexive and Institutional Achievements of Early Buddhism" in the same volume suggests a similar argument given his focus on the deliberately oral character of Buddhist culture.

The suggestion that ancient Chinese thought remained locked in nonscientific (mytho-poeic) forms has been a primary focus of attack in the work of Needham. But despite that concern, he does not unambiguously deny that there might well be significant differences in the structures of thought of ancient Greece and ancient China that might account for why modern theoretical science emerged only in the West, although, to be sure, the bulk of the explanatory weight for that development is placed on social/cultural differences between medieval Europe and ancient and medieval China. Needham, for example, after distinguishing ancient Chinese scientific thought from true primitive thought, nevertheless argues that there were two ways of advancing from primitive truth: "One was the way taken by some of the Greeks: to refine the ideas of causation in such a way that one ended up with a mechanical explanation of the universe, just as Democritus did with his atoms. The other way is to systematise the universe of things and events into a structural pattern which conditioned all the mutual influences of its different parts. . . . The Greek Democritean approach may have been *a necessary prelude* to modern science, but that does not mean that the criticism of the Chinese view as mere superstition is correct; far from it" (*The Shorter Science and Civilization in China,* 1, pp. 165–166; emphasis added). He insists that all the elements for the development of science were there (p. 191) and, in light of recent developments in physics (and in philosophy, *à la* Alfred N. Whitehead), he even suggests that Chinese bureaucratism and their organic (rather than mechanistic) outlook – *which hindered the birth of modern theoretical science* – may yet "turn out to have been a necessary element in the formation of a perfected world-view of natural science" (p. 189).

In *The Grand Titration,* Needham also acknowledges "that the Greek *praeparatio evangelica*" was an essential background for the emergence of modern theoretical science but claims that it does not in itself constitute that science (p. 50). He finds the Greek interest in proving things to be of utmost importance – including, of course, the social conditions in which this interest flourished. He writes of their assemblies "where every man was an equal citizen and every man could argue back.It was natural therefore for formal logic to develop among the philosophers of the Greek democracies. The Chinese philosophers were in a rather different position; they had indeed some important academies and societies for discussion among themselves, but for the most part they frequented the courts of the reigning feudal kings as advisers and ministers. 'The Chinese philosopher,' wrote Stange, 'could not like his Greek counterpart discuss his ideas on a political situation with an assembly of men of equal rights on the same level as himself, he could only bring his thoughts to fruition in practice by gaining the ear of a prince. The democratic method of logical argumentation was not feasible in discussion with an absolute ruler, but an entirely different method, the citation of historical examples, could make a great impression. Thus it was that proof by historical examples prevailed in Chinese history over proof by logical arguments' " (p. 243). Nevertheless, he does say elsewhere in this volume that the Chinese "were as well able to speculate about nature as the ancient Greeks, on whom is usually laid all the kudos for the establishment of the scientific world-view" (p. 148), and that lack of a break-through to modern theoretical science in China "cannot be explained by any deficiencies either of the Chinese mind or of the Chinese intellectual and philsophical tradition" (p. 191). A similarly ambiguous discussion of these issues is found in *Within the Four Seas.* He is here critical of the praise heaped on the Greeks compared to the work of the Mohists *vis-à-vis* determining "the conditions requisite for the establishment of general truth" (p. 20; see also pp. 89, 183) while yet admitting that no "Hellenic upsurge" characterizes ancient China (p. 183).

Graham, in analysing Needham's work, gives a similarly ambiguous account of the significance of the Greeks for the rise of modern theoretical science; see his "China, Europe and the Origins of Modern Science, for example, pp. 48, 61, 63. A most interesting and valuable critique of Needham's theorizing on the absence of the development of science in China can be found in Chapter 9, "The Masochist Mode of Perception in Asian Civilizations," in Feuer's *The Scientific Intellectual.*

Ben-David's study of the scientists' role in society, it might be noted here, leads him to a significantly different assessment, and he emphasizes what he sees as the uniquely central place of natural philosophy, mathematics, and formal logic of the Presocratics in the development of modern western science (*The Scientists' Role in Society*, pp. xviii, 33, 40ff). According to Ben-David, "[g]reek science can be considered . . . as the legitimate ancestor of modern science" (p. 33). A special case can be made, he insists, for Greek philosophy in a traditional culture. "[G]reek philosophy," he writes, "was different from Chinese and other traditional philosophies since it contained, or at least took cognizance of, those distinct traditions of natural, mathematical enquiry, and as a result was much more centered around logical and metaphysical problems than other ancient philosophies. . . . The marginalization of natural philosophy and mathematics and their subsumption under metaphysical and, sometimes, moral principles align the Greek case with other traditional philosophies. But the preservation of mathematical and natural philosophic traditions and the centrality of epistemological and metaphysical concerns moves it closer to modern philosophy and sciences" (p. xviii). Ben-David draws here upon the conclusions reached by Gershenson and Greenberg in their *Anaxagoras and the Birth of Modern Physics.* They see Hellenistic science, especially in Anaxagoras, as both theoretical and experimental and so (contrary to Needham) fundamentally the same as present-day physics (p. 3). It rejects everything supernatural, theological, and mythological (pp. 21, 23, 32). Furthermore, that physics is kept isolated, so to speak, from matters moral and social; its concern is purely scientific and beliefs here do not have normative moral or social tasks to fulfill. As to its modern experimental character they write: "The fact that Anaxagoras illustrated his scientific lectures with demonstrations is in itself significant. It shows that in Anaxagoras' day it was not unsual to supplement direct observation with active experimentation and that the experimental branch of natural philosophy, which was gradually to match and outstrip the purely observational branch, was already an acknowledged partner of the theoretical branch as far back as the time when rigorous scientific method was being born" (p. 37). On experimentation in ancient Greek science see also Heidel, *The Heroic Age of Science.* Though Elkana, in "The Emergence of Second-Order Thinking in Classical Greece," argues that a notion of systematic controlled experimentation had not emerged in ancient Greece (p. 62) and denies that there is a linear progress from the irrational to the rational in Greek thought (p. 53), he maintains nevertheless, that Greek thought combined reason and experiment in a fashion that is essential to scientific thought (p. 57). The essays in Eisenstadt's collection that concern "The Origin of the Axial Age in China and India" (Part IV) do not, I think put Ben-David's conclusions under any pressure.

Examination of the relation of science and religion in the East will also have to give some attention to the burgeoning popular literature in which it is argued that there is a convergence between post-Newtonian science (especially physics) and eastern metaphysics and religious belief. See especially such works as Capra's *The Tao of Physics* or Zukav's *The Dancing Wu Li Masters.* I find myself out of sympathy with much of this work but cannot take up that disagreement here.

can that difference be delineated, but the very mechanisms that gave rise to this differentiation in the thinking of the human species can also be clearly delineated.

The argument from here should be straightforward, involving only a comparison of the structure of religious thought with that of the Premilesian (i.e., the mode of thought that antedates the emergence of philosophy) and the Presocratic (i.e., the philosophic) mind. However, as the discussion of theology above makes clear, there is likely to be little agreement as to what structures of thought are to count as religious. Is one to count only what might be referred to as "primitive religious utterances," or need the initial, uncritical reflective attention paid to such utterances and the experiences of which they are the expression also be considered? And if the latter along with the former, on what grounds can one exclude the second-order reflective thought of the dogmatic and systematic theologians who attempt "to make sense" of the myths and stories that the initial reflection offered "to account for" those primary religious experiences? Even the critical reflective attention of the philosophical theologian emerges from within the religious community and would seem, therefore, to have some claim on being considered to be religious thought. In consequence of such views I shall not simply rely on direct analysis of the nature of religious thought, but rather also attempt to elucidate the nature of religious thought indirectly; that is, by means of a discussion of the nature and significance of theology both in ancient Greek thought (chapter 4) and within the framework of the Christian (religious) tradition (chapter 5).[98] The analysis here will reveal a structural similarity between Greek philosophy and theology which together account for the demise of the Olympian pantheon.[99] It will also reveal a fundamental aversion of Christianity to theology, even though Christianity ultimately embraced a wide variety of "theologies" and even, to some extent, theology itself. Though made a Christian (religious) enterprise it can be shown nevertheless that theology was, and is, fundamentally detrimental to the Christian Faith. And that irony, I

98. I have restricted myself to discussing the Christian religious tradition primarily for reasons of convenience. There is not space here to develop similar arguments to show the essentially mythopoeic character of thought in other religious traditions.

99. I do not, of course, mean to suggest that there is a simple causal connection between the rise of philosophic thought and the demise of Homeric religion, as if social, economic, and political factors were wholly irrelevant. This impression will be corrected in the discussions of Greek philosophy and religion in chapters 3 and 4.

maintain, is a clear indication of the essentially mythopoeic character of Christian (religious) thought. To put it simply, as philosophy undermines Premilesian myth so theology (a philosophic mode of thought) is destructive of the Christian (mythic) Faith.

II

Mythopoeic and Scientific Thought

DICHOTOMOUS THOUGHT?

THE ASSUMPTION that a great gulf separates the thought of some human beings from that of others has never received a great deal of support in academic circles. It has generally been agreed that, on the surface or superficial view, there appears to be a vast difference between the content and structure of the belief-systems in the modern West and tribal (traditional) cultures the world over. The majority of anthropologists, however, seem to be able to perceive far more similarity of structure on a second look and so find persuasive explanations of the thought of "the primitive" as embryonic stages of their own scientific and rational thinking. In assuming the mind everywhere and always to be homogeneous and to operate according to the same psychological laws, such early anthropologists saw themselves as a adopting a variant form of the "uniformitarian hypothesis" used to such success first by Lyell in the earth sciences and later by Darwin in evolutionary biology.[1] Although in sympathy with their intentions to apply those procedures of scientific research, analysis, and argument that had already been used to good success in sister disciplines, it seems to me that their application of that hypothesis does not dispel the obvious disparity between the "savage" and the "modern" mind. Furthermore, its proper application need not necessitate an assumption of the identity

---

1. For a general discussion of the role of that hypothesis in nineteenth-century thought see Burrow, *Evolution and Society*; also Stocking, Jr., *Victorian Anthropologists*, pp. 127, 155, 174, 225, 309, *et passim*, and Wallace's comments in this regard in his *Freud and Anthropology*, pp. 25–30.

of *thought* which, unlike the brain/mind, is subject to processes of development in addition to the purely physical/psychological conditions that set constraints on the possibilities of social development but do not necessitate them. The difference in the mode of thought is not necessarily a difference in the structure of brain or mind. What I shall attempt to do in this chapter and the next, therefore, is to show that one need neither reject the uniformitarian assumption in the study of human culture nor attempt to ignore or even downplay the vast disparity between the archaic and modern modes of thought. I shall attempt to show, in fact, that there are both significant similarities *and* vast disparities between the two, which is just what one might expect of an evolutionary approach to understanding the development of the human mind and human thought.

In this chapter I shall reevaluate the work of Lucien Lévy-Bruhl, who maintained throughout his works, including, contrary to widespread opinion, the *Carnets*, that the disparity in the content and structure of archaic and modern thought can only be adequately accounted for on the basis of a dichotomy thesis. That his work is still under attack nearly eighty years after its first publication suggests to me that there is more to it than its detractors wish to acknowledge and indicates less than full satisfaction with standard uniformitarian interpretations. That positive evaluation will be followed in chapter three by an analysis/interpretation of the emergence of philosophy and philosophical thinking in ancient Greece that shows it to be, in effect, the birth of the modern mind. The nonphilosophic thought that precedes the rise of philosophy, though not strictly mythopoeic in the Lévy-Bruhlian sense, will be seen to have more affinities with it than it does with the mature product of the intellectual revolution effected by the Milesians. The emergence of philosophy in ancient Greece therefore constitutes a kind of historical corroboration for Lévy-Bruhl's hypothesis. Tracing that development will reveal not only the differences between the philosophic mode of thought of the Milesians and the nonphilosophic mode of thought of those that precede them, but will also bring to light some of the mechanisms of change that made that development possible. The remaining chapters will, in a sense, apply the results of these analyses to the central theses regarding the irony of theology and the nature of religious thought, with particular reference to the Christian religion.

Lévy-Bruhl, as is well known, persistently maintained that there is a radical difference between the mythopoeic thinking that predomi-

nantly characterizes the thought of primitives (i.e., archaic cultures)
and the philosophic/scientific thinking that predominantly characterizes moderns. For him, the two constituted radically different modes
(structures) of thought and were therefore logically incompatible. (For
Lévy-Bruhl, the latter is, cognitively speaking, superior to the former.)
That view constitutes the dichotomy thesis (hypothesis) in the interpretation of human culture that has received not only criticism but abuse
far too long.

It appears to be widely known that Lévy-Bruhl's thesis is simply
unacceptable; that it has collapsed under the strain of incoherence and
indubitable counterevidence. Even E. E. Evans-Pritchard, for example,
a sympathetic interpreter of Lévy-Bruhl, has maintained that "[t]here
is no reputable anthropologist who today accepts this theory of two
distinct types of mentality."[2] It is also often maintained that Lévy-Bruhl
gave up the theory under the fire of heavy and persistent criticism. Any
attempt to resurrect the distinction – to rehabilitate Lévy-Bruhl – it
seems, must be doomed to failure from the start. Nevertheless, I find
myself quite unpersuaded of the truth of such a conclusion and shall
in this chapter attempt to show good reason for such scepticism. I find
some encouragement in undertaking this exercise in the judgment
of Mary Douglas – though herself opposed to a primitive/modern
dichotomy in anthropological thought – that Lévy-Bruhl quite unde-
servedly suffered neglect[3] and C. R. Hallpike's more recently
expressed intention to give Lévy-Bruhl's theories detailed consideration because of their as yet unrecognized importance and significance.[4] After a brief assessment of the prima facie grounds for

2. Evans-Pritchard, *A History of Anthropological Thought*, p. 128.
3. Douglas, *Purity and Danger*, pp. 74–75.
4. Hallpike, "Is There a Primitive Mind?" p. 269, n.5. See also on this score, T. M.
S. Evans' "On the Social Anthropology of Religion," p. 378. He maintains, and I think
correctly so, that Lévy-Bruhl has been dismissed "on the basis of grave misreadings of
his work" (p. 384). He writes: "I should also mention that, as I will hint later, my own
candidate for an early scholar whose work might profitably be resurrected but, for
reasons of its alleged deprecation of the primitive's mind, has largely been dismissed, is
Lucien Lévy-Bruhl" (p. 378).
    The question of the deprecation of such a dichotomy thesis has been raised at length
by several African thinkers and cannot simply be ignored. Okpewho sees the notion,
deriving from Lévy-Bruhl, as racist in that it places the mentality of nonwesterners at
the level of animal intelligence (*Myth in Africa*, p. 28; see also Chapter 6, "Myth, Mind
and Culture: A Review of Prejudices," especially pp. 222ff.); and Hountondji similarly

responds to the Lévy-Bruhlian notion of the prelogical (primitive) mentality as simply an ethnocentric prejudice - as does Irele in the introduction to Hountondji's work (*African Philosophy*, pp. 12, 13, 80, 157, *et passim.*). Space does not permit a detailed analysis of their respective arguments, but comment cannot be altogether avoided. It seems to me that both Okpewho and Hountondji are more dependent on the dichotomy thesis than either is able to recognize and that the latter in particular rests his apology for an "African Philosophy" on Lévy-Bruhlian grounds. Hountondji's work, especially his critique of ethnographies such as that of Marcel Griaule or Placide Tempels, indicates as much, for he portrays that "ethnophilosophy" as radically different from science and philosophy proper which in his view involve free and open debate (p. 46). For him, "philosophy is a theoretical discipline and therefore belongs to the same genus as algebra, geometry, mechanics, linguistics, etc.," and cannot be identified with an ethnophilosophy that presents a set of reasonably coherent but closed principles intended to govern the daily life of a group of people (p. 47). Indeed, he claims that "philosophy in the strictest sense, far from being a continuation of spontaneous thought systems is constituted by making a clear break from them. . . . " (p. 48). Conjectural reconstructions of "African Wisdom" decked out, as he puts it, as philosophy, belong to a wholly different genus from true science and philosophy (p. 48). Such wisdom cannot, he writes, yield a genuine philosophy: "African philosophy, like any other philosophy, cannot possibly be a collective world-view. It can exist as a philosophy only in the form of a confrontation between individual thoughts, a discussion, a debate" (p. 53).

Okpewho also seems, ultimately, to accept a dichotomy view as well, although only implicitly so. In his arguments against a Lévy-Bruhlian position, especially as he sees it reformulated in Goody (see below), he writes: "The disciplines of logic and philosophy are no more than a *relocation* in scribal culture of activities that the oral culture adequately encouraged in its peculiar circumstances" (p. 234). He immediately tries to transcend this dichotomy of the oral and the literate cultures but ends up simply denying that the latter is anything but an extension of the former. Moreover, he uses the wisdom/philosophy rejected by Hountondji as the foundation for such an argument. His argument is hardly persuasive, for it implies that science (logic) is indistinguishable from myth (p. 237).

As will become clear below, Lévy-Bruhl's thesis is exactly the opposite of ethnocentric prejudice, for it is intended to transcend the ethnocentrism of the intellectualist stance in the anthropology of the English school. It should also be noted here that Hountondji's and Okpewho's positions are mutually exclusive even though both see themselves as fighting off Lévy-Bruhl.

It needs pointing out here as well that Littleton, in the introduction ("Lucien Lévy-Bruhl and the Concept of Cognitive Relativity") to the recent reprint of *How Natives Think*, also insists that Lévy-Bruhl "thoroughly deserves to be recalled from the intellectual limbo to which he has generally been consigned" (p. v). This edition came into my hands well after this chapter had been written and so treatment of Littleton's introduction has not been included. I simply point out here, therefore, that Littleton draws attention to several positive responses to Lévy-Bruhl's work and shows its compatibility with much contemporary anthropological theory, for example, with cognitive, structural, and symbolic anthropology; indeed, he suggests that Lévy-Bruhl anticipated them. Though Littleton thinks the notion of a single primitive mentality has been rightly called into question (p. xlii) he nevertheless insists that it is quite reasonable to suggest that

reopening Lévy-Bruhl's case, so to speak, I shall proceed to an account
and interpretation of his theory of the prelogical mentality of (primitive) humankind.

THE GROUNDS FOR REVIEW

There are several good reasons for championing Lévy-Bruhl's
thought. First, despite some reports, Lévy-Bruhl himself, after much
careful consideration of the claims of his critics, held to the theory,
although with some modification, to the last. Secondly, much of the
criticism directed against his position was simply beside the point,
arising from a serious misunderstanding of his enterprise. Thirdly,
and somewhat ironically, the overwhelming extent of the reaction to
his theory and the persistence of the attacks upon it from its initial
publication to the present begs for analysis; why should a theory that is
so obviously wrongheaded receive such attention? Finally, our present
recognition of the problem that forced itself upon Lévy-Bruhl's attention leaves little room for deviation from his response. I shall comment
on each of these reasons briefly.

1 In a critique of Lévy-Bruhl's thesis in the mid-twenties, R. Allier
noted: "There is no ground for believing that M. Lévy-Bruhl is on
the point of abandoning the main element of his theory."[5] And J.
Cazaneuve more recently has pointed out that although Lévy-Bruhl
did revoke his use of the term prelogical in the *Carnets* he nevertheless
maintained that what he characterized as primitive mentality was a
permanent structure of the human mind.[6]

Lévy-Bruhl's contribution "was the discovery of a deep-seated dichotomy between two
alternative reality-constructs, thought-modes, 'logics' or whatever, one predicated on
participation and the other on the rule of non-contradiction, which can be detected in
varying proportions everywhere ... [and that] the latter mode has generally been
dominant in Western culture, at least among its elites, since well before Aristotle" (p.
xliii). My task in this chapter and the next, of course, is to persuade the reader of the
truth of this claim.

5. Allier, *The Mind of the Savage*, p. 25.
6. Cazeneuve, *Explorations in Interpretative Sociology*, pp. 20–22. On the character of
the attack on Lévy-Bruhl, Jung's assessment as recounted by Werblowsky, ("In *Nostro
Tempora*") is instructive: "As C.G. Jung once put it to me, referring to the well-known
'revocation' in the *Carnets*: 'Lévy-Bruhl allowed himself to be terrorized by the violence
of the criticisms levelled at him" (p. 132).

2 Though Lévy-Bruhl paid close attention to his critics and modified his views in light of their findings and arguments, much of the reaction to his views was simply confused and misdirected, although not often perceived as such. I have in mind here the criticism that was based on an understanding of Lévy-Bruhl's thesis as a biological-cum-psychological theory of the primitive mind.[7] Such an individualist reading of his claim seemed to imply the stupidity of the primitive – the primitive's incapacity for conceptual thought and the inability of the individual primitive to reason. This misunderstanding is still prevalent among both anthropologists and students of religion. C. Geertz, for example, suggests that Lévy-Bruhl's theory implies that primitives do not even have the capacity for intellection[8] and J. Z. Smith maintains that such a dichotomy view constitutes a mapping of the human domain that has resulted in much mischief in that it excluded recognition of the primitive as human.[9] Yet nothing could be further from the truth, for in calling primitives prelogical, as I shall elaborate below, Lévy-Bruhl did not mean to suggest that they were unintelligent or stupid – unable to think conceptually. His theory does not concern the individual's ability to reason or to make use of ideas and concepts but rather focuses

7. Evans-Pritchard made this abundantly clear in his essay "Lévy-Bruhl's Theory of Primitive Mentality," reprinted in *Journal of the Anthropological Society of Oxford* (pages cited refer to the reprint), claiming that the critics made little or no effort to grasp the ideas that lay behind Lévy-Bruhl's terminology (p. 39). "In my opinion most of this criticism is very ineffective, disproving what no one holds to be proved. It seldom touches Lévy-Bruhl's main propositions. His theory of primitive mentality may distort savage thought but it would seem better to correct the distortion than to dismiss the theory completely" (p. 42). He goes on to point out that Lévy-Bruhl's great influence on anthropological thought "is due to the fact that he perceived a scientific problem of cardinal importance and that he approached this problem along sociological lines instead of contenting himself with the usual psychological platitudes" (p. 45). On this score see also the relevant comments in n. 4.
8. Geertz, "The Growth of Culture and the Evolution of Mind," p. 61, reiterated in "Notions of Primitive Thought," p. 198.
9. See J. Z. Smith, "Map is Not Territory," pp. 294, 298, 308. The force of his criticism, however, is weakened by his earlier paper "I Am a Parrot (Red)" in the same volume, in his recognition that Lévy-Bruhl's problematic points up an important and much larger debate over rationality in general (p. 285), i.e., as to whether there are universal, contextually invariable principles of logic, rationality, and truth in addition to the contextual ones (p. 287). He maintains that historians of religion have avoided raising these issues without realizing that, in raising them, clarity must be sacrificed, so to speak, to truth and recognition given, if the evidence so indicates, to perceptions of the other that are less than flattering. However, as just indicated, this is precisely what he seems to castigate in the later essay.

on the framework – the set of categories and concepts – within which such individuals reasoned. Lévy-Bruhl's approach was precisely not psychologistic; it was an attempt to replace the psychologistic theories of early English anthropologists, who tried to explain social facts in terms of the psychological processes of individual minds, with a sociological account of individual thought in terms of collective representations. As Evans-Pritchard has put it, for Lévy-Bruhl "[t]he mentality of the individual is derived from the collective representations of his society, which are obligatory for him; and these representations are functions of institutions."[10] Different kinds of thinking, therefore, concern different social structures and not different brain physiologies. As Evans-Pritchard proceeds to explain, "as social structures vary, so will the representations, and consequently the individual's thinking. Every type of society has therefore its distinctive mentality. . . . "[11]

It is criticism of this kind, taken at face value, that is in good measure responsible for the neglect Lévy-Bruhl has suffered.

3 Given the widespread disagreement with Lévy-Bruhl and the apparent obviousness of the faults in his theory of primitive mentality, it is most surprising that he is still the focus of a great deal of attention. That "flogging of a dead horse" includes not only the apparently obligatory jibes at Lévy-Bruhl but also more elaborate repudiations of his proposals and new work designed to show their falsehood.[12] That

10. Evans-Pritchard, *Theories of Primitive Religions*, p. 79.

11. Ibid., p. 79 (my emphasis). See also his essay "Lévy-Bruhl's Theory of Primitive Mentality". Lévy-Bruhl, in a letter to Evans-Pritchard in 1934, confirms the latter's interpretation. Lévy-Bruhl writes: "When I said that 'primitives' never perceive anything exactly as we do I never meant to assert a truly psychological difference between them and us; on the contrary I admit that individual physio-psychological conditions of sensory perception cannot be other among them than among us. . . . " ("A Letter to E. E. Evans-Pritchard," (p. 121).

12. For example, see Shweder, "Likeness and Likelihood in Everyday Thought." Much previous work seemed intent on showing the similarities of primitive thought to the rational/theoretical/scientific thought of modernity, (as the discussion of the intellectualists – neo-Tylorians – to follow will show), whereas more recent work, like Shweder's, aims at showing how much modern, so-called, scientific thought is like the thinking in traditional/archaic cultures – i.e., that "[m]ost of us have a 'savage' mentality much of the time" (p. 638). He argues that "magical thinking is an expression of a universal disinclination of normal adults to draw correlation lessons from their experience, coupled with a universal inclination to seek symbolic and meaningful connections (likenesses) among objects and events. Magical thinking is no less characteristic of our own mundane intellectual activities than it is of Zande curing practices" (p. 637, also p. 647).

Lévy-Bruhl still inspires that kind of reaction ought to raise our suspicions as to the real value of his work; his critics protest overmuch. Furthermore, there is in much of the critical response to Lévy-Bruhl a profound ambiguity. Many of his critics themselves appear to espouse a kind of dichotomy view that simply echoes Lévy-Bruhl.[13] Douglas, for example, talks of distinguishing undifferentiated from differentiated thought systems[14] in which thought dominated by subjective conditions (participation?) is contrasted with that wherein there is a conscious reaching for objectivity. Douglas, therefore, although repudiating talk of prelogical societies, does not hesitate to talk about pre-Copernican societies.[15]

Evans-Pritchard admits, with Lévy-Bruhl, that the thought patterns of primitive magic and religion confront us with a real problem and he goes on to suggest a dichotomy approach to resolving it. He insists

---

Hutchins' work (*Culture and Inference*) takes a different tack in that he focuses on questions of similarity/dissimiliarity in the processes of thinking rather than on the representation of the world which is thought about. On this score, the work of Russian scholars like Vygotsky (in *Mind in Society*) and Luria, (in *Cognitive Development*) is relevant. A contrary case made on philosophical grounds can be found in Godlove, "In What Sense Are Religions Conceptual Frameworks?"

Casagrande's comment on Shweder (pp. 648–49), suggesting that Lévy-Bruhl might well be able to accept Shweder's conclusions, seems to be, despite Shweder's objection (p. 652), sound. And Lancey's claim that "while there may be a universal disinclination to use contingency information in making judgments, Westerners, as a result of formal education and circumstances related to involvement in various professional activities, probably reason correlationally more often than non-Westerners" (p. 652) is both correct and compatible with the later formulations of Lévy-Bruhl's thesis. Shweder is right to see the similarities and "overlaps" in these two kinds of thought, but he fails to see the real extent and significance of the differences between them.

Godlove's "neo-intellectualism" rests on philosophical issues that are yet (and admittedly so) open to debate. There is much with which I am in agreement, however, in his more recent *Religion, Interpretation and Diversity of Belief*, as will become clear in chapter 6. Hutchin's work, however, does require analysis, for it puts into serious question some aspects of Lévy-Bruhl's position.

13. This is a criticism lodged by Evans-Pritchard against Lévy-Bruhl's early critics as well: "Too often," he writes, "they merely repeated his views under the impression that they were refuting them" (Evans-Pritchard, "Lévy-Bruhl's Theory of Primitive Mentality," p. 39; Lévy-Bruhl held a similar view as is apparent in his letter to Evans-Pritchard referred to in n. 11). Evans-Pritchard also points out that not all the responses to Lévy-Bruhl's position were critical; see especially n. 11, on p. 58 of the above mentioned article.

14. Douglas, *Purity and Danger*, p. 78.

15. Ibid., p. 80.

on the validity of Lévy-Bruhl's essential insight but argues: "It is not so much a question of primitive versus civilized mentality as the relation of the two types of thought to each other in any society, whether primitive or civilized, a problem of levels of thought and experience."[16] Evans-Pritchard therefore recognizes two levels of thought but sees them as existent in all societies. However, unless one type characterizes primitive thought more than the other it is difficult to see how Evans-Pritchard can claim to be in agreement with Lévy-Bruhl's perception that the primitive presents us moderns with a peculiar problem.

Geertz, in an interview with J. Miller, repudiates the notion of two forms of thought that characterize different societies, yet still recognizes that in certain daily activities primitives not only invoke their practical (conceptual, scientific?) knowledge but supplement it with ritual activity that seems to constitute a different mode of thinking and a different knowledge; as he puts it, "both of these ways of thinking have been there all along."[17] In response to Miller's question, which seems to contrast two distinctly different modes of thought, Geertz seems to repudiate his critique of Lévy-Bruhl and to espouse a position not far different from his: "(Miller): Would you say that the recrudescence of mystical, occult practices that are going on in the West are the expression of a *flight* from rationality? Some attempt to reconceive the universe in terms other than technological?" (Geertz): Most certainly."[18]

Jack Goody denies "that any such simple [dichotomy] design provides an adequate framework for the examination of human interaction and development" yet refuses to adopt the opposing

---

16. Evans-Pritchard, *A History*, p. 131. This point is also stressed by Barden: "There remains the question of the primitive mentality. Although to my knowledge he never denies the validity of the notion entirely, Evans-Pritchard never uses it analytically. He compares types of commonsense between themselves, i.e. Zande and British, and Zande commonsense with science. But he finds no need for the notion of primitive mentality. Yet there is the acknowledgement that among the Azande there is no science and this gives us a further clue; *science and common sense* are not the same but there is mutual interaction between them and as science develops one hopes and expects that the grosser superstitions of unenlightened common sense will fade. . . . We should talk, then, not generally about mentalities but about specific congeries of viewpoints, interests and patterns of experience" ("Method and Meaning," pp. 127–28). (See also Barden's "The Symbolic Mentality." In this regard Littleton's comments (n. 4) are also relevant.

17. Geertz, "Notions of Primitive Thought," p. 207.

18. Ibid., pp. 209–10.

uniformitarian views.[19] He sees literate societies as radically different from oral societies and sees the former as the sources of logic and philosophy.[20] Indeed, he suggests that literacy "creates the possibility of what is almost a different kind of critical examination"[21] – i.e., a different kind of thinking that clearly distinguishes it from that found in oral contexts. I shall return to Goody's work again later in this chapter.

Further discussion of the ambiguity in the critiques of Lévy-Bruhl will emerge later in this discussion. However, it needs to be noted here that many of the critiques are themselves questionable.[22]

4 Finally, it seems to me that we cannot but agree with Lévy-Bruhl that primitive thought, regardless of how we characterize it, is radically different from modern thought and that that difference demands explanation. As Evans-Pritchard puts it, he quite correctly recognized that thought patterns of primitive magic and religion confront us with a real problem.[23] And Douglas writes that it was Lévy-Bruhl, "who first posed all the important questions about primitive cultures and their distinctiveness as a class. . . . "[24] And, as Douglas also points out, Lévy-Bruhl took up this stance in face of a contrary assumption made by British anthropologists. Allier refers to it as the assumption of the identity of mind, "a perfect unity, everywhere and always the same from the logical standpoint,"[25] and quite correctly points out that they never proved it or even discussed it; "they never even made a formal

19. Goody, *The Domestication of the Savage Mind*, pp. 226–27.

20. Ibid., p. 235.

21. Ibid., p. 240. See also p. 241: "My point is that the oral mode makes this kind of self-deception easier to carry out and less easy to detect."

22. Douglas, to whom I have already made reference, for example, talks of "pre-copernican" rather than prelogical thought; Bidney, to whom I shall pay some attention below, prefers "pre-scientific" to "prelogical"; Arieti in a brilliant discussion of creativity (in *Creativity: The Magic Synthesis*), persuasively makes the case for viewing primitive thought as "paleological"; Bergouinoux argues that traditional thought might well be referred to as "sublogical" (in "Notes on the Mentality of Primitive Man"); and Barbu, in *Problems of Historical Psychology*, talks of primitives as "pre-individualistic." Space does not permit discussion of each of these, and other, alternative formulations of an essentially dichtomous position. However, Goody's and Havelock's views of primitive thought as preliterate will receive attention below. See also n. 13.

23. Evans-Pritchard, *A History*, p. 131.

24. Douglas, *Purity and Danger*, pp. 74–75.

25. Allier, *The Mind of the Savage*, p. 20.

enunciation of it. They were content to take it for granted, looking upon it as indisputable."[26] Yet this assumption, or at least variants of it, still seems to dominate anthropology. Indeed, Geertz refers to the assumption as the doctrine of the psychic unity of mankind and claims both that it is empirically substantiated and that it is unquestioned by any reputable anthropologist.[27] Lévy-Bruhl's perception of the

---

26. Ibid., p. 20. There is obviously good justification for such an assumption having been made, given that "uniformitarian notions," so to speak, had contributed immensely in the development of other sciences in the nineteenth century – from Lyell's geology in the 1820s to Darwin's evolutionary biology. On this topic see also Burrow, *Evolution and Society*.

27. See Geertz, "The Growth of Culture and the Evolution of Mind" and "Notions of Primitive Thought." However, see also his "The Cerebral Savage"amd "The Way We Think Now."

It seems that theories making sense of the assumption (doctrine) of the unity of the human mind fall into two classes. In the one the assumption is hard to distinguish from the original Lévy-Bruhlian formulation of it, for it grounds contemporary structural anthropology which denies vast intellectual differences amongst human persons, primitive or modern.Neo-intellectualists like R. Horton and structuralists like C. Lévi-Strauss will receive some attention below. Similar views, but with interesting variations, are expressed, however, by Sperber in his "Is Symbolic Thought Prerational?", where he argues that symbolic thought is built on a *prior* rational processing. Rationality is not progressively acquired by transcending symbolic thought, but rather overloading the rational device triggers the symbolic processing (see also his "Apparently Irrational Beliefs") Turner in his *Life Before Genesis*, also argues against the notion that archaic/ traditional thought is symbolic and therefore non- or irrational. He castigates that view as ethnocentric, particularly so in his review of a recent translation of Lévy-Bruhl's book on *Primitive Mythology*.

Dupré (in *Religion in Primitive Cultures*), in a more philosophical vein, argues a similar point: "When we spoke about mythic thinking we did not say that this mode of thinking is the expression of a pre-human form of life or that it prevents man from conceiving adequately the empirical world. On the contrary, we emphasized the fundamental character of mythic thinking as the foundation of mythopoeic as well as of all rational acts, including those of reflective thinking. Mythic thinking as it is understood here, is not a deficiency of man's reasoning processes but the enactment of mythicity as the foundational unity of mythos, logos and being at once" (pp. 315–316).

In its other form, the identity thesis is substantiated by arguing/showing that/how primitive modern thought really is – a line of argument, as I have already shown, taken up by scholars like Evans-Pritchard, Shweder, and Hutchins, among others. Although the arguments of such scholars are often persuasive on first reading, they are fundamentally misdirected, for they dissolve rather than (re)solve the original problem, i.e., they deny what seems, as Gellner suggests, the undeniable: "The biggest, most conspicuous single fact about the human world is the Big Divide between what may roughly be called the industrial-scientific society and the Rest" ("An Ethic of Cognition," p. 175).

problem is apparently wrongly praised and his, and our, perception of the oddness of primitive thought and expression is illusory. I shall argue, however, that the praise is well-deserved, that Lévy-Bruhl, as Malcolm Crick has suggested, recognized both unity and diversity in humankind, and that he was clearly bent on examining the diversities within that unity; diversities that were, and still are, all too easily glossed over.[28]

THE LÉVY-BRUHLIAN THESIS STATED

Early English anthropology since E. B. Tylor had attempted to explain the differences of belief between primitives and moderns on the basis of the assumption of the identity of the human mind across all cultural boundaries. As Lévy-Bruhl put it: "For lack of proceeding by a comparative method, philosophers, psychologists and logicians have all granted one common postulate. They have taken as the starting-point of their investigations the human mind always and everywhere homogeneous, that is, a single type thinker, and one whose mental operations obey psychological and intellectual laws which are everywhere identical."[29] Given such a Kantian assumption, the explanation for divergence of primitive from modern thought could only be proffered in terms of concepts such as mental weakness, confusion, illusion, mental hallucination, childish trust in analogy, ignorant use of principles, etc.[30] Those following the lead of such scholars, Lévy-Bruhl com-

---

28. The glossing over occurs out of "charity," as Gellner puts it (in his "Concepts and Society") to "the other" which will show "the other" in the most flattering light possible; that will show apparent absurdities, ultimately, to be quite rational claims. This may be inspired by a healthy criticism of the ethnocentric bias of the observer/scholar, but it can, as Gellner points out, lead to error in interpreting/understanding "the other." He insists "that the over-charitable interpreter, determined to defend the concepts he is investigating from the charge of logical incoherence, is bound to misdescribe the social situation. To make sense of the concept is to make nonsense of the society. Thus the uncharitable may be contextual in the . . . deeper and better sense" (p. 140). I have suggested that this is an error to which students of religion in particular are prone, as can be seen, for example, in J. Z. Smith referred to in n. 9.
See also Malcolm Crick, *Explorations in Language and Meaning*, p. 164, regarding the matter of diversity in unity.
29. Lévy-Bruhl, *How Natives Think*, p. 346.
30. Ibid., pp. 35, 36, 45, 58, 61, *et passim*. Evans-Pritchard, *Theories*, refers to such interpretations of archaic thoughts as "if I were a horse" theories.

plains, could only observe the new empirical data gathered "with prejudiced eyes."[31] He argues, however, that if one does not assume that the question can be answered in only one way, that an understanding of the anthropological data may in fact yield quite a different picture: "Let us then [he writes] no longer endeavour to account for these connections either by the mental weakness of primitives, or by the association of ideas, or by a naive application of the principle of causality, or yet by the fallacy *post hoc, ergo propter hoc*; in short, let us abandon the attempt to refer their mental activity to an inferior variety of our own."[32] Lévy-Bruhl himself proceeds, then, with quite a different question in mind, one obviously not till then seriously entertained: "Do the collective representations of the communities in question arise out of higher mental functions identical with our own, or must they be referred to a mentality which differs from ours to an extent yet to be determined?"[33] And he answers it in the affirmative, maintaining that only a thesis of difference will do, although not implying thereby an absolute difference in the types of thought considered.[34] The imme-

---

31. Ibid., p. 21. It is interesting to notice here how Lévy-Bruhl's comments anticipate the understanding of the role of theory in the sciences in Kuhn's *The Structure of Scientific Revolutions*, and Hanson's *The Patterns of Discovery*.

32. Ibid., p. 61.

33. Ibid., p. 7.

34. In his letter to Evans-Pritchard (n. 11) he admits that he over-emphasized the differences between primitive and modern modes of thought but in defence of doing so says: "My intention was to introduce the idea (which seemed to me to be new), that there is a *real difference* between primitive mentality and that of more developed civilizations, particularly those of the West, and consequently, I was not obliged to give the most complete picture of this primitive mentality, including in it what is common to our own – but insist continually on that which is characteristic of it and constitutes the specific difference. . . . I have done this '*on purpose*': I intended to bring fully to light the mystical aspect of primitive mentality in contrast with the rational *aspect* of the mentality in our societies" (pp. 118–19). The similarities that exist between the two modes of thought had, he insisted, been brought to light by other anthropologists to the neglect of this significant difference.

It is obvious, furthermore, that an *absolute* difference would imply incomprehensibility between cultures which would be, as Runciman puts it (in "The Sociological Explanation of 'Religious' Beliefs"), self-defeating, "since it would mean that the anthropologist could not express, and therefore could not discover in the first place, what is the untranslatable belief which he claims the members of the alien culture to hold" (p. 73). Crick (*Explorations in Language and Meaning*) makes the same point in an effort to show that Lévy-Bruhl was not concerned with absolute differences but rather with diversities in an assumed unity: "A totally different mind would just be unintelligible to us, so we could not have any warrants for recognizing it as a mind. . . . Completely different standards

diately apparent differences of intellection between primitives and moderns arise because of two rather significantly different modes of thought – the primitives being possessed, so to speak, of a prelogical or mystical mentality. "I have been able to show," writes Lévy-Bruhl, "that the mental processes of primitives do not coincide with those which we are accustomed to describe in men of our own types. . . . "[35] He rejects, therefore, the notion of the "savage philosopher."[36]

---

of reasoning simply could never show up . . ." (p. 164). Hollis also argues that point in his "The Limits of Irrationality" (p. 216), showing that without that assumption translation from one culture to another would not be possible. See also Gellner, "Concepts and Society."

Godlove ("In What Sense Are Religions Conceptual Frameworks?") also argues this claim, intent on showing that it implies more than most of us have been willing to see, namely, that all dichotomy theories are misleading.

35. Lévy-Bruhl, *How Natives Think*, p. 4. Lévy-Bruhl also shows how the practical activities and institutions of primitive society are more coherently accounted for in terms of his theory of primitive mentality; see especially part III, "Institutions in Which Collective Representations Governed by the Law of Participation Are Involved."

36. Ibid., p. 66. Boas in *The Mind of Primitive Man* challenged Lévy-Bruhl's thesis because, he claimed, there existed evidence to show the primitive mind to be capable of being like that of the philosopher (see pp. 104, 114) and he therefore reiterated the doctrine of the unity of the human mind (p. 122). His claim, however, is not wholly unambiguous, for he also shows that there are considerable differences between primitive and civilized cultures that must be countenanced (see pp. 122, 201, 202, 238, 240, 243). Radin, however, in *Primitive Man as Philosopher*, is, as the title suggests, more forceful in his attack on Lévy-Bruhl, amassing evidence to support the notion of independent and critical thought by individuals within particular archaic cultures. (See also chapter 3, "Psychological Types, the Man of Action and the Thinker" in his *The World of Primitive Man*.)

Kluckhohn talks of "The Philosophy of the Navaho Indians," seeing in their thought an "implicit philosophy" (p. 357). He seems fully to support Radin's view: "The publication of Paul Radin's *Primitive Man as Philosopher* did much toward destroying the myth that a cognitive orientation toward experience was a peculiarity of literate societies" (p. 356). However, he does also admit that some thought forms among primitives look very much like Lévy-Bruhl's *participation mystique* (p. 360). Malinowski, as Bidney points out, seemed to have held a similar view but saw that mind as tied in tandem with "another mind," so to speak, in other matters: "Malinowski . . . seeks to combine the rationalistic theory of Frazer and Tylor with the mystical, prelogical interpretation of Lévy-Bruhl, and therefore holds that the native mind is both rational and irrational in different contexts of experience. The native is said to be empirical and rational in his secular, everyday experience and practice, but irrational, emotional, and prone to wishful thinking in times of individual and social crisis when his rational knowledge proves to be inadequate" ("The Concept of Meta-Anthropology," p. 330).

It is of some interest to note here that Hountondji's analysis of Radin's critique puts Radin into the same camp with Lévy-Bruhl. Radin, he admits, shows the possibility "of

a plurality of opinions and beliefs, of theoretical individuality in 'primitive' societies,"
yet claims that Radin himself shows unmistakable signs "that he still believes in an
essential difference between Western and other cultures, even if the difference is dis-
placed, determined in a new way" (Hountondji, *African Philosophy*, p. 79; see also p. 80
for a fuller description of that contrast). As I have already noted above, it seems to me
that Hountondji's critique of Griaule and Tempels puts him into that camp. However,
given a proper interpretation of Lévy-Bruhl – which I do not think Hountondji possesses – that does not militate against his argument that such "primitives" as, for example,
the Africans, have the *capacity* to think like moderns. Okpewho's criticism of Redfield's
"Thinker and Intellectual in Primitive Society" has similar overtones (*Myth in Africa*, pp.
230, 237), although Hountondji, I suspect, would be in agreement with Redfield's
suspicions of the ethnography of people like Griaule and Tempels. There is no need,
however, to elaborate on these differences of interpretation here. Suffice it to say that
Hountondji's work, contrary to appearances, is really very much in support of the Lévy-
Bruhlian thesis I am putting foward here.

Other work on African thought and African philosophy is also germane here; see, for
example, Wiredu, *Philosophy and An African Culture*; Hallen and Sodipo, *Knowledge,
Belief and Witchcraft*; and the essays in Wright's, *African Philosophy*. See also Abraham's
comments in chapter 2 – "Paradigms of African Society" (espec. pp. 103–13) – of his
The Mind of Africa. Adequate treatment of all the issues raised in these and other works
would require a book to itself and so cannot be delved into further here.

It must be admitted that all cultures/societies exhibit abstraction, a matter clearly
shown by Fairservice in his *The Threshold of Civilization*, pp. 21–22. But, even as the title
of his work suggests, Fairservice sees great transformations of society as a result of
differences of degree of abstraction between what he calls enactive, ikonic and symbolic
cultures (p. 208). Given that the later stages grow out of those preceding them, there is
no mystery as to why the evidence Boas and Radin find for the existence of the
philosopher/intellectual in primitive society should be there: "Civilization as culture at
a symbolic level will include enactive citizens, and enactive culture will have citizens
whose cognitive level reaches a degree of symbolic cognizance" (p. 52). (See also here,
Goody, *The Domestication of the Savage Mind*, especially chapter two, "Intellectuals in Pre-
Literate Societies.") Furthermore, Radin's evidence can also be recognized without
challenge in a Lévy-Bruhlian context if one sees that modern rational thought, as
characteristic of modern as opposed to mythopoeic/primitive society, is not something
that is done by the individual alone, but rather as a part of a critical communal activity.
For the latter to emerge, the potentiality of Radin's primitive philosopher must be there.
I treat this matter at greater length in chapter 3. This same point is made by Redfield
in his "Thinker and Intellectual in Primitive Society": "It is the existential human
individual who has the quality of mind that Radin has made us recognize in primitive
society" (p. 35). However, he is essentially in disagreement with Radin. Writing of the
Dogon he says: "If to think long and deeply about the nature of the world and its origins
as tradition has proposed explanations to one, is to be a philosopher, Ogotemmeli is a
philosopher. He is not, if a philosopher is one who struggles with intellectual problems
in abstract terms and offers solutions of some originality" (p. 39; see also p. 45).

There is much of value on this topic in Marshak's *The Roots of Civilization*. He finds
the roots of writing and modern science to go back at least to Upper Paleolithic times
and claims that archaeological evidence exists to show that "the same basic cognitive
processes that appear later in science and writing" were already then in use (p. 58). He

Space does not permit a detailed accounting and illustration of the structure of primitive thought as Lévy-Bruhl perceived it.[37] We must, however, look at the two essential qualities that he suggested characterized it: namely, that it is prelogical, in that it takes little or no account of the law of noncontradiction characteristic of modern thought; and that it is governed by the law of participation.[38] Primitive thought, therefore, although it makes use of abstractions and concepts, is little given to critical reflection and analysis. Primitive mentality, with its acceptance of a supernaturalism, adopts an "agentic" view of the world that stands in stark contrast to the "causal" understanding of the modern mind. And primitive perceptions of space and time are qualitative and preclude the quantitative perceptions of modern (scientific) thought. Little doubt is left in Lévy-Bruhl's account that the two modes of thought are, logically speaking, mutually exclusive.[39]

---

does recognize, however, that their writing and science is not like ours and that there are therefore differences, though he insists that the differences are not in the way the human brain functions (p. 60). Given the sociological character of the Lévy-Bruhlian hypothesis, therefore, there is no necessary conflict between Marshak's findings and the claims being made here. Marshak's comments in chapter 14, "The Step Towards History" (pp. 341ff.) and the "Postscript" (pp. 369ff.), seem to indicate the same.

Of some interest in this connection is the older work by Levy, *The Gate Of Horn*, to which I shall have occasion to refer in chapter 3.

37. A more extensive treatment of Lévy-Bruhl can be found in Cazaneuve, *Explorations*. See also Schlagel's *From Myth to the Modern Mind*, vol. 1, *Animism to Archimedes*, especially chapter 2, "Anthropological Conceptions of Primitive Mentality." I am in essential, though not total, agreement with his understanding of Lévy-Bruhl.

38. Lévy-Bruhl, *How Natives Think*, p. 323.

39. It would be helpful to the reader (and prudent for the writer) to point out that the discussion in this book does not necessarily assume that the world of thought is exhausted by the types discussed here. There is evidence to suggest the possibility of intermediate types of thought between the two extremes of the primitive and the modern, and good theoretical reason to ground expectation of their existence. Gellner ("The Savage and the Modern Mind") is perhaps right to suggest that much of human history is occupied by civilizations whose thought patterns fall between these extremes. Despite this, however, Gellner sees good analytical grounds for "thinking away this enormous middle ground" but to do so wittingly, and in this I agree with him. I also follow him in making use of a further tacit assumption to the same end, namely, "that there is one homogeneous kind of modernity and one homogeneous kind of savagery" (p. 163). These are not taken as self-evident truths and can – and should – be put under critical scrutiny in further assesssments of the questions under consideration here. It should be noted as well that not everyone would agree with the conclusion in this paragraph; see, e.g., Evans-Pritchard (*A History*), who claims: "Lévy-Bruhl is also wrong in supposing that there is necessarily a contradiction between an objective causal expla-

Lévy-Bruhl's work, as I have already indicated above, was attacked almost immediately, and under the pressure of attack he subjected his thesis to revision.[40] In the final analysis, it is true, he came to acknowledge that, like his colleagues in the English tradition, he too had made the facts speak a special language; that he had crammed the facts into a procrustean theoretical bed. Whereas he could boldly state in 1910 that "Primitives see with eyes like ours, but they do not perceive with the same minds,"[41] in 1938 he admitted that "the logical structure of the mind is the same in all known human societies."[42] Nevertheless, he still maintained, and I think correctly so, that "there is a difference between the primitive mentality and ours: not only that of the cultured,

---

nation and a mystical one. It is not so. The two kinds of explanation can be, as indeed they are, held together, the one supplementing the other; and they are not therefore exclusive" (p. 129). But this seems to be mere assertion; there are here important philosophical and epistemological assumptions that need full discussion, which Evans-Pritchard does not offer. Furthermore, it must be recognized that Lévy-Bruhl was quite aware that the two modes of explanation could, socially, supplement each other, even if they were logically incompatible – a possibility to which Evans-Pritchard seems oblivious. Gellner brings this out clearly in a passage relevant to this essay in his "A Wittgensteinian Philosophy of (or Against) The Social Sciences," which is worth quoting at length: "Quite unwittingly, Louch has provided us with a highly simplified ideal type of certain types of thought. I shall call it Traditional/Primitive Thought, or TP for short. I do not wish to be credited with any crude theories, or any theories at all, concerning the historical or other distribution of TP, or with any assumption to the effect that TP, is wholly or permanently in possession of the thought of any group, or wholly and permanently absent. All I do require for my argument is that TP should be an ideal type recognizably approximated by many actual ways of thought, and be seen to be logically incompatible with another style, which I shall call the Generalising/Scientific, or GS for short. The two are logically but not socially incompatible. In other words, they can co-exist in the same person, at the same time, and even applied to the same phenomenon, but the contents of a TP explanation will be inconsistent with that of a GS one" (pp. 86–87). (For further development of the implications of this "grand opposition," as he calls it, see his "Tractatus Sociologico-Philosophicus").
     40. The Revision is documented in a further five volumes, plus a posthumous volume of notes: *Primitive Mentality, The Soul of the Primitive, Primitives and the Supernatural, Primitive Mythology, L'Experience mystique et les symbols chez les primitifs*, and *The Notebooks on Primitive Mentality*. An interesting and plausible account of the nature of that revision – seeing primitive thought as magical rather than prelogical – can be found in O'Keefe's *Stolen Lightening*, pp. 86–90. It leaves Lévy-Bruhl's position on the contrast between primitive and modern thought untouched, however, although it highlights modern rather than primitive thought as peculiar (p. 88.)
     41. Lévy-Bruhl, *The Notebooks on Primitive Mentality*, p. 49. As will become obvious below, not all would agree with Lévy-Bruhl's "capitulation" here.
     42. Ibid., p. 49.

scientific man with a critical mind, but also that of the average person. . . . "[43] For Lévy-Bruhl, then, the facts require recognition of a diversity in unity when it comes to providing a theoretical account for the prima-facie differences of thought in archaic and modern societies. Not only does Lévy-Bruhl not deny the logical/physiological unity of mind in humankind, he also recognizes a continuity between the primitive and modern. Although seeing the modern mind (i.e., modern thought), as a development beyond the primitive, he nevertheless also sees that primitive mentality as still present to a degree in every human mind, only, as he puts it, "more marked and more easily observable among 'primitive people' than in our own societies. . . . "[44]

Having rejected the notions of "prelogical minds" and "a law of participation" he did not, however, abandon the concept of participation itself. Rather than explicating it in terms of logic, he invoked the

43. Ibid., p. 101. Certainly Evans-Pritchard noticed this (*A History*, p. 130), pointing out that for Lévy-Bruhl Christianity and Judaism were also superstitious – i.e., prelogical and mystical.

44. Sieber's *The Mirror of Medusa*, attempts to show a much stronger parallel between primitive and modern thought in this regard. His argument in a sense reverses that of Lévi-Strauss and the general anthropological view of primitive mentality. He writes: "it has been the practice in anthropology, perhaps beginning with Emile Durkheim, to deny vast intellectual differences among men, whether archaic or modern. This idea is central to structural anthropology, which contends that primitive thought strongly resembles technological thought. We seem to have reached the conclusion that primitive man already possesses the mental sophistication that we like to claim for ourselves. We have not, however, examined the opposite perspective that modern man may also apply the kind of superstitious logic long associated with primitives" (p. 12). Although he tries to develop a theory that sees superstition as a universal human activity, he does not altogether deny the distinction between primitive and modern scientific thought; he does not, that is, argue that they are identical (p. 34).

That, however, does seem to be argued for by Sewell in her *The Orphic Voice*, in which she maintains, against the likes of Lévy-Bruhl and Cassirer, that science is structurally similar to poetry and myth (pp. 13, 15, 19, 20, 38, *et passim*). She writes: "The human organism, that body which has the gift of thought, does not have the choice of two kinds of thinking. It has only one, in which the organism as a whole is engaged all along the line. There has been no progression in history from one type of thought to another" (p. 19). Sewell sees Bacon's attack on Aristotle and logic as the striving for a postlogical myth (a view of Bacon differing sharply from that presented by Jones in his *Ancients and Moderns*.) Something of Sewell's notion here seems to characterize much of the "new" philosophy of science from Polanyi and Kuhn and on, although that "subjectivist" stance among philosophers is not nearly so alive today. It must be noted, however, that Elias has come to a somewhat similar view on the relation of science (reason/dialectic) and poetry in his recent *Plato's Defense of Poetry*. I take a substantially different view of Plato, as will be seen in chapter 3.

notion of the "viewpoint of the knowledge of objects," as he puts it. When knowledge involves participation, he suggested in his notebooks, the understanding achieved "entails an important part of affective, not cognitive elements."[45] In fact, it appears as if this notion is already hinted at in the last chapter of *How Natives Think* entitled "The Transition to Higher Mental Types." He there raises the question as to the origin of myths, surmising them to be the products of a primitive mentality, "which appear when this mentality is endeavouring to realize a participation no longer directly felt – when it has recourse to intermediaries, and vehicles designed to secure a communion which has ceased to be a living reality. . . . "[46] The differences in mode of thought between primitives and moderns for Lévy-Bruhl, therefore, is both real and very important, but they are clearly epistemological differences and not purely logical ones, nor are they differences of brain physiology or differences of ontology. On that basis his position is quite plausible and has, indirectly at least, been perceived to be so. I shall show that Lévy-Bruhl did not stand alone in holding to a dichotomy view in accounting for the prima-facie differences of thought between primitives and moderns. Indeed, in many of his critics, it will become apparent – even as I have already indicated above – a similar view is readily adopted as explanatory of these differences. Furthermore, I will also show that much contemporary anthropology similarly adopts the dichotomy view, but now more carefully and forcefully argued, with auxiliary theories reinforced by

45. Lévy-Bruhl, *The Notebooks on Primitive Mentality*, p. 100.
46. Lévy-Bruhl, *How Natives Think*, p. 330. It is important to take notice here of the distinction between true prereflective primitive thought and the reflective, ordering primitive thought to be found in the "structuring" of myths. On this matter see especially Vernant's essay "The Reason of Myth." I discuss this matter further in chapter 3. A different kind of intelligence, not dealt with in this book, is also given scrutiny by Vernant, together with Detienne, in their *Cunning Intelligence in Greek Culture and Society*. It is an intelligence in contrast to that of the philosophers whose wisdom is concerned with the world of ideas. They write: "It is an intelligence which, instead of contemplating unchanging essences, is directly involved in the difficulties of practical life with all its risks, confronted with a world of hostile forces which are disturbing because they are always changing and ambiguous" (p. 44; see also, however, pp. 47, 305, *et passim*). However, see also Elkana's "The Emergence of Second-Order Thinking in Classical Greece." Although Elkana sees no linear progression from "cunning reason" to "epistemic reason," he nevertheless sees a direct connection between them. He writes: "It was exactly this approach [i.e., of cunning reason – *metis*] that developed the awareness of alternatives, which today is considered a basic characteristic of scientific thought" (p. 51).

confirming evidence not available to Lévy-Bruhl. The discussion of these matters will necessarily be merely indicative rather than exhaustive.

Lévy-Bruhl's hypothesis, although castigated in some respects by E. Cassirer, was, on the whole, virtually reproduced in Cassirer's own philosophy of symbolic forms. As early as *Language and Myth*, he insists that there are two modes of conception, mythic and discursive, which "represent entirely different tendencies of thought"; tendencies that are opposed. [47] Furthermore, the latter, referred to as reason by S. K. Langer in the introduction to this work, emerges out of the mythic and is not humankind's primitive endowment.[48]

This theme is developed in full in Cassirer's philosophy of symbolic forms and is especially clear in his *Mythical Thought*. Like Lévy-Bruhl, Cassirer sees myth as a form of primitive thought that, although in one sense a preparation for modern thought and modern knowledge, is yet in tension with it; the two are incompatible. Unlike those in the English intellectualist tradition in anthropology, however, Cassirer did not see this mythic thought as a mode of misunderstanding but rather as an archaic mode of understanding.[49] His ambivalence towards that archaic mode of understanding is obvious, as it is in Lévy-Bruhl, for he sees reason's emergence from mythic thought as a triumph over a kind of immaturity and yet is grateful for mythic thought as the origin of reason. Furthermore, he could not really bring himself to believe that mythic thought was irrational and for that reason felt Lévy-Bruhl to be essentially in error. He argued that, if one really understood the basic premises and presuppositions of primitives, their utterances/claims would not really appear to be illogical and irrational. That Lévy-Bruhl is guilty of such a charge, however, is highly questionable, as I shall point out below.[50]

---

47. Cassirer, *Language and Myth*, pp. 90–91.

48. Langer, "Introduction" to Cassirer, *Language and Myth*, p. ix. See also her essay "On Cassirer's Theory of Language and Myth." One might, given adequate time, fruitfully analyse Langer's own work on this and related subjects.

49. See Langer, "On Cassirer's Theory," and Strenski, "Ernst Cassirer's *Mythical Thought.*

50. However, on this score, see Bidney, "The Concept of Meta-Anthropology," p. 324; and Gellner, "Concepts and Society," pp. 132–33.

Evans-Pritchard, to whose work I have already adverted above, seems to have directed his theoretical work on primitive culture to undermining Lévy-Bruhl's thesis of the prelogical mentality. He did not, however, thereby espouse the intellectualism of his anthropological forebears such as Tylor, Frazer, et al. Like Lévy-Bruhl, he rejected the intellectualist/rationalist focus on literal understanding of the apparently illogical expressions of primitives, but unlike Lévy-Bruhl, he invoked the notion of the symbolic. In this position he was more akin to Cassirer although without the latter's Hegelian concern for "the progressive triumph of reason in history."[51] Consequently, "the symbolic" still stands in contrast and, I suggest, in tension with "the logical."

Evans-Pritchard and the symbolist school more generally, seem to affirm Lévy-Bruhl's later description/characterization of the primitive mind as one granting more importance to the affective meaning of symbols and concepts, and in so doing, they implicitly recognize a radical contrast between primitive and modern thought. This becomes immediately obvious, for example, in Mary Douglas who, contrary to intellectualist/rationalist presuppositions, insists that anthropologists must "remember that it is a practical interest in living and not an academic interest in metaphysics which has produced these beliefs . . . ," for in that perception "their whole significance alters."[52] She continues: "The anthropologist who draws out the whole scheme of the cosmos which is implied in these practices does the primitive culture great violence if he seems to present the cosmology as a systematic philosophy subscribed to consciously by individuals. We can study our own cosmology – in a specialised department of astronomy. But primitive cosmologies cannot rightly be pinned out for display like exotic lepidoptera, without distortion to the nature of a primitive culture."[53]

Other symbolist positions that focus attention on meaning more than on the function that primitive symbolic expression performs, also sit in the dichotomy camp in this debate. John Beattie, who shows some sympathy for Lévy-Bruhl in his quest to understand traditional

---

51. See Strenski, "Ernest Cassirer's *Mythical Thought*," p. 374. However, on this score, see also Barden, "Method and Meaning," pp. 127–28, for a different assessment of Evans-Pritchard. See also n. 16.

52. Douglas, *Purity and Danger*, p. 89.

53. Ibid., p. 91. See also n. 4 to chapter 1.

societies on their own terms, argues: "We do the grossest injustice to the subtle allusive and evocative power of language if we require all meaningful verbal expression to conform to the rules of syllogism and inductive inference. Coherent thinking can be symbolic as well as scientific, and if we are sensible we do not subject the language of poetry to the same kind of examination that we apply to a scientific hypothesis."[54] Traditional cultural complexes, therefore, must not be read as cognitive structures but rather as structures of expression.[55] As Beattie puts it, the symbols express humankind's "fundamental dependence on the natural world which he occupies and of which he is a part. We have seen that much ritual and religious behaviour translates uncontrollable natural forces into symbolic entities which, through the performance of ritual can be manipulated and dealt with. Ritual is a language for saying things which are felt to be true and important but which are not susceptible of statement in scientific terms."[56]

Not only is this symbolist gloss on Lévy-Bruhl's work not essentially different from his position, it is a variant of the dichotomy theory it critiques but one that has less cogency than the original. That much is clearly established in Ernest Gellner's critique of Evans-Pritchard in his "Concepts and Society." As Gellner points out, such a view is so charitable with respect to apparently contradictory statements in primitive contexts that it would also have to apply to the apparent absurdity of Lévy-Bruhl's theoretical claims. As Gellner sees it, "[i]f it be adopted as a principle that people cannot mean what at some level (e.g., implicitly through their conduct) they know to be false or absurd, then this principle must be applicable to Lévy-Bruhl too."[57] Such a principle, however, is then obviously too strong, for it means necessarily, "that no reasonably viable society can be said to be based on or to uphold absurd or 'pre-logical' doctrines."[58] It would be quite *arbitrary* and make nonsense of our original perception that some cultures make assertions which, prima facie, are quite contradictory and absurd. That

---

54. Beattie, *Other Cultures*, pp. 68–69.
55. Ibid., p. 71.
56. Ibid., p. 239. It is obvious that such expressionism is a kind of instrumentalism and hence functionalistic. It is not, however, reductionistic in the same sense as are the functionalist positions referred to above (see p. 227).
57. Gellner, "Concepts and Society," p. 133.
58. Ibid., p. 133.

kind of hermeneutic method forgives too much and precludes our ever arriving at an understanding of "the other." He writes:

> I do not wish to be misunderstood: I am *not* arguing that Evans-Pritchard's account of Nuer concepts is a bad one. (Nor am I anxious to revive a doctrine of pre-logical mentality *à la* Lévy-Bruhl.) On the contrary, I have the greatest admiration for it. What I am anxious to argue is that contextual interpretation, which offers an account of what assertions "really mean" in opposition to what they seem to mean in isolation, does not by itself clinch matters. It cannot arrive at determinate answers (concerning "what they mean") without doing a number of things which may in fact prejudge the question: without delimiting just which context is to be taken into consideration, without crediting the people concerned with consistency (which is precisely what is *sub judice* when we discuss, as Evans-Pritchard does, Lévy-Bruhl's thesis), or without assumptions concerning what they can mean (which, again, is precisely what we do not know but are trying to find out.)[59]

Furthermore, a persuasive rebuttal to the symbolist approach to understanding primitive cultures is contained in the recent renaissance of the old intellectualist approach to be found in the neo-Tyloreanism, so to speak, of Robin Horton.[60] Horton, in "African Traditional Thought and Western Science," argues that taking traditional systems of religious thought as they are understood by their sponsors is to understand them, in a serious sense, as theoretical thinking. Primitive religious myths, he maintains, originate as attempts to explain and control the environment in which the community concerned exists. And this casts serious doubt on the dichotomy approaches to understanding primitive thought, for it can make much more sense of what has until now appeared quite senseless.[61] "Like atoms, molecules and

59. Ibid., p. 136.
60. Horton has attacked this problem with persistence, and no analysis of the issues concerned can ignore his treatment of it. I list here some of his major essays: "African Traditional Thought and Western Science i, ii" (the two papers, abridged, were reprinted in Wilson's *Rationality*); "Neo-Tylorianism: Sound Sense or Sinister Prejudice?"; "Lévy-Bruhl Among the Scientists," *Second Order* 2 (1973); "Lévy-Bruhl, Durkheim and the Scientific Revolution" in Horton and Finnegan, *Modes of Thought*, see also his "Introduction" to that volume; "Material-Object Language and Theoretical Language"; "Tradition and Modernity Revisited," (with a reply to a response by M. Hollis); and "Social Psychologies: African and Western," a companion essay to the republication of Meyer Fortes's *Oedipus and Job in West African Religion*.
61. Horton, "African Traditional Thought," p. 152.

waves," he writes, "the gods serve to introduce unity into diversity, simplicity into complexity, order into disorder, regularity into anomaly."[62] For Horton, then, primitive persons can quite legitimately be understood as philosophers and/or scientists. Using a Popperian distinction, he does admit that traditional cultures are "closed," whereas scientific or modern cultures are "open," but he maintains that this dichotomy does not mimic those he criticizes, because the distinction between open and closed is not an essential one since both types of cultures still seek explanations and differ merely "in the idiom of the explanatory quest."[63] There is, he suggests, an awareness of alternatives in the explanatory quest that characterizes posttraditional cultures and has contributed to the tremendous development and growth of science in modern times.

Although Horton stresses continuity between primitive and modern thought, his use of the Popperian open/closed dichotomy seems to soften his critique of symbolist approaches. He draws back from any such suggestion in his later work, however – or at least appears to do so. In "Lévy-Bruhl, Durkheim and the Scientific Tradition," for example, he points out that Durkheim's work shows there to be a far more intimate connection between primitive and modern mentalities than Lévy-Bruhl had suspected,[64] and he insists that, in the light of recent empirical evidence, Durkheim's work has been far more prophetic and insightful.

In reviewing the treatment his own thesis has received in more than ten years of debate and discussion Horton in fact repudiates his own Popperian dichotomy, seeing it as "far too contrastive to do justice to the facts."[65] He further maintains that his continuity thesis, following Durkheim's lead, has remained virtually undamaged, although he does reformulate it to some degree. He admits, for example, that there are still contrasts between primitive and modern thought but sees the contrasts only in light of a common cognitive core shared by both types of culture.[66] In a later work that common cognitive core is identified, following the work of P. F. Strawson, with the "everyday material-object framework" that is taken to be common to primitives

62. Ibid., p. 134.
63. Ibid., p. 152.
64. Horton, "Lévy-Bruhl, Durkheim and The Scientific Revolution," pp. 267–68.
65. Horton, "Tradition and Modernity Revisited," pp. 211, 226.
66. Ibid., p. 228.

and moderns alike.[67] He then argues, however, that two levels of theory emerge from that common framework, namely, "primary theory," which is roughly equivalent to our commonsense, everyday discourse which is the same from community to community, and "secondary theory," which is a theoretical formulation that differs from community to community. While the latter transcends the former it is still also dependent on it,[68] making the former the ultimate source of criteria of truth on both the everyday and theoretical levels.

Horton grants that on the level of secondary theory primitives are more consensual whereas moderns are competitive, but he denies that that difference undermines the continuity thesis he has taken over from Durkheim. Similarly, he admits that at the level of secondary theory primitives opt for personalistic understanding (interpretation) whereas moderns invoke impersonal – causal-explanations, but he asserts that the contrast is insignificant, because each "is concerned above all to show order, regularity and predictability where primary theory has failed to show them."[69] That contrast, however, as the discussion to follow will show, is of considerably greater significance than Horton cares to recognize or acknowledge.

Horton's distinction between primary and secondary theory is reminiscent of a similar distinction of kinds of science in another representative of modern intellectualist anthropology – that is, Lévi-Strauss. In *The Savage Mind* Lévi-Strauss argues that, like modern western persons, primitives are also motivated by other than merely survival needs; that they are also motivated by purely theoretical interests, a desire to construct conceptual frameworks; and that consequently they have elaborate categorial systems of plants, trees, animals, etc., that are not simply tied to taming the physical environment. As he puts it in a later volume, "they [i.e., the primitives] are moved by a need or a desire to understand the world around them, its nature and their society. On the other hand, to achieve that end, they proceed by intellectual means, exactly as a philosopher, or even to some extent a scientist, can and would do."[70]

Though Lévi-Strauss, like Horton, seems to reject the Lévy-Bruhlian dichotomy thesis, there are ambiguities in his own position that, as

67. Horton, "Material Object Language and Theoretical Language."
68. Ibid., p. 230.
69. Horton, "Tradition and Modernity Revisited," p. 237.
70. Lévi-Strauss, *Myth and Meaning*, p. 16.

with Horton again, indicate a lack of success. For even Lévi-Strauss admits that this kind of primitive thinking is scientific only in a very limited sense, since it differs radically from modern western science as we commonly understand it. It is, he says, both different from it and inferior to it because of what he calls its "totalitarian ambition" that requires everything to be understood if anything is to be understood. Consequently: "myth is unsuccessful in giving man more material power over the environment. However, it gives man, very importantly, the illusion that he can understand the universe and that he does understand the universe. It is, of course, only an illusion."[71] As Robert Zimmerman has quite correctly observed, Lévi-Strauss has confused one element of science, namely that of classifying and ordering, with the essential aspect of science as explanatory and theoretical.[72] Abstract, theoretical, scientific thinking is characteristic of modern society but not of primitive societies. Consequently, it appears that Lévi-Strauss has reintroduced the very distinction he set out to transcend, by talking of a logic of the concrete, characteristic of primitives, and of a logic of abstract, theoretical science, characteristic of moderns only.[73]

It is obvious from this discussion that the claims of Lévi-Strauss and Horton that the human mind is everywhere the same and operates in a similar fashion encounter serious problems. For each, a new dichotomy – two kinds of theory; two kinds of science – replaces the old, but it functions as did the old.

An excellent general account of the intellectualist/symbolist debate, emerging from an encounter between Horton and the author,[74] can be found in John Skorupski's *Symbol and Theory: A Philosophical Study of Theories of Religion in Social Anthropology*. Although Skorupski's original encounter with Horton was a defence of a symbolic (and therefore dichotomous) understanding of primitive religious thought, the later work is much more sympathetic to the new intellectualism. Nevertheless, Skorupski's final verdict is a far cry from victory for that view: "The 'Lévy-Bruhlian' character of religious thought," he writes, "remains

71. Ibid., p. 17.

72. Zimmerman, "Lévi-Strauss and the Primitive."

73. Goody, for example, sees Lévi-Strauss as guilty of ethnocentrism, in his *Domestication of the Savage Mind*, p. 8. See also his (with I. Watt), "Literate Culture."

74. Skorupski's parry is found in his "Science and Traditional Religious Thought." Horton responded with "Paradox and Explanation: A Reply to Mr. Skorupski."

unaccounted for by intellectualism: the classic issues of interpretation and explanation it poses remain wide open."[75]

Although recognizing the dissatisfaction with Lévy-Bruhl's understanding of primitive mentality, I have also shown that much of the criticism he has suffered has been misdirected and that the perspectives on primitive thought proposed as alternatives to his have often been found to be even more seriously flawed than the original. However, pointing out the weaknesses of the opposition is not in itself a justification of Lévy-Bruhl's position. There is much recent work, however, that does lend weight to a modified dichotomy view, such as Lévy-Bruhl came to hold towards the end of his life.[76] I shall limit discussion

75. Skorupski, *Symbol and Theory*, p. 221.

76. I have already intimated above that not everyone agrees with Lévy-Bruhl's modifications to this theory; there are some, that is, who do not accept the "doctrine of the unity of the human mind," and try to build a case for a more radical diversity. Needham, for example (in *Belief, Language and Experience*), maintains that the general intellectualist finds support only in an uncritical use of the interpretive concept of belief which takes for granted the existence of "a human mind" that is the same in all periods of time and all places. Such an "axiomatic approach," he insists, further presumes that it is the Aristotelian thought processes of the European mind in their clearest embodiment that constitute "the standard mind," whereas there may exist equally valid forms of ideation that are quite different and that may be the result of genetic differences or of the development of different culture-related logics. To acknowledge this possibility in a genuine comparative study of cultures, he concludes, seriously weakens the claims of the intellectualists: "The premises of an absolute conception of human experience against which cultural styles of thought and action can be objectively assessed, disintegrates; and its place is taken by an apprehension of conceptual relativity in which variant representations of man and his powers confusedly contend" (p. 185). I have subjected Needham's views to examination in a review-article in *Philosophical Studies* 22 (1974). A position similar to Needham's but concerned with "religious thought" is to be found in the work of W. C. Smith – especially in his *Belief and History* – and in Bellah's, *Beyond Belief*. I have considered those positions in my "The Role of Belief in the Study of Religion."

Jaynes, on the other hand, unhesitatingly argues a biological thesis. Crudely summarized, there are radically different forms of thought, both in the evolutionary development of humankind as well as in individual persons, both past and present, and likely so in the future, as a result of brain "malfunction." These modes of thought are, paradoxically, both complementary and working at cross-purposes. Although his thesis, as expressed in *The Origin of Consciousness*, makes for enjoyable reading, it is hardly persuasive. A similar kind of argument, although not concerned directly with the matter here but with some relevance, can be found in Koestler's "Is Man's Brain an Evolutionary

here to the more interesting and persuasive aspects of that recent work.

Within a few years of Lévy-Bruhl's death several scholars working within a Lévy-Bruhlian inspired dichotomy framework produced ground-breaking discoveries in understanding the cultural life of the ancient Near East, their results being published under the title *Before Philosophy: The Intellectual Adventure of Ancient Man.*[77] Even though some of the essays contained in the volume are critical of the stronger formulations of Lévy-Bruhl's thesis, they nevertheless maintain that there is an obvious and radical distinction between primitive and modern minds. H. Frankfort, for example, writes: "Myth is a form of poetry which transcends poetry in that it proclaims a truth; a form of reasoning which transcends reasoning in that it wants to bring about the truth it proclaims; a form of action, of ritual behaviour, which does not find its fulfilment in the act but must proclaim and elaborate a poetic form of truth."[78] Frankfort then sets out to provide a kind of anatomy of this mode of thought – which he refers to as mythopoeic. And that structure clearly resembles Lévy-Bruhl's perception of the primitive mind, for it involves, *inter alia,* (1) constant reference to supermundane powers and beings (agents), (2) qualitative concepts of time and space, (3) a radically different – personalistic/agentic – notion of causality, and iv a failure to distinguish between appearance and reality. That mythopoeic and modern thought are mutually exclusive, is clearly brought out by Frankfort: "the cosmologies of mythopoeic thought are basically revelations received in a confrontation with a cosmic 'Thou'. And one cannot argue about a revelation; it transcends reason."[79]

As is to be expected, the Frankfort group has come in for a good deal of criticism, but the best and latest research on and interpretation of ancient Near Eastern culture seems rooted in the same theoretical framework, as I shall show in some detail below (chapter 5).

Mistake?" One might also consult Sagan's *The Dragons of Eden.* Views of this physical/physiological kind ought not, however, to be wholly abandoned – especially in light of split-brain research. See, for example, Maclean's *A Triune Concept of Brain and Behaviour,* and other interesting developments such as the holographic theory of mind – for example in Pribram's *Languages of the Brain* or Pietsch's, *Shuffle Brain.* See also Wilbur, *The Holographic Paradigm.*

77. H. and H. A. Frankfort (et al.), *Before Philosophy.*

78. Ibid., p. 16.

79. Ibid. p. 262.

Jean Piaget's structuralism is another source of support for the dichotomy view, especially as it is used by C. R. Hallpike in his very impressive study of primitive cultures in *The Foundations of Primitive Thought*. Piaget's research on the cognitive development of the individual reveals an epigenetic series of levels of mental development from sensori-motor and pre-operational, through concrete-operational, to formal ways of thought. A detailed theoretical account of that structure is provided by Jean Piaget in his *Biology and Knowledge*. The argument it contains, especially as interpreted by Hallpike, suggests that primitive thinking is to be equated with the thinking of the child and therefore differs from modern thought to the same degree that the thinking of the child at the pre-operatory (or possibly concrete-operational) stage differs from the adult at the formal stage. In this form much of the essential thrust of the Lévy-Bruhlian thesis is retained, as even the harshest of critics is ready to admit: "The theory may be too neat," writes G. S. Kirk, "but it leads to a more than usually acceptable version of the 'childhood of the race' idea."[80]

Hallpike argues convincingly that only a clear theory of learning and of cognitive growth will help resolve the question as to "modes of thought." Such a theory must attempt to understand how thinking develops in relation to the total environment. Cognitive growth, he maintains, is only one particular aspect of a general organic adaptation to the environment, and neither hereditary characteristics nor environmental structures but rather the interaction between the two complexes accounts for the patterns of growth in organisms, including cognitive growth. From such an interactionist perspective it follows that, since the environment of traditional societies is not as cognitively demanding as that of modern western societies, individuals within them will "stabilize," as he puts it, at a level of development below that of formal thought. In fact, he argues, primitives are usually found to be at the pre-operatory stage of thought.[81] This means that primitive thought, although radically different from modern thought, is not absolutely different; it is thought "based on an incomplete logic rather than on a different logic from that which we know. . . . "[82] Such a view

80. See Kirk, *Myth: Its Meaning and Functions*, p. 276 n. 42.

81. Hallpike, *Foundations of Primitive Thought*, p. 24.

82. Ibid., p. 489. Arieti, in *Creativity: The Magic Synthesis*, uses the term "paleological" to describe it. The term is, I think, for reasons spelled out in chapter 3, apt. The same notion is taken up by Goldstein in his "Concerning the Concept of 'Primitivity'."

appears to account for the final position that seems to have been adopted by Lévy-Bruhl in his notebooks, namely, that all persons, primitives and moderns alike, seem to operate, in varying degrees, in both modes of thought.[83] We have here a theory of duality in unity that has a wide range of supporting evidence; the doctrine of the unity of the mind in regards to its potentiality/capacity is seen still to allow for radically different – even mutually (logically) exclusive – modes of thought. Indeed, Hallpike goes so far as to claim that, "it is worth observing that if we substitute the term 'pre-operatory' for 'pre-logical' in his [i.e., Lévy-Bruhl's] work, many of his observations on primitive thought have some justification."[84] There is no doubt in Hallpike's mind, therefore, that Piaget's concepts and categories offer by far the best analytical tools in accounting for the differences in the ways of thinking between primitives and moderns. As he puts it in the conclusion to his study: "It has been shown in detail that primitive thought generally conforms to Piaget's criterion of the advanced stages of pre-operatory thought at the level of collective representations. But it has been a consistent theme of this study that pre-operatory thought is not absurd or mistaken, but rather of limited generality and much more restricted to the phenomenal appearance of things than our own."[85]

Recent attention to changes in what Goody has referred to as "the technology of the intellect" seems to lend even further support to a

83. Hallpike, *Foundations of Primitive Thought*, p. 33.

84. Ibid., p. 50. It is interesting to note here that Piaget, in a conversation with Bringuier (*Conversations With Jean Piaget*), actually refers to the mode of thought of the child at the preoperational level as prelogical. Bringuier is so surprised by Piaget's response that he remarks in a footnote: "The very tranquillity of his comments, its matter-of-fact tone, were probably what brought me face to face with what it meant – brought it home to me. Clearly, the child's reasoning did not rest on an inarticulate or poorly formulated logic; it wasn't a clumsy attempt at adult logic. It owed nothing to that logic. It rested instead on something else, another world – a world that Piaget had been exploring for a long time. From what he said, I sensed the dimensions, the true perspective, of his research – or at least I believed that I did" (p. 33). There is also some suggestion in the work of Piaget and his colleagues that what holds for the child moving into adulthood holds also for "humankind"; see, for example, the ninth conversation entitled "Games for Children and Scholars: Toward a Comparative History of Individual Intelligence and Scientific Progress."

85. Hallpark, *Foundations of Primitive Thought*, p. 489. Two recent studies of medieval society based in part on Piaget's work present further support for the dichotomy thesis presented here. I became aware of these studies too late to incorporate them into my anaylsis. See Radding, *A World Made by Man*, and Le Pan, *The Cognitive Revolution in Western Culture*.

Lévy-Bruhlian view of the primitive mind, despite the fact that Goody's own views on that score are somewhat ambiguous. In *The Domestication of the Savage Mind* Goody takes up the Lévy-Bruhlian question as to how modes of thought have changed, but he questions the categories in terms of which that question has been tackled by others. He does not wish to deny that there are differences in thought or mind between primitives and moderns but argues that "great divide theories" use a binary we/they set of categories which are ethnocentric and misleading: "We speak in terms of primitive and advanced," he writes, "almost as if human minds themselves differed in their structure like machines of an earlier and later design."[86] Despite the disclaimers, however, which, significantly, are frequently interjected into Goody's analysis, he does argue that the advent of literacy has brought about great changes in that it has in fact brought about changes of cognitive structures in human societies. Indeed, Goody even claims that literacy is responsible for the emergence of logic and philosophy[87] which, presumably, did not exist up to that point.[88] Goody himself has a

86. Goody, *The Domestication of the Savage Mind*, p. 1.

87. Ibid., p. 44.

88. I think it worth remarking here that Goody gives credit for that emergence of philosophy and logic to Thales and the Milesians (i.e., to the Presocratics generally, as he does, more ambiguously, however, in his essay with Watt entitled "The Consequences of Literacy"), because I argue, in the chapter to follow, that it is precisely in pinpointing a revolution of thought to a particular period in history, that provides a kind of empirical support to the Lévy-Bruhlian thesis. Goody, especially in the earlier ("Consequences") essay, claims to reject the Lévy-Bruhlian dichotomy (pp. 43, 44, 67) and yet rejects the "over-reaction" to Lévy-Bruhl as well (p. 67), and talks of taking up a position that recognizes, "somewhat along the lines suggested by Lévy-Bruhl" (p. 44), the general differences that exist between literate and nonliterate societies. Indeed, it is for that reason that Goody is taken to task by Street in his *Literacy in Theory and Practice*, wherein he writes: "Where Lévy-Bruhl's . . . version of the 'great divide' theory claimed differences in cognitive *capacity* between members of different cultures, those appealing to literacy simply claim differences in cognitive *development*. The suggestion is no longer that a culture has acquired such technological skills as literacy because it is intellectually superior, as earlier racist theories had argued. Rather, it is claimed that a culture is intellectually superior because it has acquired that technology" (p. 29). It is obvious from this passage, however, that Street misreads Lévy-Bruhl (i.e., in a psychologistic vein) and that he fails to see what vast effects differences in cognitive development can have (although not altogether so, as can be seen in his remarks about the social and political – i.e., bureaucratic – advantages that literacy provides [p. 119]). Furthermore, he misreads Goody and Watt in attributing to them a sharp dichotomy (p. 47, *et passim*). Street sees their reliance upon the example of classical Greece as weak, since literacy was not invented in Greece (p. 50), as if they were ignorant of that fact, and he fails to see that

dichotomy view, although he does not see a contrast between primitive and modern but rather between oral and literate societies.[89] Writing makes speech objective (i.e., depersonalized, abstract), in that it makes it a visual concern as well as an aural one, and he admits that in doing this there is created the possibility of a different kind of rational/critical examination of thought – i.e., the development of a kind of sceptical thinking not possible without writing.[90]

Goody is aware of the paradox of his verbal rejection of the grand dichotomy thesis and his continued invocation of dichotomies in his work, and particularly the dichotomy of his contrast between utterance and text,[91] but he does not see that as indicating a "great divide" between types of cultures and modes of thought. His argument that there is the possibility of communication between literate and illiterate persons is not sufficient however, to persuade one of the identity of the structures of thought in archaic/traditional/primitive societies on the one hand and modern/philosophic/scientific societies on the other.

Goody's later work seems to support such a critical interpretation of his position, especially his essay on "Thought and Writing," inspired, it appears, by the work of Soviet psychologists and ethnologists. He acknowledges more freely here that changes of the means of communication subsequent to the emergence of speech may have important implications for the structure of ideas within a society; that such change may lead to the development of a special cognitive style.[92] Writing affects the cognitive processes in important ways which generate cultural differences that he sees as bearing a striking similarity to earlier dichotomies – (i.e., Lévy-Bruhlian dichotomies like primitive/advanced, simple/complex, etc.) – assumed to exist between domesticated and savage thought.[93] The change is summed up adequately

---

it is, although only in part, because of the peculiar nature of that literacy as "alphabetic literacy" that they make these claims. On that particular issue Goody and Watt rely heavily on the work of Havelock; see, therefore, Havelock's recent "The Alphabetic Mind," which, of course, was not then available to them. See also Goody's recent general and synthetic treatment of some of these issues in his *The Logic of Writing*, and *The Interface Between the Written and the Oral*.

89. Goody, *Domestication of the Savage Mind*, p. 43.

90. Ibid., pp. 37, 43. Goody emphasizes that written language is not simply a visual representation of the oral, but rather a *different* kind of communication (see pp. 127–28).

91. Ibid., p. 151.

92. Goody, "Thought and Writing," pp. 120–21.

93. Ibid., pp. 129–30.

when he writes: "If we presume some functional relation between language-using and the higher psychological functions, there is an apriori case for assuming that further changes in the mode of communication might affect internal cognitive processes. In terms of the development of human society, and hence of human potentialities as well as achievements, the most important subsequent change is from oral to written language, a shift which of course adds to rather than replaces the cultural equipment available to a society."[94]

In fact, Goody perceives the possibilities of effect on internal cognitive processes in the strongest possible terms in suggesting possible psychological correlates for the differences: "The different implications of oral and written communication for cognitive development may also have important psychological correlates, arising out of the hemisphere differences in the brain which influence the processing of sensory material."[95]

Others have similarly noticed radical differences between oral cultures and cultures built around the act of writing. Walter Ong's work, for example, and especially his *Orality and Literacy: The Technologizing of the Word*,[96] focuses attention on "the modern discovery of primary oral cultures" that seems to echo Lévy-Bruhl's discovery of a prelogical mind. Ong argues that we are only now beginning to realize that "it takes only a moderate degree of literacy to make a tremendous difference in thought processes."[97] Ong's work is also replete with binary contrasts, including formulaic/nonformulaic thought patterns and oral/literate noetic structures, although this does not constitute a naive restatement of the original Lévy-Bruhlian dichotomy of the prelogical and logical mind.

The work of Eric Havelock also recognizes a contrast of cultures and modes of thought generated by the birth of literacy and the concomitant revolution in what he calls "the technology of education." As early as *The Crucifixion of Intellectual Man* and *The Liberal Temper in Greek Politics* Havelock writes about "civil war" in western culture, connecting that with "the ascendancy of intellectual man," which in turn is linked to the emergence of literacy.[98] It is in his *Preface to Plato*,

---

94. Ibid., p. 120.
95. Ibid., p. 130.
96. See also his *The Presence of the Word*; and *Interfaces of the Word*.
97. Ong, *Orality and Literacy*, p. 50.
98. In *The Crucifixion of Intellectual Man*, pp. 23–24.

however, that he stresses "the great transition," as he puts it, *away* from the poetic and *towards* the conceptual. As he states it: "The poetic experience is the function of a faculty which accepts a constant wandering and contradiction in physical reporting; one which is alien to number and calculation."[99] Consequently, for Havelock, the modern mind is the result of a conversion "from the image-world of the epic to the abstract world of scientific description. . . . "[100] And this is a process that he sees coming to fruition in Plato's theory of forms, the net effect of which is "to dramatise the split between the image-thinking of poetry and the abstract thinking of philosophy."[101] He concludes, therefore, that the new idiom of discourse in Plato (although, admittedly, prefigured in earlier writing), ushered in a new development – the emergence of the nonmythic "Greek and European mind."[102]

The force of Havelock's claims finds even further support in the essays, written over a period of twenty years, in his *The Literate Revolution in Greece and Its Cultural Consequences*,[103] devoted to analysing the effects of the introduction of the alphabet into early Greek culture. Space does not permit an analysis of that material, but a brief mention of two claims made (and substantiated) in those essays is important, for they seem fully to support a Lévy-Bruhlian approach to understanding the differences between traditional and modern societies. First, Havelock sees the development of the Greek alphabet as "a piece of explosive technology, revolutionary in its effects on human culture, in a way not precisely shared by any other invention."[104] It created "the alphabetic mind"[105] which alone is the foundation for the emergence of philosophy and the modern sciences. Secondly, although a new mind emerges, later antiquity never wholly discarded the "oral habit" and

99. Havelock, *Preface to Plato*, p. 239.

100. Ibid., pp. 258–59.

101. Ibid., p. 266. In the chapter to follow I shall argue that the split emerges with the Presocratics. Others who have argued such a split see it as coming much later (as Havelock sees it coming with Plato). Reiss, more recently (in *The Discourse of Modernism*) argues a radical difference between a "discourse of patterning" (an episteme of resemblence) and an "analytico-referential discourse" but sees it emerging only after the seventeenth century. He does, however, see the Presocratics as "precursors" to that development.

102. Havelock, *Preface to Plato*, p. 267.

103. These essays deserve close and detailed examination which cannot, however, be given here.

104. Havelock, *The Literate Revolution in Greece*, p. 6.

105. Ibid., p. 7.

in consequence never fully recognized the new emergent reality. Furthermore, although a revolutionary invention, the spread of the use and effects of the alphabet was drawn out over many generations and was simply too gradual for participants in the process to be aware of its significance. This said, a strong case for seeing the emergence of the modern mind in ancient Greece can be made.[106]

A FURTHER REFORMULATION

It appears from this lengthy discussion that there is no unanimity as to how to account for the prima facie differences between primitive and modern patterns of thought, although the fact of the manifest dissimilarity of those patterns is granted by all.[107] It also seems to be widely accepted that the early, and stronger, formulation of Lévy-Bruhl's thesis is a failure, but it is also agreed that his critical questioning of long-standing assumptions in the study of primitive cultures was on target. Moreover, the devastating criticisms of the theories of the symbolists and the critiques of the neointellectualists (i.e., neo-Tyloreans) makes Lévy-Bruhl's revised thesis much more attractive. His view of modes of thought, *not as two absolutely different enterprises*, but rather as two kinds of activity of one mind, with different qualities of thought predominating in any particular society, seems to account for the ethnographic facts more persuasively than any of the alternative proposals. The emergence of one mode of thought from the other implies neither the (logical) compatibility of the two nor the necessary disappearance of the first upon the arrival of the second.[108] What does seem to be implied, however, is that their mutual coherence – should they both persist through time – can be maintained only by the one being made subservient to the other. By the dominance of one mode of thought over the other, then, it is obvious that both can coexist, even

106. See, for example, Havelock, "The Alphabetic Mind," in which he claims that the alphabetic and nonalphabetic mind are in conflict throughout the history of Greek culture, (pp. 139, 144). Graham's recent book, *Beyond the Written Word*, is based on Havelock's work, and, with some qualification of Havelock's thesis as he understands it Graham argues that the foundational scriptural texts of religious traditions are fundamentally mythopoeic in character. See also, in more specific terms, Kelber's *The Oral and the Written Gospel*.

107. Gellner refers to this fact as "the biggest, most conspicuous simple fact about the human world"; ("An Ethic of Cognition," p. 175).

108. See n. 39.

if they are logically incompatible, but only one controls or organizes the analysis and understanding of the majority of enterprises/practices within each specific culture/society.[109] The reformulated Lévy-Bruhlian thesis finds a good deal of empirical support, as I have shown above, in the work of psychologists like J. Piaget and in contemporary research into the discovery/emergence of writing and its cultural consequences. In the chapter to follow I shall argue that this Lévy-Bruhlian theory best accounts for – explains – the emergence of the Greek philosophic/scientific tradition that is the soil from which our modern scientific culture springs. Philosophical support for that account is persuasively set out by E. Gellner in his "The Savage and the Modern Mind,"[110] a brief description of which I provide here.

109. According to Reiss (*Discourse of Modernism*) such a dominant mode of thought or episteme is always accompanied by a dominant occulted epistemic practice (p. 11). His analysis suggests much, but examination of his claims and their implications cannot be taken up here.

110. Gellner's position finds support in Horton and Finnegan, *Modes of Thought*, from Lukes, in "On the Social Determination of Truth," which is, in turn, an attack on the essay by Barry Barnes, "The Comparison of Belief-Systems: Anomaly Versus Falsehood," which proposes a "symbolist" stance with respect to the understanding of other cultures. Lukes' understanding of Lévy-Bruhl as a "symbolist," however, seems to me a misreading of Lévy-Bruhl's work. Tambiah's paper ("Form and Meaning of Magical Acts: A Point of View") makes use of the notion of analogy in understanding nonwestern modes of thought but with greater subtlety than one finds in Barnes. Tambiah insists that we must recognize that magical acts, for example, are not pervaded by a scientific intentionality, yet he argues: "Although we should not judge their *raison d'être* in terms of applied science, we should however recognize that many (but not all) magical acts are elaborated and utilized precisely in those circumstances where non-western man has not achieved that special kind of 'advanced' scientific knowledge which can control and act upon reality to an extent that reaches far beyond the realm of his own practical knowledge" (p. 226). Modern thought for Tambiah, therefore, is both different from and yet also an advance beyond archaic thought.

The remaining essays in the Horton and Finnegan volume (with the exception of the introduction and Horton's essay on Lévy-Bruhl and Durkheim already referred to above), though concerned with thinking in western and nonwestern societies, do not directly impinge on the question of "modes of thought" as I have structured it here – or at least not significantly so. Finnegan's "Literary versus Non-Literary: The Great Divide?", for example, has only limited relevance, for she seems to suggest that those who argue for a significant difference between oral and literate cultures imply that the expression of insight and understanding is necessarily dependent upon writing (pp. 118, 122). That, however, is clearly not the case, as has already been shown above. Wolfram's essay, "Basic Differences of Thought," however, focuses helpfully on the question of what kind of differences of thought might qualify as basic. And Jenkins's

According to Gellner there are four crucial distinctions between the primitive and the scientific mind. First, there is the use of idiosyncratic norms in primitive thought that is both cognitive and moral at the same time. "A traditional belief-system contains at least one general vision of 'what is normal,'"[111] whereas in scientific society the cognitive base-lines are not at the same time the framework of a social and moral order. The scientific outlook is mechanistic and therefore is in conflict with traditional society's provision of a meaningful world-picture through its use of idiosyncratic norms – its "bending of the regularity expectations in the interest of the local status-system. . . . "[112]

A second crucial distinction is to be found in the low cognitive division of labour in primitive societies, accompanied by a proliferation of roles for the individual in that society. Gellner argues that "the enchanted vision works through the systematic conflation of descriptive, evaluative, identificatory, status-conferring, etc. role of language [and that] a sense of the separability and fundamental distinctness of the various functions, [originally and innocently introduced as a neutral analytical device], is the surest way to the disenchantment of the world."[113] Once concepts have become tools for explanation, they cannot be allowed, on pain of the loss of coherence and efficiency, to be tools for other purposes. Gellner illustrates this point by showing how empiricist thought has discouraged use, for example, of the same concept to be applied to matters in the world and to the transcendent. It discourages what he calls systematic boundary-hopping. "Orderly and regular conduct," he writes, "is exacted from concepts, as it is from people."[114]

"Religion and Secularism: The Contemporary Significance of Newman's Thought" in some sense provides support for Lévy-Bruhl's suggestion (referred to in chapter 1) that "religious thought" is mythopoeic in character and therefore significantly different from modern or scientific thought.

111. Gellner, "The Savage and the Modern Mind," p. 170.

112. Ibid., p. 172. There are some interesting parallels to Gellner on the issues of meaning and knowledge (truth) to be found in the first volume of Arendt's *The Life of the Mind, Thinking*. In the introduction she writes: "To anticipate, and put in a nutshell. *The need of reason is not inspired by the quest for truth but by the quest for meaning. And truth and meaning are not the same thing*" (p. 15; emphasis in the original). She does not, however, deny all connection between "thinking's quest for meaning and knowledge's quest for truth" (p. 62).

113. Ibid., p. 174.

114. Ibid., p. 176.

The diffused and persuasive quality of the entrenched clauses of the intellectual constitution of the primitive mind, Gellner suggests, is a third crucial distinction between it and modern scientific consciousness. Gellner recognizes that *all* societies have such entrenched or sacred (i.e., untouchable/unquestionable) claims, but he also insists that they are much more extensive and numerous amongst primitives: "Fewer hostages are given to fortune; or, looking at it from the other end, much less of the fabric of life and society benefits from reinforcement from the sacred and entrenched convictions."[115]

The fourth and final distinction between the savage and the modern mind is what Gellner refers to as "the diplomatic immunity of cognition," by which he means that ever greater areas of truth acquire autonomy from "the social, moral and political obligations and decencies of society." In primitive societies cognition is subject to the same kinds of obligations and sanctions as are other kinds of conduct, whereas in modern society this is not so – truth and knowledge are not controlled according to the effects they may have. Such autonomy, however, does not mean that they are philosophically neutral for they (i.e., truth and knowledge) can and often do come into conflict with the entrenched clauses of older traditional belief-systems.

This description of the chasm between the primitive and the modern mind is, I suggest, entirely consistent with the general conclusion about the nature of the primitive mind required of us after the foregoing discussion; and it is also, I think, philosophically persuasive.[116] I will not, however, rest content with the argument as it stands with Lévy-Bruhl. I shall provide for it a groundwork of empirical evidence in the process of pinpointing, so to speak, the (historical) emergence of the modern mind in the intellectual developments of ancient Greece. The argument of the chapter to follow will show that, with the development of the philosophy/science of the Milesian thinkers and their successors, we also have the development of that chasm between the savage and the modern mind pointed to by Lévy-Bruhl.

115. Ibid., p. 178.
116. There are, however, a number of general problems regarding rationality in general that are left unresolved. On this score see especially the essays in Wilson, *Rationality*. In particular, see Lukes, "Some Problems About Rationality" and Hollis, "The Limits of Irrationality."

III

Religion and Philosophy in Ancient Greece

IN THE PRECEDING CHAPTER I attempted to defend a Lévy-Bruhlian account of the great divide that separates and distinguishes the content and structure of the belief-systems in the modern West from those in archaic/tribal cultures. There is, I argued, a chasm that separates the savage from the modern mind. I shall contend here that the emergence of philosophy with the Greeks corroborates such a view. Indeed, a review of the history of the interpretations of that process of emergence will all but demonstrate that we have with the Greeks *the historical origins* – the birth – of the modern mind. The thinking of the Presocratics will be seen to constitute a revolution of such magnitude that from this point on we find the Greeks to be in two minds; Greek philosophy, in (progressively) abandoning the medium of myth, created a mode of thought that transcends the essentially mythopoeic thinking of the traditionally religious Greek mind. Philosophy does not, however, simply replace religion in ancient Greece, it only emerges as another and alternative "form of life." And it will become apparent that the two modes of thought/forms of life are logically incompatible.[1]

---

1. It is interesting to note here, *vis-à-vis* the Lévy-Bruhl thesis, the change in the concept of *phronein* in the history of Greek usage. Onians, in *The Origins of European Thought*, points out that "In later Greek φρονεῖν has primarily an intellectual sense, 'to think, have understanding,' but in Homer it is more comprehensive, covering undifferentiated psychic activity . . . involving 'emotion,' and 'conation' . . . " (p. 14). That is, the concept the later Greeks used, or that we ourselves use, to refer to intellectual awareness,

has a far richer meaning involving feelings and emotion in Premilesian usage – in, for example, Homer. Onians maintains that there is in the earlier usage a primal unity between perception and cognition on the one hand and action on the other. There is a complex reality of the knower and the known embodied in the action of the organism. In consequence, earlier thought is less detached than later thought which implies a change in modes of thought with that development. Onians writes: "Where cognition and thought are so bound up with feeling and tendency to act, the relation of moral character, and of virtue to knowledge, is closer than where cognition is more 'pure.' How emotional and prone to physical expression of their emotions Homer's heroes were we have seen. Greeks like Aristotle and we today have apparently attained to greater 'detachment,' power of thinking in cold blood without bodily movement, as we have to a sharper discrimination and definition of the aspects and phases of the mind's activity" (p. 18). It is with this knowing self as detached, as spectator, that persons came to identify themelves as distinct from the world and values. The thought of Homeric persons is explicitly compared to the thought of Lévy-Bruhlian primitives (p. 20). He admits that there is no such reality as purely cognitive thought but that there is a significant difference of degree in the impurity of the cognitive thoughts of Homeric and post-Homeric persons, although he seems to read the transition of thought in distinctly negative tones: "Most of us are, perhaps, inwardly calmer and outwardly more restrained than '*les primitifs*,' and we have learned to differentiate conceptually, to analyse a complex state of mind into abstract elements with separate names which create the illusion of separate existence. We lack terms like φρονεῖν for the complex unity which is the reality" (p. 20).

Guthrie reminds us in his *The Greek Philosophers* of "how close were the Greeks in early times, and many of the common people throughout the classical period, to the magical stage of thought" (p. 12). And, like Onians's, Guthrie's talk of magical thought, and "the law of sympathy" are compared to Lévy-Bruhl's categories. Although Guthrie thinks Lévy-Bruhl's distinctions too exaggerated, he sees some point in the comparison, for it is only when we see this "odd" character of the earliest/religious Greek thinkers that we can really appreciate the overwhelming and revolutionary character of the Milesian achievements (see also his *A History of Greek Philosophy*, vol. 1, p. 40). It is an emancipation (*The Greek Philosophers*, p. 16). The Presocratics are not "primitives" – superior medicine-men with a dash of rational thought thrown in – but new kinds of thinkers altogether. Guthrie admits that the emergence of this new mode of thought (see *The Greeks and Their Gods*, p. xii) is not sudden but rather slow and gradual (*A History*, vol. 1, p. 1), but that it is, nevertheless, something quite new. This justifies us in calling Thales the first European philosopher, for one sees in Thales and the other Milesians the abandoning of mythological solutions and their replacement with intellectual solutions (ibid., p. 44). This modified Lévy-Bruhlian interpretation of Guthrie's can also be seen in his use of the Frankfort thesis (see chapter 5) in his history of Greek philosophy (ibid., pp. 28, 40–41). It should be noted here, however, that even though Guthrie seems to support the thesis I shall be developing in this chapter, he does not, nor do I, "condemn" myth as false in itself. He even goes so far as to refer to Plato's use of myth as "genuine myth" (ibid., p. 2), although he does not set out how that is distinguished from myth that is not genuine. Although I do not condemn myth, I do wish to make it very clear that I do not consider it possible that myth and science can, *logically*, coexist in the same mind. This does not mean that they can never appear side by side in the same society

The difficulties in assessing the meaning and significance of the Presocratics – and particularly that of the Milesians – are well known, given the availability of their views in mere fragments or preserved in later doxographical accounts of their thought. This is bound to give rise to a wide range of interpretations, as will become clear in the ensuing discussion, and yet there seems to have been a general agreement in the early decades of this century that we have with the Milesians entered into a new stage of thought in the history of humanity. I shall review that literature very briefly, as well as objections raised against this thesis. A further consideration of the response to that debate in subsequent years, and particularly since the 1950s will, however, confirm the original "revolutionary-shift-in-thought" hypothesis that is so congenial to a Lévy-Bruhlian understanding of the nature of the human mind.

An early, and almost belligerent, espousal of this dichotomy thesis is to be found in John Burnet's *Greek Philosophy: Thales to Plato*. Not only does Burnet refuse to countenance any connection between theological/mythological patterns or modes of Greek thought and the emergence of Greek philosophy and science, he suggests that the notion of divinity had been effectively removed from Ionian thought long before Thales' appearance on the scene. Greek science, he maintains, springs on the scene *de novo* and is completely independent of religion and myth.[2]

Eduard Zeller similarly argued that the Milesians broke what he refers to as the shell of myth – that is, they broke away from the condition of the reliance of thought upon something other than itself.[3] Although there may still be some reliance on or allusions to cosmogonic myths for imagery and concepts in their own attempts to account for

---

or even in the same mind but that they do so in spite of the logical inconsistency. See, e.g., Adkins' comments in his "Greek Religion," p. 385 and Farnell, *The Evolution of Religion*, pp. 30–31).

For a significantly different reading of the Milesians see Finkelbergh's critique of Guthrie in his "On the Unity of Orphic and Milesian Thought." Finkelbergh does not, however, deny that a radical distinction between Greek religious thought and Greek philosophy exists. Rather, he simply dates the emergence of the latter as a later elaboration of Milesian thought (see n. 147.). His argument, therefore, does not put in question the distinction being argued here, but only the date of its emergence amongst the Greeks.

2. Burnet, *Greek Philosophy*; see especially pp. 28–29.
3. Zeller, *Outlines of the History of Greek Philosophy*.

the world, he emphasizes the fact that their accounts are no longer merely repetitions or a continuation of the stories of the activities of the gods.

A similar position is taken by Theodor Gomperz in the first volume of his history of ancient philosophy, in which he argues that the Milesians undermined the conception of the universe as "a playground of innumerable capricious and counteracting manifestations of Will" and replaced theogony with cosmogony. This "impulse to simplification," as he refers to it, is a result of the imagination that "actually outstripped the results of modern knowledge."[4] And Leon Robin in his *Greek Thought and the Origin of the Scientific Spirit* refers to the work of the Milesians as a miracle and writes of Greece as creating human reason. Thales, although he is in some senses a continuator of the theogonywriters for Robin, is the first of the philosophers because he transformed "the methods of research"; he introduced "something quite new in respect both of Eastern science and of the old cosmogony" in replacing narrative accounts of the world with reasoned accounts.[5] I shall make much of this change in the spirit of inquiry throughout this book.

In a less radical but essentially similar vein, F. M. Cornford argued in his *From Religion to Philosophy* that with the Milesians one sees for the first time the unaided use of reason and the discovery of nature.[6]

---

4. Gomperz, *The Greek Thinkers*, vol. 1, pp. 44, 46.

5. Robin, *Greek Thought*, p. 37; see also p. xii.

6. Cornford, *From Religion to Philosophy*; see especially pp. 138–39, 195). It should be noted here that Burnet, in the last edition of his *Early Greek Philosophy*, accused Cornford of the error of having derived science from mythology in the latter's *From Religion to Philosophy*. Cornford does not admit to error but insists that "derivation" is the message of his book and maintains that the book would have little interest if it were not. However, he goes on to argue that what he meant to say in the volume is that one cannot "read" the Ionians as if they were "pure intelligences," having no past and therefore thinking without a cultural/social context. Nevertheless, Cornford does argue in this volume that philosophy emerges from religion, with the suggestion that it gains an independence from it – an argument that seems to be rejected by him in later work. See here also Thomson's comment on the Burnet/Cornford disagreement in chapter 8, "The Milesian School," of his *Studies in Greek Society*, vol. 2, pp. 156–172. (In a monograph, *From Religion to Criticism*, De Deugd, I should note, reads Cornford quite differently. His conclusion, however, is most ambiguously stated in that he claims that Cornford both attributes and denies a "revolutionary" quality to Presocratic thought and does not further analyse Cornford's "claims" but rather simply adopts them. Following a brief quotation from Cornford he writes: "This is as much as saying that the new and revolutionary steps

Cornford's position regarding the significance of the Milesian revolution in thought, however, was not to remain the same, as I shall shortly indicate. Nor is Cornford the only one to have questioned this general sentiment about the Milesians that he himself had been instrumental in creating. A vehement rejection of this position is to be found persuasively argued in Roy Kenneth Hack's *God in Greek Philosophy to the Time of Socrates*. No advance of the thesis of this chapter is likely to be adequate, I suggest, until that argument and others like it are properly assessed.

MYTH AND PHILOSOPHY:
CONTINUITY HYPOTHESES EXPLORED

According to Hack the concept of divinity was never effectively banished from the Ionian understanding of the world. He sees that as an indication of an essential continuity between the mythopoeic-like thought of the Premilesian thinkers and the philosophers of Ionia. He admits that if the term god had been used by the Ionians in a non-religious sense, their thought would then in fact constitute a chapter in the history of western science. But that would make of the Milesian experiment "a strange and hostile prelude to the profoundly religious systems of Plato, Zeno, and Epicurus."[7] Furthermore, it would require one to believe that the main current of Greek thought had changed direction, radically, twice in a period of less than three centuries, which he considers a ludicrous proposal.[8] Consequently, he attempts to provide an explanation for this persistent but false view of the

---

which the pre-Socratic philosophers took were not so drastic as to eradicate the spirit that once permeated Greek life. As a matter of fact, we encounter the continuation of a basically religious outlook – a heritage of no mean proportion" [p. 25].)

   The Burnet position has not entirely given way to the more anthropological interpretation. Fränkel, for example, in *Early Greek Poetry and Philosophy*, still talking of the appearance "as if by miracle" (p. 255) of pure philosophy with the Ionians, writes: "Shortly after the beginning of the sixth century, probably even before Pherecydes had lit the wretched lantern of his theological cosmogony, there arose in Ionian Asia Minor the daystar of pure philosophy, to bring a light which was to illuminate the world for centuries, or for millenia" (p. 252). Their ideas "are independent and self-supporting and are destined continuously to beget new departures in thought" (p. 254). The view to be set out here is neither wholly with the anthropological school nor with the 'miraculous' one.

   7. Hack, *God in Greek Philosophy*, p. 2.
   8. Ibid., p. v.

development of Greek thought. He writes: "Many philosophers, inspired by natural and harmless pride in the achievements of the man whom they recognize as the founder of their profession, represent the birth of philosophy as a kind of miracle. According to them, Thales the Milesian suddenly shook himself free from the bonds of myth and legend, from the irrational theogonies and cosmogonies current in the seventh century and created philosophy. . . . Thales himself has thus become a mythical figure, and the gradual processes of history are cancelled in order to make room for a new legend, which is the legend of Thales."[9]

Hack's positive argument begins with an analysis of the concept of the divine in Homer and Hesiod. He maintains that neither poet works simply within the framework of an anthropomorphic personal polytheism. Admitting that such anthropomorphic deities do in fact play a large role in their poems, he insists that they are merely one element in the intuition of divinity. There is, especially in Homer a personal and an impersonal Zeus with the latter characterizing divinity chiefly in terms of the possession of power – a power that is preeminently causal and hence the source of all events, of the world. This, he goes on to claim, is a kind of speculative thinking which is continuous with that of the Milesians and other Presocratics. Therefore, the philosophers did not eliminate God/the gods from their accounts of the world but rather were primarily interested in and employed a nonanthropomorphic conception of divinity to form their explanations of the world and its history. The Presocratics and their successors were therefore, according to Hack, both scientists and theologians, as the poets were theologians with cosmological interests. It is only because of the influence of modern prepossessions that the two vocations are now seen to be mutually incompatible. The driving force of Greek philosophy is quite obviously the conviction that only a divine reality can explain the universe and that, although the demand for an explanation generated what we might call science, this was a science carried on only within the framework of a more important theology.[10]

9. Ibid., p. 38.
10. Ibid., pp. 147–48. Solmsen, in arguing, in his *Plato's Theology*, that Greek physics, unlike modern physics, never adopted a position that excluded divine casuality *ab initio*, makes the same point: "The study of the Presocratic physicists has suffered a good deal from the unconscious retrojection of the modern concept of science. With the early Greek physicists the problem of the true nature of the deity was not only of fundamental importance but actually one of the problems which gave the impulse to their enquiry"

Hack's position, despite its superficial attractiveness, suffers several critical ambiguities that leave the argument less than cogent and therefore unpersuasive. The use of the concept of God, for example, is riddled with ambiguity in both Homer and the Presocratics. Furthermore, the nature of the relationship of the thought of the Milesians to their social, cultural, and intellectual context (their *Sitz im Leben*) is left entirely unclear. Hack does little to clear up the nature of the connection between the thought of the Milesians from the mode of thought that precedes them, and on the surface at least they appear to have no common basis. I shall look at each of these criticisms in turn.

As to the matter of the gods, two issues will be of concern: the first relates to the definition of the word divine (god, *theos*) in early Greek literature, and the second raises the matter of the twofold Zeus in Hack's account of Homeric religion. There is some truth in Hack's claim that it is anachronistic to call the Ionians materialists and to refer to them without qualification as scientists. It is quite true that the Ionians solved their problems with respect to the origin of motion in the universe by assuming their primary "world-stuff" to be alive and so to move of itself and that they applied the epithet god to that stuff.[11] But it is also important to recognize that despite the use of this appellation it had, as Guthrie puts it, "nothing whatsoever to do with the gods or cults of popular religion."[12] That use of the concept of god becomes explicable, as it has been argued, when it is recognized that for the early Greeks the concept has primarily a predicative force or function. The concepts of god, divinity and the immortal are equivalents. As G. M. A. Grube puts it, to say that something is a god is to say "that it is more than human, not subject to death, everlasting . . . [and that] any power, any force we see at work in the world, which is not born with us, and will continue after we are gone could thus be called

(p. 54). Greek physics, that is, provided a new conception of cosmic gods as spiritual or semi-spiritual beings who could account for the physical world rather than political gods tied inseparably to the city-state as were the gods of the "Olympian dynasty" of Homer (see pp. 40, 52) and implicated in the crisis of the city-states (see pp. 53–54).

11. Guthrie, *The Greek Philosophers*, p. 118.

12. Guthrie, *A History*, vol. 1, p. 2. In quite a different context George Thomson makes the same point: "The worlds of Milesian cosmology are described as gods because they move, but they are none the less material" (p. 147). Such a change, at least with respect to the notions of "soul," is already evident in the Homeric poems. See Thomson, *Aeschylus and Athens*, pp. 147–52. See also Thomson's *First Philosophers*, p. 154.

a god, and most of them were."[13] Guthrie in his history of Greek philosophy, and elsewhere, maintains that "everlasting life is the mark of the divine and of nothing else" and therefore is characteristic of the eternal stuff of the Milesians out of which the world is made.[14]

An explanation of the world or of some aspect of the world, that makes use of the words god/gods (*theos/theoi*) is not necessarily, therefore, a "theological"/religious account of the world – it could well be a wholly materialistic explanation forced to make use of "*theos/theoi*" as alone adequate to characterize the new substance which the Milesians refer to as *physis* (matter) – a substance that is not dead/inert and subject only to mechanical motion from outside itself. This matter is not a materialist substance but rather something to which the term hylozoist is appropriately applied.[15] That oddity of *physis* forces us to admit, with Guthrie and others,[16] that the Milesian reference to the divine reveals "some unconscious relic of mythological thinking" but not to conclude, as does A. H. Armstrong, that "this hylozoism . . . is not yet very far from primitive animism . . ."[17] and that the Milesians are "really closer to the myth-maker than to the true scientist."[18] Guthrie argues far more convincingly that, even though the references to the divine can be seen as a relic of the ineradicable animism or animatism of the Greeks, there is still a crucial difference between the Milesians and their contemporaries, namely, in their approach, "their critical spirit and determination to fit them [i.e., the references to the divine] into a rational and unified scheme."[19] Milesian thought constitutes the first attempt "to explain the variety of nature as the modification of something in nature,"[20] and it therefore transcends the mythopoeic thought of its predecessors. Guthrie leaves no doubt about this matter when in the summary of his analysis of Thales' thought he writes: "The evolution of the cosmos in these mythical

---

13. Quoted in Guthrie, *The Greek Philosophers*, pp. 10–11.

14. Guthrie, *A History*, vol I, p. 68. See also his *The Greeks and Their Gods*, p. 115. The same point is repeatedly made by Furley in his *The Greek Cosmologists*, vol. I, pp. 81, 86, 140, 162.

15. Guthrie, *A History*, p. 64.

16. Ibid., p. 66; see also Onians (n. 1).

17. Armstrong, *An Introduction to Ancient Philosophy*, p. 3.

18. Ibid., p. 5.

19. Guthrie, *A History*, vol. 1, p. 66.

20. Ibid., p. 68.

accounts proceeds in sexual terms. It is achieved by the mating and begetting of a series of pairs of powers imagined in human form, and how near these stories are to the primitive is easily seen in Hesiod's description of the mutilation of Ouranos by his son Kronos and of the birth of Aphrodite. Granted that the Milesians had the ground prepared for them by these myths, it is more important to reflect that they abandoned the whole mythical apparatus of personal agents and . . . tried to explain the variety of nature only in terms of something in nature itself, a natural substance."[21]

It is in this light, I suggest, that one must understand Guthrie's earlier comment in *The Greeks and their Gods*, where he maintains that the spirit of the age and class of the Ionian philosophers was "materialistic." He might rather have spoken of that spirit as naturalistic which would, less contentiously, reveal Ionian interests to be a religiously disinterested this-worldliness. For that is his intent, as can be clearly seen when he writes: "The gods had been politely shelved, and divine explanations of the origin and nature of the world were no longer tolerable. The question was raised, and raised for the first time, whether man's intellect could solve these problems without recourse to myth."[22]

It is obvious from all that has thus far been said that the question of the role of the gods in explaining the world is a nonstarter with the Milesians – for them "the gods had been shelved." However, given the hylozoist character of *physis*, later "theological"/religious developments of Milesian thought were possible, as I shall point out below, but were not, in point of fact, a quality of Milesian thought itself. Guthrie refers to this notion as involving "the birth of religious concepts which, crude and ungainly as they still are, contain remarkable possibilities

---

21. Ibid., p. 70.

22. Guthrie, *The Greeks and Their Gods*, p. 132. Similar caution is required in reading Guthrie's claim in his later history of Greek philosophy that the Ionians do not exclude the possibility of divine agency in accounting for the monistic substance out of which our world "is fashioned" (see especially his *A History*, vol. 1, p. 4). The nature of Ionian disinterest in religion will be treated at some length in the chapter to follow. See also here Stokes who recognizes (in his *One and Many in Presocratic Philosophy*) the force of the argument that the Greeks were more scientific than their neighbours, but says that the argument that shows that to be so, does not account for the monism that characterizes their thought. "It accounts well for the abolition of personal and arbitrary intervention in natural processes; but it would not even begin to suggest a reason why that abolition should be accompanied by the postulation of a single material for everything and by the commencement of an argument as to which material should be selected" (p. 39).

of development."[23] He suggests that it provides the impetus, wholly unexpected, that allows for the later adoption of the Chthonic god(s), even though religion in general is in decline and is so, at least in part, because of the influence of the thought of the Milesian physicists.

Some attention must now be focused on Hack's claims regarding the twofold Zeus in Homer. According to Hack there is in Homer both a personal and an impersonal Zeus, the latter being invoked and developed by the Presocratic philosophers. There is no question but that there are at least two main strands of tradition entwined in the notion of Zeus. That they conform to the neat dichotomy suggested by Hack, however, is somewhat doubtful. The two main strands in fact constitute two main types of religion amongst the classical Greeks, the one linked to the humbler and at times oppressed pre-Achaean inhabitants of the land and the other carried into the land by the newcomer invading it. The former are the Chthonic gods associated with "dark and orgiastic" phenomena but concerned with the soul of the human person as potentially divine, whereas the latter, the Olympian gods of Homer, are immortals who outclass humans who are required only to please the gods in order to avoid their wrath. Guthrie in his account of *The Greeks and Their Gods* summarizes the matter succinctly as follows: "In describing the dual character of the historic Zeus, it becomes clear that the contrast between Aegean and Homeric cults was, generally speaking, a contrast between a religion of the soil, a worship of the fertility of the earth not unmixed with magical practices to secure its continuance, and a religion of the sky whose chief god was the sender of lightning upon those who displeased him."[24] No doubt is left that in both traditions – in both Olympian and Chthonic types of religion – we have to do with personal gods: "The Olympian taught of gods intensely personal, strong, wilful, possibly honest but by no means invariably so. Man entered into contracts with them because it was his only hope. The Chthonic cult brought us from this human, comprehensible and business-like atmosphere of daylight to gods who were surrounded with an air of mystery."[25]

Hack may be right to claim that the Milesians did not, in an antireligious frame of mind, intend to dismiss the gods, but there is little question, I think, that since the Homeric gods were powers of nature

23. Guthrie, *The Greeks and Their Gods*, p. 144.
24. Ibid., pp. 52–53. See also Otto, *The Homeric Gods*, especially chapters 2 and 4.
25. Ibid., p. 256.

they therefore became vulnerable, as Solmsen points out, "as soon as speculation offered alternative explanations of the physical world and the processes and events in it."[26] Furthermore, Hack is also right in claiming, and he finds support for the claim in Solmsen,[27] that not only did the fifth-century philosophers not intend to divest the universe of gods, they in many instances were anxious to reestablish them as the principles directing cosmic processes. Solmsen concludes, however, that for the most part they were unsuccessful, since entities in the world, after the Milesian revolution in thought, appeared to operate merely by mechanical laws. Consequently, writes Solmsen, "it happened for the first time in the history of thought that materialism seemed to dethrone religion"[28] in that, in field after field of research and thought, divine causality was replaced by natural causality.[29]

However, the decline of the Homeric gods does not imply the decline of religion *per se*. Guthrie has argued, for example, that even with such a decline the religion connected with the Chthonic spirits and gods always remained nearer the hearts of the common people, and that since they were not directly connected with the virtues of the *polis* they provided the foundation for the survival of religion. And he further maintained,[30] as did Solmsen before him,[31] that this form of religion received an unexpected impetus from the speculations of the physical philosophers. This does not, however, confirm Hack's analysis of a continuity of thought between the Presocratics and the Premilesians on the basis of a supposition about an impersonal Zeus. This only shows the vitality of the *theological quest* – recently emerged – to reestablish religion by reinterpreting the meaning of the philosophy of the Ionians. Solmsen therefore rightly points out that the Greeks themselves no longer recognized religion as existing *de jure* and that, especially for the intellectuals, a "theology" was needed to provide religion with a theoretical foundation. Consequently, "every position thus gained would in some way or other inevitably bear the marks of its origin in a fight against the enemies of tradition. It would be fortified by arguments and theories."[32] Plato's argument from motion to God

---

26. Solmsen, *Plato's Theology*, p. 29.
27. Ibid., p. 37, n. 27.
28. Ibid., p. 29.
29. Ibid., p. 31.
30. Guthrie, *The Greeks and Their Gods*, p. 144.
31. Solmsen, *Plato's Theology*, p. 40.
32. Ibid., p. 38.

involves precisely such a reinterpretation of the element of the divine in the *physis* of the Milesians. His concept of soul as motive power, though, is far richer than the hylozoist matter of the Milesians and gives an automatic priority to the notion of personal agency – even if immanent in matter – to that of matter and so constitutes a *revision* of the philosophy of the Milesians that attempts to turn back the clock on their discovery of the possibility of nonpersonal or impersonal explanation. The interpretation is therefore, in effect an attempt to bring about a counterrevolution in the development of philosophy.[33]

M. P. Nilsson, especially in his *A History of Greek Religion*, seems to espouse a view of Homeric religion that would confirm Hack's interpretation, or, stated more precisely, support assumptions Hack makes about Homer's understanding of a twofold Zeus. Like Hack, Nilsson does find in Homer both personal gods and the more general notion of divine powers: "The idea of 'power,' was living, although without a name, among the people of Homer; it remained still living to the Greeks, and they afterwards coined abstract expressions 'the divine', 'the god-like' . . . to denote it. This conception alone could answer to the idea of a divine cause in all the details of human life, and in the human heart; the anthropomorphic gods could not do so, for the process of specializing and individualizing had set up narrow limits for them."[34] The concept of power therefore supplemented the explanation of unexpected events or unintended results of human behaviour that was provided by invoking the concept of the intervention of the gods. Indeed, that notion, in obtaining a unique generality, brought it very near to the idea of fate (*moira*), although for the most part it remained a daimon that represents a portion of the supranormal power manifested in phenomena that were otherwise inexplicable.

Nilsson's thesis, although superficially similar, is in fact radically different from, and in essence opposed to, that of Hack. It is true that Nilsson sees in this distinction the origin of Ionian science – as does Hack – but, whereas Hack sees the thrust towards science deriving from a move from anthropomorphism to abstract thought about divine power, Nilsson sees the origin of science to be the rationalizing of the animistic and primitive notion of divine power in the anthropomor-

33. This notion is developed further by Solmsen in *Plato's Theology*. See also, however, comment of this kind in Robin, *Greek Thought*, p. 129 and Finley, *The Ancient Greeks*, p. 129.

34. Nilsson, *A History of Greek Religion*, p. 166.

phism of Homer. Nilsson writes: "The humanizing of the gods penetrated deep down among the people notwithstanding the resistance
of popular belief. Homer's anthropomorphism gave rise to the first
criticism of religion, and for the development of the Greek mind it had
an importance the full extent of which has never been realized. For
this humanizing of the gods served to ward off the conception of divine
power as the magical, wonder-working agency which prevails in many
religions: . . . Under this all-compelling magical power of the gods man
bows in fear and terror, but from its fetters the Homeric humanization
of the gods delivered the Greeks. They could henceforth of their own
accord and by their own efforts find order and coherence in the world.
From this origin came Greek science."[35]

Both Hack and Nilsson see a two-stage religious evolution in Homer,
but each assesses the temporal direction of that evolution differently.
For Hack, the general notion of divine power is the result of rational
thought and the anthropomorphism of Homer belongs to a naive,
earlier stage of religious development. Nilsson, however, persuasively
argues that the general notion of divine power derives from the primitive notion of power such as mana. An expression of that power is a
daimon and the expression has only the individuality of its particular
moment conferred upon it. As Nilsson puts it: "a *daimon* represents a
portion, adapted to the accidental manifestation of the moment, of
the supranormal power recognized by man in phenomena which he
believes himself unable to explain from his ordinary experience."[36]
According to Nilsson, then, the old (primitive) belief in power survived
in Homer (and Homer's Greece) but was developed in a way peculiar
to the Greeks, namely by rationalization of that belief, through the
tendency to personify these powers, into anthropomorphism.

Not only does Nilsson's position differ from Hack's on the order of

---

35. Ibid., pp. 178–79. Hadas makes a similar claim in his article on "The Supernatural," in which he talks of the purposefulness of Homer's neglect of the Chthonians who
were not expected to be rational. Hadas writes: "But when gods are imagined in the
shape of sensitive humans, men expect their ordinances shall be humanly intelligible"
(p. 41). Jaeger, on the other hand, does not see Homer as quite that rational although
he does insist that for Homer life is still governed by universal laws (*The Theology of the
Early Greek Philosophers*, p. 51). He also sees the Homeric epic as containing "the germ
of all Greek philosophy," (p. 53). Therefore, like Hack, Jaeger sees greater continuity
between Homer and the Milesians than do I. He writes: "when we contemplate Homer
and the later Greeks in one broad survey we cannot help seeing the underlying identity
of spirit" (p. 55). See also Finkelbergh's argument to this effect referred to in n. 1.
36. Nilsson, *A History of Greek Religion*, p. 166.

the evolution of Greek religious thought, but, even more importantly, Nilsson's evaluation of the significance of that development stands in direct opposition to Hack's understanding of Homer. For Hack, the evolution of Greek religious thought is one of continuous, orthogenetic elaboration; talk of divine power is merely a sophisticated generalization of the implicit meaning of the anthropomorphic gods. For Nilsson, the two stages of Greek thought rest on entirely different foundations and are therefore in tension with each other – the earlier stage resting on naive, primitive notions of magical power and the later on an incipient rationalism that interprets that power: "Rationalism succumbed to the temptation of representing the influence and intervention of the gods in a visible form credible to ordinary reason."[37] In rationalizing the myth which Homer inherits (i.e., primitive gods much more akin to magical power), argues Nilsson, he (Homer) takes the first step toward the overthrow of religion,[38] not, as Hack would argue, toward its establishment and elaboration. This is foreshadowed, Nilsson points out, in the tension between power understood as fate (*moira*) and the anthropomorphism that attends the personification of such powers, that personification being not a late and advanced development of thought but rather, as Nilsson puts it, "the bastard descent of 'power' and the god."[39] One cannot consider the gods subject to *moira* and, at the same time, claim that the gods – especially Zeus – are all-powerful. Hack evades this problem by conflating the foundations of the two stages of Greek thought, making Zeus identical with power; confusing personification in Homer with a later development of abstraction. Nilsson's view that in Homer logic imposes a problem on religion is, I think, the more persuasive argument: "The belief in 'power' which had to compensate for that which was lacking in the gods, was refashioned into belief in Fate which, consistently developed, would remove the gods from their thrones."[40] Nilsson sees the legacy of Homer, therefore, to be a contradictory one and one in which religion was ultimately dissolved.[41] That matter, however, will be left for discussion in the chapter to follow.

37. Ibid., p. 160.
38. Ibid., p. 178.
39. Ibid., p. 172.
40. Ibid., p. 178.
41. It is of importance to note here Nilsson's reliance on the thought of Lévy-Bruhl, even though his interpretation of Lévy-Bruhl is not wholly correct. On both points see McGinty, *Interpretation and Dionysus*, pp. 106–30, 231.

Before leaving the matter of the twofold Zeus, I shall refer briefly to a later, fifth-century, theological development that at first glance seems to support Hack's interpretation. Leon Golden[42] maintains that in Aeschylus, Zeus can only be understood in a nonanthropomorphic way. Aeschylus, he argues, is clearly not a naive, primitive, religious thinker but rather a rationalist who sees Zeus simply as an (the) ultimate causal agent in the universe. Zeus is therefore a *symbol* of a physical and spiritual force that governs the universe and is known only in terms of the effects he produces in the world.[43] The suggestion here, of course, is that Aeschylus represents an advance beyond the anthropomorphism of earlier thought. Golden also suggests that such a development depends to a great extent upon the developments in the thought of the Presocratic philosophers, together with the scientific and technological advances which they fostered.[44]

Despite his quoting Nilsson in support of his interpretation[45] and maintaining that this Aeschylean notion of Zeus is sophisticated – free from absurdity and self-contradiction – there are problems with Golden's view. His description of Zeus in Aeschylean thought raises at least two problems which I can but illustrate here. The first concerns Golden's notion that Zeus constitutes a first cause that is unpredictable[46] and mysterious.[47] In a key passage Golden writes: "The tracing back of all of the proximate causes of human actions and natural events leads to a mysterious first cause that is beyond the ability of the human intellect to comprehend. This first cause the chorus is willing to call 'Zeus, whatever its name may be,' and it is clear that the Zeus who is described in these terms is an impersonal force or power who is in no sense represented in anthropomorphic terms."[48] Thus, although events have proximate causes of which the human intellect can usually be quite clear, Zeus is nevertheless an ultimate cause and one that, because of limitations of human reason, must forever elude the "mind of man." And "man," the human person, must "almost of necessity" maintain a faith in it.[49] This however, makes Zeus indistinguishable

42. Golden, *In Praise of Prometheus*.
43. Ibid., see pp. 109, 117, 119, 126.
44. Ibid., pp. 14–15.
45. Ibid., p. 123, n. 30.
46. Ibid., p. 46.
47. Ibid., pp. 118, 122.
48. Ibid., p. 118.
49. Ibid., p. 122.

from the primitive notion of power referred to by Nilsson and is not the advanced notion suggested by Hack.

The second problem in Golden's account concerns consistency, for even though Zeus is the ultimate cause of all things, Zeus, in the "humanism and rationalism" of Aeschylus (which Golden sets out to defend in his own work), must ultimately defer to human power. This is obvious especially in the *Prometheus Bound*, in which we see that Zeus will someday have to bend his knee to Prometheus who stands as symbolic of human persons and society. Golden claims that this weakness of Zeus, like his absolute power, is also an indication that Aeschylus is no naive, primitive religious thinker. "I submit," he writes, "that if Aeschylus were a naive, primitive religious thinker, he would never have authorized the transfer of authority for solving difficult moral problems from the gods to a human agency relying on reason and wisdom. Aeschylus' solution as given here actually heralds the breakdown of naive religious thought. It places in the hands of man the ultimate responsibility of deciding moral questions in human society while recognizing the existence of an ultimate divine cause of all events in the world. It is a solution, also, that is in harmony with the action of the *Prometheus Bound* where it is predicted that Zeus, who symbolizes the totality of power in the universe, must eventually yield to Prometheus who represents the force of human intellect and civilization."[50]

It is odd, to say the least, to claim Aeschylus to be rational because of his purification of religion by conceiving of Zeus as an impersonal force governing the universe and, at the same time, as rational because of his awareness that that impersonal power *must* eventually yield to the force of the human intellect which implies, of course, the breakdown of religion. Aeschylus has certainly inherited Homer's contradictory legacy. However, in the final analysis the religious world view gives way to a new mode of humanist/rationalist thought.[51]

A further matter in Hack's discussion needs to be mentioned here. Hack's account of the exhaustion of Greek theological thought in the atomists and in the ensuing scepticism of the period of the sophists does not fit well with his thesis of the continuous elaboration and

---

50. Ibid., p. 125.

51. Eric Havelock, it seems to me, sees in Prometheus a similar opposition to religion in his *The Crucifixion of Intellectual Man*. But the humanism Havelock sees in Aeschylus is a darker humanism that adopts "intellectual man" as the foundation of society (p. 24) and yet has a deep distrust of the intellectual powers of humankind (p. 51).

development of theology from Homer and Hesiod through the Milesians and down well into the fifth century. His admission that in the fifth
century BCE we encounter persons who proclaimed that the ultimate
divine reality did not exist, or if it did exist, could not possibly be
known,[52] seems more likely the result of the degeneration of a once
dominant theistic/"theological" paradigm that has radically and steadily, even if only slowly, eroded over a period of time. As Solmsen points
out, the emancipated study of a thing's nature could lead to a surer
understanding of it in the sense of the power to predict its behaviour,
which seemed wiser than consulting an oracle from the gods on the
matter.[53] The passion for argument and the confidence in reason –
whether the cause or the effect of the transcendence of religious
thought – is correlative with it.[54]

That there is an overlapping of terminology, and especially of religious language, between the Milesians and their predecessors is the
last point that needs comment with respect to Hack's thesis. There
is no doubt, and in this one cannot help but agree with Hack, that the
Milesians did not shake themselves entirely free from the vestiges of
myth and legend. Since no philosopher thinks in a vacuum, this is
hardly to be expected. As Guthrie has put it, no one could be expected
"at one bound [to] free themselves from the mass of traditional ideas,
some enshrined in poetry and others absorbed less perceptibly from
popular lore, amid which they had grown up."[55] But it is a *non sequitur*
to argue on that basis that no fundamentally new element could have
been introduced into the thought-domain. As has already been made
clear in the foregoing discussion, Guthrie recognizes in the Milesians
a radical shift in thought that, even though its emergence is not sudden
but rather slow and gradual,[56] is nevertheless fundamental. The religious concepts, the myth and the legend still to be found in Thales
and the other Presocratics are therefore vestigial remains and not
primary doctrine.[57]

---

52. Hack, *God in Greek Philosophy*, p. 142.

53. Solmsen, *Plato's Theology*, pp. 31–32.

54. Solmsen expands on this idea and its development in the later Presocratics and
Sophists in his *Intellectual Experiments of the Greek Enlightenment*. See also Finley, *Four
Stages of Greek Thought*.

55. Guthrie, *The Greeks and Their Gods*, p. 138.

56. Guthrie, *A History*, p. 1.

57. See e.g., Onians, *The Origins of European Thought*, pp. 248, n. 3, and 252–53, *et
passim*. See also n. 1 above. A similar understanding is to be found in Thomson's *Aeschylus
and Athens*, p. 158.

As will already have become clear in this analysis, Hack does not stand alone in holding what might be referred to as the continuity thesis in accounting for the developments in Milesian/Presocratic philosophic thought. Cornford, like Hack, has argued that science derives from magical and religious thinking, although his final position seems a good deal more ambiguous. In his *From Religion to Philosophy*, Cornford seems to have foreshadowed Hack's position in arguing the importance of the concept of *physis* in Dorian thought, for *physis* is, he insists, substance, soul, and the divine and not the neutral stuff or matter of modern physics. He writes therefore: "The importance of this attribute, 'divine,' as applied to the primary physis is overlooked by historians of philosophy; yet it can hardly be overemphasized. Philosophy is the immediate successor of theology, and the conceptions held by philosophers of the relation between the ultimate reality and the manifold sense-world are governed by older religious concepts of the relation between God and the human group or Nature."[58] In rejecting the supernatural, the Milesian school "strikes a new note, unheard before,"[59] but it is not on that account purely scientific. In stripping their accounts of the universe of theological elements they were not presenting purely rational explorations of natural facts, but were rather going behind that religious phase of development and quite unconsciously reproducing the pretheological, Shamanic, mode of thought that gives rise to the poets: "as we shall see, when the Milesian philosophers quietly left the Gods out of their scheme of things, and supposed themselves to be dealing straight with natural facts, what really happened was that they cleared away the overgrowth of theology and disinterred what had all the time persisted underneath. Hylozoism, in a word, simply raises to the level of clear scientific assertion the primitive savage conception of a continuum of living fluid, portioned out into the distinct forms of whatever classification is taken to be important. What the Milesians call *physis* has the same origin as what the savage calls *mana*."[60]

And yet Cornford can talk of a "scientific temper,"[61] "the scientific tradition,"[62] and of "Milesian science."[63] It may have its roots in a

---

58. Cornford, *From Religion to Philosophy*, p. 135.
59. Ibid., p. 42.
60. Ibid., pp. 88–89. See also his "Introduction" to his *Greek Religious Thought*, pp. xx–xxi and his *Principium Sapientiae*, p. 153.
61. Cornford, *From Religion to Philosophy*, p. 156.
62. Ibid., pp. 152, 155.
63. Ibid., p. 185.

magical art, but when faith in magic weakens, a new notion of causality emerges that he refers to as "a critical moment in the pre-history of science."[64] Therefore, although starting with the ambiguous notions of *physis*, that scientific tradition develops a conceptual model of reality that is radically incompatible with its original meaning.[65] The Milesians, as he puts it, start down the road that leads to Leucippus, Democritus, and the philosophy of atomism. And "these atomists succeeded in reducing *physis* to a perfectly clear, conceptual model, such as science desires, composed of little impenetrable pieces of homogeneous 'matter,' with none but spacial properties – tiny geometrical solids, out of which all bodies of whatever shape or size, could be built up."[66] *Physis* had therefore lost all its ancient associations. The archaic system with its element of arbitrariness is replaced with a closed system, thoroughly ruled by necessity.[67]

Cornford's later assessment of the relationship of the Premilesian thinkers and the earliest philosophers is more clearly in support of Hack's thesis. After an analysis of the thought of Epicurus in his (posthumous) *Principium Sapientiae* he writes: "It is hard indeed to suppose that the earlier Ionians had established a genuinely scientific method if it could be so entirely ignored by those who adopted atomism."[68] The philosophers, unlike the medical thinkers, according to Cornford, simply neglected to check their claims either empirically or by experiment. They were therefore no less dogmatic than the seers, poets, and prophets who preceded them.[69] The theogonies of the poets and the cosmogonies of the philosophers both, therefore, enshrine myths of great antiquity, and neither is the outcome of immediate observation. Both retain the sacred character of religious revelation. Ionian rationalism was a moral response, Cornford insists, that did not abandon the myths but rather defended them via allegorical interpretation.[70]

64. Ibid., p. 140.

65. Ibid., p. 142. This is captured clearly by J.-P. Venant in his essay "The Formation of Positivist Thought in Archaic Greece": "The emergence of philosophy was, as Cornford has shown, a historical fact with its roots in the past, growing out of the past *as well as away from it*" (p. 365, emphasis added).

66. Cornford, *From Religion to Philosphy*, p. 144. See also, however, pp. 142, 158–59.

67. See here Cornford's "Unwritten Philosophy," pp. 40–42.

68. Cornford, *Principium Sapientiae*, p. 30; see also p. 155.

69. Ibid., pp. 63–64.

70. Ibid., p. 106. See on this score also Finkelbergh ("Orphic and Milesian Thought"), as well as n. 147.

The philosophers are successors of the Seer-Poet that only *our* obses-
sion with the nineteenth-century "conflict of religion and science" can
obscure.[71]

After discussing Anaximander's system of the world he asks: "Is the
Milesian cosmogony the work of rational inference based on observation and checked by at least rudimentary methods of experiment? Or
are its features to be referred to an attitude of mind uncongenial to
natural science as we understand it?"[72] And he answers: "when we
look more closely at the Milesian scheme, it presents a number of
features which cannot be attributed to rational inference based on an
open-minded observation of facts."[73] Recognition of this should "dispel
the illusion that the common field of cosmogony was originally occupied by the poets and then suddenly invaded by prosaic rationalism
having a quite independent origin than the thought of the poets,
namely, the direct observation of phenomena."[74]

Cornford does admit here, however, that no reader of the Milesians
can fail to be struck by the rationalism that does seem to distinguish it
from mythical cosmogonies and insists that this difference must not be
underrated.[75] Indeed, he further insists that this achievement of the
Ionians "has become the universal premise of all modern science."[76]
"But," he proceeds, "there is something to be added on the other side.
If we give up the idea that philosophy or science is a motherless Athena,
an entirely new discipline breaking in from nowhere upon a culture
hitherto dominated by poetical and mystical theologians, we shall see
that the process of rationalization had been at work for some considerable time before Thales was born."[77] Although this is not as belligerent

71. Ibid., p. 107. See also p. 29 and his comments regarding the conflict between
science and religion.

72. Ibid., p. 186.

73. Ibid., p. 188. There seems, however, to be some doubt in Cornford on this point
for later statements regarding Anaximander's cosmology conflict with the claim made
here (see, e.g., p. 200). Further statements at pp. 201 and 228 seem to reverse this again.

74. Ibid., p. 143; see also pp. 201, 228.

75. Ibid., p. 187.

76. Ibid., p. 188.

77. Ibid., p. 188. The ambiguity that characterizes *Principium Sapientiae* is also to be
found in Cornford's "Mystery Religions and Pre-Socratic Philosophy." Cornford there
maintains that in the Presocratics we witness the birth of science and yet also that it is
continuous with earlier mythical modes of thought (see especially pp. 522–23 and 538).
Cornford seems here to foreshadow the position taken by Kirk to be discussed below
(see also Vernant, "Formation of Positivist Thought").

a view as Hack's, the gap between poet and philosopher seems to have dwindled in his view almost to the point of vanishing.[78]

Cornford's position as described above is extremely ambiguous and hardly constitutes firm support for Hack's thesis. This conclusion seems well supported in Guthrie's appendix to the posthumous volume of Cornford's essays. "The danger of ending with this inadequate summary," he writes, "is that it may convey the false impression that the earliest Greek philosophers (*and of ancient peoples it was only among the Greeks that this transition from myth to philosophy was achieved*) did no more than repeat the lessons of myth in a changed terminology."[79]

A further weakness in Cornford's argument concerns his view of the nature of science, especially as it emerged in *Principium Sapientiae* – a view that is essentially positivist and verificationist. For him the medical thinkers are the chief explorers of scientific thinking because they deduce their theories, if at all, directly from empirical observation *and*, because for him, influence of that tradition cannot be traced in the Milesians.[80] The philosophers, as I have pointed out above, have convictions regarding the cosmos that are not only not derived from experience but are also beyond rational proof. Hence his criticism of Epicurus as not experimental and as working not out of a practical motive but rather from a religious quest for peace of mind.[81] Thus Cornford writes: "For all his exaltation of the senses as the criterion of truth, Epicurus' procedure in this field of the imperceptible is essentially similar to the despised Plato's. . . . "[82] He concludes his analysis more generally as follows: "What we claim to have established so far is that the pattern of Ionian cosmogony, for all its appearance of complete rationalism, is not a free construction of the intellect reasoning from direct observation of the existing world."[83]

With an alternative view of the nature of science as something more than the generation of theories from unprejudiced observation, however, a quite different picture of the Ionians will emerge. I have in mind here K. Popper's falsificationist view of science as being a procedure of

---

78. In this I find myself in agreement with Vlastos in his "Review of F.M.Cornford: *Principium Sapientiae*" especially p. 55. See also Guthrie's introduction to the *Principium Sapientiae* and Cornford's essay, "Silent Philosophy" in his *The Unwritten Philosophy*."
79. Cornford, *Principium Sapientiae*, p. 259; emphasis added.
80. Ibid., p. 186.
81. Ibid., p. 21.
82. Ibid., p. 155.
83. Ibid., p. 201.

"conjectures and refutations." Science, in this view, is not an inductive process of forming theories from observation but rather the creative development of conjectures/theories/accounts for the world which then are tested against one's own experience in/of the world. In such a view there is both a creative rational component as well as an experimental one. Cornford argues rather that we have two diametrically opposed theories of knowledge – one empirical and one (*anamnesis*) that provides convictions that are "beyond the domain of rational proof."[84] And yet he seems to see the possibility of some interaction between the two that comes close to embodying a Popperian understanding of the nature of science: "The ultimate truth, in fact, is directly revealed to the intelligence; the witness of the senses is called in afterwards. They cannot positively confirm the truth about a reality which is altogether beyond their range. We are satisfied that their testimony does not contradict the pronouncement of intellect. The senses serve not as the source, but as the *criterion* of truth."[85] From such a viewpoint the Ionians – as Popper has pointed out[86] – are in fact very much scientific thinkers. Certainly the atomists, whom Cornford sees as the fulfilment of the Ionian project, represent such a science, as he himself admits in his essay on "Greek Natural Philosophy and Modern Science," where he writes: "Atomism, which has recently borne astonishing fruit, might not have been thought of, if Democritus had not allowed his reason to outrun his senses, and assert a reality which the senses can never perceive, and no means of observation then existing could verify."[87] Popper, of course, would talk rather of testing or falsifying the theory. And insofar as such theories were open to criticism they were rational and therefore scientific. Cornford himself admits as much in "The Unwritten Philosophy," in suggesting that the history of philosophy in the early period is "a bit like the record of a debate . . . "[88] which constitutes a work of abstraction and elimination.[89] Indeed, it is on the basis of precisely such a view of Ionian philosophy that he draws the following conclusion in that essay: "Finally there may come a time

84. Ibid., pp. 58, 63.
85. Ibid., p. 63.
86. This will be treated below.
87. Cornford, "Greek Natural Philosophy and Modern Science" (p. 85). It seems to me that a similar case could be made in terms of Cornford's analysis of Presocratic thought in his "Mystery Religions and Pre-Socratic Philosophy," pp. 538, 553, *et passim*.
88. Cornford, "Unwritten Philosophy," p. 32.
89. Ibid., p. 41.

when rational thinking consciously asserts itself, and the foremost
intellects of the race awaken out of the dream of mythology . . . they
demand literal, matter-of-fact truth. This happened in sixth-century
Ionia and what the Western world calls philosophy or science was
born."[90]

In his *Before and After Socrates* Cornford maintains that Socrates
effected a revolution in turning attention from external nature to the
study of persons and society. Although I agree with Cornford that we
have a radical development in Socrates, I think it more reasonable to
see that change of thought as a counterrevolution.[91] Certainly this is
the position, and with some justification, of Benjamin Farrington in

---

90. Ibid., p. 42. See also his "Mystery Religions and Pre-Socratic Philosophy," p. 538.
Shiel's position in *Greek Thought and the Rise of Christianity* seems to be taken over directly
from Cornford. Greek philosophy, he maintains, even though unemotional and rational
can be shown nevertheless, to have had "permanent roots in the non-rational" (p. 18),
for it "grew out of primitive religious attitudes and permanently retained traces of them"
(p. 24). Vlastos in a review of Cornford's *Principium Sapientiae* concludes that, even
though the Ionians may have failed to understand the experimental method and that
their ideas arose out of a particular set of social conditions, "we must still give them
credit for laying the conceptual foundation on which nearly two millenia later, more
skilful hands than theirs, equipped with better tools, intellectual and technological, could
build the enduring edifice of natural science" (p. 55). "This," he continues, "was their
great bequest to the intellectual heritage of mankind, and this they did not derive from
their religious sources" (p. 55). Indeed, going back to their religious roots was a denial
of the fruits of this revolution. See here, for example, Murray, *Five Stages of Greek Religion*,
especially the chapter on "The Failure of Nerve." See also Altizer's *Oriental Mysticism and
Biblical Eschatology*, pp. 36–37, 44; and Vernant, "Formation of Positivist Thought," pp.
348, 355.

91. Cornford refers to this as "a Copernican revolution of another kind" ("Mystery
Religion and Presocratic Philosophy," p. 578), and he is well aware of its devastating
effect on the philosophy of the Ionians and their successors. He writes: "Hitherto
philosophy had been looking backward to find the beginning of things. Socrates turned
it around and bade look to the end – the good for which the world existed, not the
source from which it came. The effect on physics was disastrous. For the first time
in Greek thought there emerged the doctrine of a benevolent creator, the Mind of
Anaxagoras, set to the task of designing a world upon a perfect model. This hypothesis
cuts the heart out of speculation by providing a complete answer to every question. Why
does this happen, rather than that? Because it is for the best. When the why is known,
the how matters little. To Plato the 'science' which dealt with the sense-world was no
science, but a plausible myth. Not even the genius of Aristotle could secure a permanent
foothold for the study of truth, unprejudiced by the cult of virtue or the pursuit of
happiness" (p. 578).

his *Greek Science: Its Meaning for Us*[92] wherein he denies that Socrates really marks the advent of a new epoch in human culture in the way that the Milesians do. Socrates' reaction to the materialism of the physicists, especially as it emerges in the *Phaedo*, for example, is not at all a revolution but rather merely a variation on a theme – it is a return, although in a modified form, to what might be termed agentic or mythic thinking. The agentic thinking of the poets was a thinking in terms of the transcendent agency of the gods, whereas that of Socrates is the immanent agency of the self.

Despite my agreement with Farrington on this matter, it seems to me that his great attachment to the meaning of the Milesian revolution for us moderns blinds him to recognizing that the Socratic move is not simply a capitulation to myth and a total rejection of the naturalism of his predecessors. As Cornford attempts to show, Socrates finds it hard not to admit the greatness of the discoveries of the Ionians – that is, their naturalist over against a supernaturalist-like view of the world; their espousal of causal (i.e., non-agentic) accounts of material phenomena in the universe and of the universe as a whole. What Socrates reacts to is what that view eliminates when it is applied to the whole of reality, including the spiritual aspect of persons. That kind of reductionism Socrates simply rejects as counterintuitive. His argument that a study of the world beginning with persons would never have reached so (intuitively) incredible a conclusion is therefore the beginning of an attempt to halt what we might well call the process of the disenchantment of the world, begun by the Milesians and reaching its peak with the atomists. Socrates' anxiety over the degeneration of the poetic/ "theological" paradigm of order[93] therefore provides a foundation for a hybrid kind of thinking that combines philosophy/science with myth which later is used to great advantage by Plato, as I shall clearly show in the next chapter. I think the essential character of this process is aptly captured in the title of the seventh chapter of E. R. Dodds' *The Greeks and the Irrational*: "Plato, The Irrational Soul and the Inherited Conglomerate," in which he sees Plato as heading a "counter-reformation," as he puts it, combining the "tradition of Greek rationalism with

92. See also Kahn, *Anaximander and the Origins of Greek Cosmology*, pp. 204, 206.

93. I adopt this locution from Eric Voegelin whose analysis of the thought of the Greeks is ultimately tied to an analysis of their social and political order. See his *Order and History*, vol 2.

the magico-religious ideas whose remoter origins belong to northern shamanistic culture."[94]

So as not to mislead, it should be emphasized that Dodds' reference to ideas whose origins are to be found in northern shamanistic culture must involve the assumption that that culture is very much their *remoter* origin. Any view of the birth of philosophic thought that sees rationality bursting miraculously and full-blown onto the scene of human history at the time of the Milesians, totally distinct from the form of thought that precedes it, is naive and historically inaccurate. Hack's indignation at the implication in some histories of philosophy that myth in Homer and Hesiod is of the same order as that of "ignorant savages," is not wholly inappropriate, as I have already intimated above.[95] There can be no doubt but that there is a kind of continuity in Premilesian and Milesian thought that ought not to be lightly passed over. Hesiodic myth, for example, is not merely a reworking of Greek traditional stories of the gods but rather, in a quasi-philosophic way, attempts to provide a reasonable and comprehensive picture of the workings and history of the universe. As Voegelin puts it, philosophy as a "new form [of thought] begins to disengage itself from the myth, toward the end of the eighth century, in the work of Hesiod inasmuch as in his *Theogony* the myth is submitted to a conscious intellectual operation, with the purpose of reshaping its symbols in such a manner that a 'truth' about order with universal validity will emerge."[96] Hesiod's work therefore constitutes "the first great document of both the awakening and the effects of speculation,"[97] although Voegelin reserves for Heraclitus the honour of being the author of "the first piece of methodical philoso-phizing in Western History."[98] Voegelin maintains that the style of intellectual adventure undertaken by the great Milesians is the same as that of Hesiod – a claim I think open to serious question, even in terms of his own later claims – but he does admit that with them the elimination of the mythical personnel from speculation proper was

94. Dodds, *The Greeks and the Irrational*, p. 209. This seems also to be the essence of Despland's *The Education of Desire*, in which he sets out to defend Plato's strategy/ programme. I show the inconsistencies involved in this exercise in a critique of his analysis of Plato and the philosophy of religion in the following chapter.

95. Hack, *God in Greek Philosophy*, p. 39.

96. Voegelin, *Order and History*, vol. 2, p. 126.

97. Ibid., p. 167.

98. Ibid., p. 209.

established.[99] This break with myth is a crucial development; an all-important assertion of the autonomy of reason, so to speak, from mythopoeic modes of expression, and consequently from mythopoeic modes of thought. In this the Milesians are opposed to the poets and are, as Hussey claims, of another mind.[100] Thus Hussey, even though recognizing, as does Voegelin, a continuity of thought between Hesiod and the earliest Presocratics, maintains that "there is a great gulf, created by a revolution in thought."[101] And even Voegelin recognizes the revolutionary import of the Milesians for the subsequent history of Greek philosophy, when he acknowledges that "neither Heraclitean analysis of the soul, nor even the speculation of Parmenides in spite of the fact that it is embedded in a *mythos*, can well be imagined without the Milesian background."[102]

99. Ibid., p. 167.

100. Hussey, *The Presocratics*, p. 16. My interpretation of Hussey quite clearly differs from that of Zaehner in his *Our Savage God*, in which the Presocratics appear very Hindu (chapters 2 and 3). There are moments, however, where Zaehner seems to see contrasts to which I draw attention here; see pp. 13, 111, 145–46, 163.

101. Hussey, *The Presocratics*, p. 13.

102. Voegelin, *Order and History*, vol. 2, p. 167. Finley, in his *Four Stages of Greek Thought*, sees the continuity going back not only to Hesiod but also to Homer: "If the purpose of the early stories was at bottom to clarify an otherwise chaotic world, this bent of mind was natively intellectual. The journeys of Odysseus, though they seem real and apparently move through actual places, are in substance analytical of experience. . . . This aim towards clarification is crucial . . ." (p. 98). However, Finley, like the others, recognizes that a radical intellectual change occurred in Greek thought, although he points to Thucydides as the first thoroughgoing analytical writer (p. 69). That intellectual change, he writes, was concerned with "the change from verse to prose, from shape to concept, from story to analysis, from mythological to conceptual ways of thinking" (p. 58).

It is important to note that, although Finley speaks of four stages of thought, his thesis is really much closer to the dichotomy view I have been setting out here. In his final chapter on "the rational mind," for example, he refers to Plato's struggle with the "two faiths" (p. 107) and his attempting to see them as one. The two faiths are those of sensibility and mind; or "our bright impressions of the world" which is that of Homer's mythological world and that of "our wish to simplify and explain the world" which is a post-Homeric, post-Hesiodic quest for a nonmythological understanding of the world: "[After mythology] another kind of world came into existence, a world of concepts rather than figures, of prose rather than verse, of analysis rather than myths. It is, accordingly, possible to divide Greek thought into two periods, the mythological and the conceptual" (p. 35; see also p. 108). Little (*Myth and Society in Attic Drama*), however, points out that something of this transition of thought can also be found in the emergence and growth of Athenian drama. Athenian drama, as he puts it, reveals "a turning point in which

Hack's argument that the notion of divinity was never effectively banished from the Ionian and later Presocratic scheme of the world is in one sense quite correct.[103] His further claim that to fail to emphasize this matter constitutes a wilfully wrongheaded interpretation of the significance of Milesian thought and an arbitrary rejection of the essential continuity of Greek thought from its earliest beginnings, is not persuasive.[104] Even the theology of the Presocratics itself can be seen as revolutionary. Hussey's discussion of the Milesians, for example, shows how their new theology (what for Hack would be their emphasis on the impersonal Zeus and for Cornford a return to *moira*) initiated a new cosmology. The core of the Milesian revolution of thought, as Hussey puts it, is "the development of a reformed theology based on general principles, and . . . [a] correlative vision of a universe governed by universal law," which freed thinking from "the entrenched belief in the arbitrary power of an uncoordinated multiplicity of gods."[105] Cosmology for the Milesians is no longer a mere sequence of events without any internal necessity. Although Hussey does not claim that the Milesians represent an essentially materialistic culture (i.e., as revealed in their cosmology), he does nevertheless maintain that "the last and greatest representative of the Milesian tradition [namely Democritus] was the first explicit materialist."[106] The atomists went beyond the Milesian view in removing from their list of ultimate constit-

---

were forged the instruments of organized thinking which have controlled the advance of civilization since. This organized thinking was a selective process dependent on adequate terms and definitions, which prepared the way for the social philosophy of the fourth century" (p. 11; see also pp. 4, 19, 71). This, Little maintains, constitutes a secularization of myths "which were originally invested with all the religious mystery of belief" (p. 19). Little, like Finley, finds Plato to be struggling to keep two disparate worlds together in a single frame: "The tone of Plato's dialogues is itself dramatic and, thought borrowed not from tragedy but from the more realistic Sicilian mime, preserves the organic form and high social purpose of tragedy. Indeed, Plato's own thought remains still a compound of the mythological and the logical. Just as Euripides continued to use the old characters and myths to embody new ideas in a visible form upon the stage, Plato, who constructed a system of social philosophy with the use of only one technical term, still had recourse to myth-making to clinch emotionally what his logic had failed to make clear" (p. 10). Further comment on Plato's ambiguous relation to the Milesian revolution is made below and especially in n. 154 and in the section on "Plato's Reactionary Rationalism" in chapter 4.

103. Hack, *God in Greek Philosophy*, p. 2.
104. Ibid., p. 38.
105. Hussey, *The Presocratics*, p. 29.
106. Ibid., p. 148. See also pp.142, 146.

uents of the universe everything mental but were in essential agreement with the Milesian intention in searching for a fully impersonal/
impartial account of the universe. Consequently, and wholly persuasively, Hussey concludes: "It is to philosophers and scientists whether
professional or amateur, that the Presocratics speak, though they
themselves are, in the strict sense, neither philosophers nor scientists,
but by their efforts brought about the birth of both philosophy and
science from less formal ways of thinking."[107]

Even more recently Jonathan Barnes in his massive *The Presocratic
Philosophers* argues that the Presocratics had one supreme characteristic in common, namely, rationality, and that it is not only often misun-
derstood but "sometimes mistakenly denied."[108] He admits that this
does not imply the rejection of the supernatural or involve the repudia-
tion of all things divine and superhuman, and in this he admits room
for theology – a matter I shall subject to examination in chapter 4.
However, the Presocratics, he insists, replaced unargued fable with
argued theory and substituted reason for dogma.[109] As he puts it in
his discussion of the astronomy of Anaximander, science can only exist
if the gods do not capriciously interrupt the operation of the world:
"That there is no transcendental, divine, or capricious intervention in
natural processes is a presupposition fundamental to the very enterprise of science."[110]

107. Ibid., p. 154.
108. Barnes, *The Presocratic Philosophers*, p. 4.
109. Ibid., p. 4.
110. Ibid., p. 25. Emlyn-Jones, however, argues that the hylozoism of Anaximander
and other Milesians indicates an inheritance from the prephilosophical world (*The
Ionians and Hellenism*, p. 125), and that in consequence, even though Anaximander's
reaction to the poetic tradition was to remove the personal and arbitrary elements,
Anaximander did not lose the poetic outlook (p. 128); philosophy and science, that is,
did not dissipate myth (p. 119). Nevertheless, Emlyn-Jones is not as ambiguous in his
assessment of the character of Ionian thought as is Cornford. He refers, for example,
to the Ionians as effecting an "intellectual revolution" (p. 6) and maintains that we see
in them "the modern world in the making" (p. 6). In tracing the Ionian origin of Greek
philosophy he contrasts myth and reason and argues that with Thales and his successors
"something entirely new entered human consciousness" (p. 98). The origins of speculative thought "took the form . . . of a transition from myth to reason: that is, from a view
that the world was created and organised by the personal impulses of powerful deities
towards an attitude which saw the universe as the product of impersonal forces working
in a predictable manner" (p. 116). In this, of course, Emlyn-Jones is in entire agreement
with Guthrie, and he boldly refers to this contribution of the Ionians as wholly original:
"Amid all the uncertainties associated with the study of archaic Greece, one point stands

THE MILESIAN REVOLUTION:
THE DICHOTOMY THESIS REFINED

This contrast of slow, continuous development of the Greek mind and a sudden revolutionary shift of thought within the Greek tradition has been with us for some time. But the overwhelming support, as the discussion thus far suggests, is on the side of the dichotomy view.[111] The remainder of this chapter will be taken up with several more recent contributions to the debate, in which the argument is further nuanced and refined and consequently made even more persuasive. I begin this rehearsal with Bruno Snell's *The Discovery of the Mind*.

According to Snell: "primitive man feels that he is bound to the gods; he has not yet roused himself to an awareness of his own freedom. The Greeks were the first to break through the barrier, and thus founded Western Civilization."[112] But for Snell there is also a wide divergence between Greek and Oriental religion as regards arbitrary power, so that the difference between Greek religion and Milesian thought is less drastic than Snell's comment above might suggest.[113] In a later chapter, "From Myth to Logic," he corrects the impression given and brings out the slow emergence of logical thinking in the development of similes and metaphors in the Greek poets. Despite that continuity he still maintains, however, that there is a difference of consciousness in and with the rise of the Milesian philosophers. It is worth quoting Snell directly on this: "The problem [of the significance of the emergence

---

out firmly: the discovery of an intellectual or scientific outlook on the world was the achievement of the Ionians. It was their greatest gift to Hellenism, and indeed the only gift from Ionia ever genuinely acknowledged by the recipients. The Ionians set themselves against an accumulated weight of myth and tradition in order to go behind man's immediate experience and explain it. In this way they were wholly original" (p. 109).

111. However, one still sees hesitancy in the acceptance/adoption of such a clear and unambiguous statement of the matter. Burkert, for example, in *Structure and History in Greek Mythology and Ritual*, talks of myth as dominating Greek civilization and suggests that "we see rational language and thought struggling for emancipation from myth without ever arriving at a radical separation" (p. xii). He goes on, in the conclusion to his study, to draw our attention to the fact that modern science fiction seems to repeat ancient mythical patterns of thought. Nevertheless, Burkert also argues that logical and rational thought "definitely destroyed mythical thinking" (see pp. 24–25).

112. Snell, *The Discovery of the Mind*, pp. 31–32.

113. Ibid., p. 32; Snell writes: "The Greek god does not burst forth in a storm cloud to strike man with his thunder, nor is the worshipper awed into a sense of insignificance by the terror which his god inspires in him."

of logic] is comparable to that of the soul which did, in a certain sense, exist even for Homer, but of which he was not cognizant, whence it did not really exist. Logic, in that same sense, has been in existence ever since men have talked and thought; the reason why it did not, at first, find expression in speech was not that logic did not exist but that it was implicit and understood. As soon, however, as it is discovered and intrudes into consciousness, human thinking undergoes a radical change, and this mutation is particularly apparent in the comparisons, the images which make up language."[114]

After delineating some striking differences and similarities between mythical and logical thought Snell concludes: "Thus it is evident that mythical and logical thought are not co-extensive; many aspects of myth remain inaccessible to logic, and many truths discovered by logic were without precedent in myth. Outside of the causal explanation of nature, to speak of a polarity of myth and logic is not quite correct, for the additional reason that myth refers to the content of thought, logic to its form. Nevertheless it is better to retain the two terms, because they effectively describe two stages of human thought. They do not exclude each other completely; there is room in mythical thought for much that is logical and vice versa, and the transition between the two is slow and gradual – in fact no transition is ever fully completed."[115] Although the transition may never be fully completed we do nevertheless have, after the Milesians, a new way of thinking, a way that is nonagentic in orientation and hence primarily causally oriented and naturalistic. In attempting to account for the world without invoking the gods (at least the anthropomorphic ones), there is a beginning of the disenchantment of the world, as has already been intimated above. The point is succinctly made by G. E. R. Lloyd in his *Polarity and Analogy: Two Types of Argumentation in Early Greek Thought*. Of Thales' idea of the world he writes: "[It] is a rational account, a logos, first in that it omits any reference to anthropomorphic gods or the supernatural, and secondly, in that it is based on a certain positive analogy between the effect to be explained (why the earth is 'held up') and an effect that is observed elsewhere (solid objects being 'held up' when they float)."[116]

---

114. Ibid, p. 213.
115. Ibid., pp. 223–24. For a similar position see Dodds, *The Greeks and the Irrational*, p. 179.
116. Lloyd, *Polarity and Analogy*, p. 308.

According to Snell, then, this transitional thought provides the foundations of science, although it is not in itself science. That awareness of the thought of the Milesians as scientific in character is confirmed, he insists, in that it eliminated much in life, as does modern science, sweeping aside a great deal of what he refers to as the fullness of experience.[117]

Popper's controversial essay on "Back to the Presocratics" draws a like conclusion about the work of the early philosophers, but is much less pessimistic about its significance for human/humane existence. Popper champions the Milesians as the founders of scientific rationality and, although there are problems of detail in his interpretation of the Milesians that might be questioned,[118] his account of their rationality in terms of the development of a "critical attitude" and a "tradition of criticism" persuasively reinforces the view of a revolution in thought achieved by them. It should be noted here that Popper argues that the Milesians constructed not empirical theories of the world but rather "critical and speculative" theories.[119] They are therefore not the founders of modern science but rather the founders of modern scientific rationality. That a theory did not originate in empirical observation is not important, he insists, but it is important that it have explanatory

117. Kirk expressed a similar sentiment, talking of myth as "adulterated"reason (*Myth: Its Meaning and Functions*) as does Findlay in *Plato*, pp. 411–12. Finley, (*Four Stages of Greek Thought*) talks of the "visionary mind" as one of "full consciousness" wherein meanings are within human grasp but which are given up in the pursuit of special intellectual powers. Mythology made meanings possible, conceptual thinking seems to destroy them (see chapter 2). Havelock's *The Crucifixion of Intellectual Man* sets out the conflict between modes of thought by showing that the "scientific world-view" is not really a view in the time honoured sense of providing a framework of meaning for our lives. But science, despite this shortcoming and even though it may kill us, "will not allow us to retreat" (p. 9). Consequently knowledge is, according to Havelock, the special burden of the age, as is indicated in the title of his first chapter: "The Bitter Fruit of the Tree of Knowledge." The Presocratics, therefore, provide the foundation for a "tragic humanism" (represented in the Prometheus myth), for there is a "civil war" between mythology and science. Since modern western civilization is built upon the ascendancy of "intellectual man," we too have that "civil strife."

118. See, for example, Kirk, "Popper on Science and the Presocratics." Popper responded with a further paper on the matter as did Kirk: see Popper, "Kirk on Heraclitus, and on Fire as the Cause of Balance," which appeared, in part, in *Mind* n.s. 72 (1963) and was reprinted in his *Conjectures and Refutations*, as "Historical Conjectures and Heraclitus on Change"; and Kirk, "Sense and Common-sense in the Development of Greek Philosophy."

119. Popper, "Back to the Presocratics," p. 140.

power and that it be open to and capable of standing up to criticism and to tests.[120] Popper concludes: "The early history of Greek philosophy especially the history from Thales to Plato, is a splendid story. It is almost too good to be true. In every generation we find at least one new philosophy, one new cosmology of staggering originality and depth. How was this possible? Of course one cannot explain originality and genius. But one can try to throw some light on them. What was the secret of the ancients? I suggest that it was a *tradition – the tradition of critical discussion.*"[121]

Some more recent work on early Greek philosophy by Lloyd, confirms this Popperian kind of understanding of the significance of the Milesians. That agreement is first expressed in his response to the Popper-Kirk controversy[122] and is more fully taken up in his *Early Greek Science: Thales to Aristotle.*[123] In two other works, *Polarity and Analogy: Two Types of Argumentation in Early Greek Thought*, and *Magic, Reason and Experience: Studies in the Origins and Development of Greek Science*, both of which were written as a contribution to the debate over the supposed difference between traditional/primitive and modern modes of thought, his conclusions are essentially the same. Both works deserve detailed examination but I shall have to content myself with simply reporting his conclusions. In the former volume he argues that the thought of the philosophers marks a very definite break with earlier thought and he writes: "They are for the first time cosmological theories, presenting conceptions of the cosmos as a unity: they are

120. Ibid., p. 140.
121. Ibid., pp. 148–49.
122. Lloyd, "Popper versus Kirk."
123. Lloyd, *Early Greek Science*; see especially pp. 10, 12, 13, 15 *et passim*. The following passage is very Popperian in tone: "The history of Milesian views about the primary substance is chiefly remarkable for the way in which the awareness of the problems grew from one philosopher to the next. Anaximander's suggestion that the primary substance is undifferentiated seems to counter an obvious objection to Thales' postulate of water – that is, how can its opposite, fire, have come to be. Anaximenes' theory of condensation and rarefaction gives a clearer account of the changes that affect the primary substance than Anaximander's idea that a seed separates off from the Boundless. As is usual in the history of science, their actual theories strike a later age as childish – they already appeared so to Aristotle. But the measure of their achievement is the advance they made in grasping the problems. They rejected supernatural causation and appreciated that naturalistic explanations can and should be given a wide range of phenomena . . . " (p. 23; see also p. 142). Furthermore, Lloyd's analyses of other scientific but nonphilosophic texts, namely the texts of the *Hippocratic Corpus*, confirm this kind of view of the Milesian development.

subject to rational criticism and debate: and where pre-philosophical myths tend to refer to arbitrary personal deities, the philosophers adopted their political, biological and technological images to express the notions of order and rationality themselves. If we may say that the types of images in the philosophers broadly resemble those which can be found in earlier beliefs and myths, these images now become the vehicle for the expression of original and important theories about the nature of the cosmos."[124]

In the latter volume, after warning against exaggerating the extent to which the critical approach typified Greek thought (even Greek empirical/scientific thought as found in the texts of the *Hippocratic Corpus*) and even though denying that Greek philosophy and science are the product of a wholly different mentality in the sense of using a different logic, he still maintains that this development is a unique turning-point in the history of thought.[125] The comparative evidence

124. Lloyd, *Polarity and Analogy*, pp. 414–15.
125. Lloyd, *Magic, Reason, and Experience*, p. 264. See also Lloyd's *Science, Folklore and Ideology* and his inaugural lecture, *Science and Morality in Greco-Roman Antiquity*. Though cautiously, he holds here essentially the views expressed in earlier publications. In his most recent, *The Revolution of Wisdom*, the tone of caution is continued but he nevertheless still talks about the "displacements of mythology" and contrasts Greek scientific documents with those of Egypt and Babylonia (p. 57). He writes: "My theme has been that one of the striking and distinctive features of much of early Greek thought, particularly when we contrast it with what we know from some other ancient civilizations, relates to the degree of overtness of innovation and of the contestability of tradition" (p. 102). He concludes as follows: "The distinction between science and myth, between the new wisdom and the old, was often a fine one, and the failures of ancient science to practise what it preached are frequent; yet what it preached was different from myth, and not *just* more of the same, more myth" (p. 336). For a similar argument, see Furley, *The Greek Cosmologists*, section 5 of chapter 11 entitled "The Progress of Rationalism," pp. 163–68.
Humphreys criticizes Lloyd's timidity regarding the break between *mythos* and *logos*. In his " 'Transcendence' and Intellectual Roles," he objects to Lloyd's understanding of the nature of mythical thought in the Greeks and maintains that Lloyd overemphasizes the continuity between myth and rational argument (p.303 n. 26). Humphreys' interpretation of a more radical distinction between these two modes of thought is based on Bernstein's distinction between restricted and elaborated speech codes in "On the Classification and Framing of Educational Knowledge." Humphreys concludes: "If this is a valid approach, the early Greek philosophers were not merely making explicit the 'informal logic implicit in primitive or archaic thought' . . . but were trying to make propositions that were self-evident because of their linguistic form, rather than depending on confirmatory information embedded in the context of communication" (p. 304). Humphreys further elaborates on Bernstein's distinction between speech codes in his

shows, he insists, that the central element in that development is the general scepticism and critical inquiry directed at fundamental issues.

Recent histories of science chart a similar development in Greek thought, and I shall refer briefly to three such accounts. S. Sambursky in his *The Physical World of the Greeks* talks of the Milesians as having effected (created) a scientific revolution[126] that "opened up a new era in the history of systematic thought. . . . "[127] Indeed, according to Sambursky it is that cosmos of the Presocratic philosopher that is the "rock from which our own cosmos has been hewn."[128] He admits that some continuity between the Milesians and their predecessors exists[129] but argues that we have with the Milesians the beginning of the severance of *mythos* and *logos* that is completed in the seventeenth century. Two brief quotations make Sambursky's stance clear: "Greek science's achievement of independence through the struggle of logos against mythos is in many respects similar to the birth of modern science from the assault on petrified medieval scholasticism. With the study of nature set free from the control of mythological fancy, the way was open for the development of science as an intellectual system."[130] "Greek science and modern science alike have their origins in a revolutionary departure from what preceded them. The Milesian school opposed logos to mythos, while Galileo and the investigators of the seventeenth century set science free from the swaddling bands of the Church and made it an independent sphere of human thought."[131]

Georgio de Santillana's *The Origins of Scientific Thought*, although recognizing Milesian thought to be a theology and a theodicy,[132] maintains that it also lays the foundation for a natural philosophy in that the Milesians did not, like their predecessors, trace everything that happened back to the gods. "What made the Ionian way 'physical,'" he writes, "is that the cause of things is no longer imagined in a dramatic or mythical way, but as some kind of primordial – and stable –

"Evolution and History;" also in *Anthropology and the Greeks*, especially pp. 265–73. See also Gernet's "The Origins of Greek Philosophy," upon which Humphreys draws.

126. Sambursky, *The Physical World of the Greeks*, p. 18.
127. Ibid., p. 31.
128. Ibid., p. 276.
129. Ibid., p. 274.
130. Ibid., pp. 18–19.
131. Ibid., p. 255.
132. G. de Santillana, *The Origins of Scientific Thought*, p. 42.

substance."[133] In this "the light of reason has dispelled Chthonian darkness."[134]

S. Toulmin and June Goodfield's *The Fabric of the Heavens* is a slightly ambiguous affirmation of the line of argument I have thus far set out. Toulmin and Goodfield on a number of occasions refer to the procedures of the Milesians as resting on faith[135] but do still insist that Milesian thought is the product of purely intellectual types (not prophets)[136] and that it was a rational impulse and motive that lay behind their inquiries.[137] I can best summarize their position by quoting their response to the question as to the novel element to be found in Presocratic/Milesian thought: "Perhaps the best way of putting it is to say they transformed our whole manner of understanding natural phenomena. By their definition, the philosopher was a man who related the visible changes in nature to the permanent principles underlying them, showing in this way why the events happened as they did. The mythologist or magic worker might have an intuitive 'feel' for the moods of nature, a familiarity born of long practical experience, and his advice might often be effective for this very reason. . . . But the natural philosopher was not satisfied until he could back up his explanations by arguments. He must have a theory."[138]

According to Peter Gay in *The Enlightenment: The Rise of Modern Paganism* the rise of science meant a recovery of the programme of classical antiquity as against Christianity.[139] The modern Enlightenment, like the enlightenment of the ancient Greeks, accepted the intellect as the only avenue to truth. Consequently, science was taken to be a revolt against superstition and the formation of a disenchanted world-view. The Christians, it was generally felt, were caught in a

133. Ibid., p. 22.
134. Ibid., p. 40.
135. Toulmin and Goodfield, *The Fabric of the Heavens*, pp. 66, 79.
136. Ibid., pp. 56, 68.
137. Ibid., p. 57.
138. Ibid., p. 69. It is often claimed that one does not understand what mythology is all about because there is no "communion" with nature and so, consequently, no "intuitive feel" for it. Such a claim is made, for example, by Jacobsen in his *Toward the Image of Tammuz*: "For our modern inability to understand myth is very largely our inability to 'commune' with matter and the powers that inform it. . . . There is, then, truly no other way toward understanding myths either as myths or as literature other than the laborious one of trying to recapture the lost unity of the human soul with the universe as matter and phenomenon" (pp. 60–61).
139. Gay, *The Enlightenment*, p. xi.

myth[140] for by philosophy (science) they meant "not so much a technical discipline as a stance toward the world, a critical freedom."[141]

The essential elements of this programme were understood to be criticism and power – the first adopted from the Ionians who were taken to constitute the first enlightenment since it was a move from myth to reason:[142] "In magical thinking," writes Gay, "mind is inhabited by a demon and the world is constantly, bewilderingly, alive; in philosophy the demon is exorcised and the confusion is reduced to laws."[143]

Brian Easlea's *Witch-Hunting, Magic and the New Philosophy: An Introduction to Debate of the Scientific Revolution 1450–1750* makes it plain that that revolution was not, as the Enlightenment philosophers perceived it to be, a straightforward triumph of reason over prejudice and irrationality. Easlea maintains, and with some justification, that the revolution must also be seen to have intimate dependence upon the fortunes of the social forces in society, especially the highly stratified society of Europe in that day. Nevertheless, scientific mechanism is still triumphant even in Easlea's account.[144]

If scholarship were able not only to exhibit the differences that exist between the thought of the poets and the philosopher but also to show *how* that critical attitude of the philosophers came to be, the dichotomy thesis elaborated here would be considerably strengthened. Are there "mechanisms of change and transformation," so to speak, that would explain the rise of this tradition? There are a few such works, I think, that suggest such mechanisms can in fact be found to have been operative. I shall advert to only a few of them here.

Havelock's *Preface to Plato* confirms this kind of dichotomous reading of the development of Greek thought, although Havelock sees the originator of the revolution to be Plato rather than the Presocratics. Indeed, he refers to the Milesians as a "Preplatonic" attempt to achieve

140. Ibid., p. 151.
141. Ibid., p. 159; see also pp. 212, 229, *et passim*.
142. Ibid., pp. 72, 81.
143. Ibid., p. 185.
144. It must be acknowledged here, however, that Foster has argued that the scientific revolution of the seventeenth century is due specifically to the impetus provided by the Christian doctrine of creation. See his "The Christian Doctrine of Creation and the Rise of Modern Natural Science" and "Christian Theology and Modern Science of Nature I & II." There is some merit to this argument but it does not hold the field as the only reasonable position. Space does not permit extended criticism here. However, for alternative views see, among others, Goldstein's *The Dawn of Science*.

conceptual thought.[145] He does not deny that Hesiod and the Presocratics mark the *beginning* of the "great transition" in thought but
maintains that its chief and most important architect is Plato;[146] they
are precursors, "proto-thinkers," only.[147] Plato's attack on *mimesis* in
the *Republic*, according to Havelock, is the first direct, conscious
attempt to accelerate an intellectual awakening – an attempt to bring
about a conversion from the Homeric state of mind.[148] The contrast
he draws is that between poetry and science: "The poetic experience
is the function of a faculty which is the antithesis of science; it is a
condition of opinion which accepts a constant wandering and contradiction in physical reporting; one which is alien to number and calculation."[149] The image-thinking of poetry is radically different from the
abstract thinking of philosophy. Havelock accounts for this shift in
thought in terms of the emergence of alphabetic writing and the conse-
quent decline of the oral culture of Homer: "As a method of preservation the acoustic technology of epic had been rendered obsolete by the
technology of the written word."[150]

A full account of Havelock's argument and supporting evidence
cannot be provided here.[151] In any event, a claim similar in many
respects is made by J.-P. Vernant, and to this I shall give some attention

145. Havelock, *Preface to Plato*, p. 298.
146. Ibid., pp. 99, 267.
147. Ibid., p. 295. Finley, *Four Stages of Greek Thought*, also sees Plato as the true
author of the new conceptuality that *replaces* "the old half-sensate reliance on myth" (p.
97). Finkelbergh, "Orphic and Milesian Thought," though insisting "on the unity of
Orphic and Milesian thought" nevertheless sees the speculative pantheism of the Milesians as the origin of Greek philosophy. That speculative pantheism, he argues, was
ultimately subject to a nonreligious development. Consequently, he writes, "the differences between Orphic and early Presocratic thought acquire significance only when
viewed from the standpoint of the ultimate results of the historical development of the
latter" (p. 334).
148. Havelock, *Preface to Plato*, pp. 177–78.
149. Ibid., p. 239.
150. Ibid., p. 293.
151. That account would also have to take into consideration Havelock's "Pre-literacy
and the Pre-Socratics"; *Prologue to Greek Literacy*, and "The Alphabetization of Homer."
These and other essays have been reprinted in Havelock's recent *The Literate Revolution
in Greece*. This volume with its lengthy introductory essay is a very important contribution
to this debate. Other major works of importance by Havelock include *The Crucifixion of
Intellectual Man*, *The Liberal Temper in Greek Politics*, and *The Greek Concept of Justice*. See
also his more recent essay, "The Alphabetic Mind." Essays of relevance on Havelock's
work can be found in Robb, *Language and Thought*, vol. 1.

below. However, a comment is required on Havelock's attribution of the revolutionary shift of thought to Plato rather than to the Milesians. That claim is seriously weakened in Havelock's recognition that Plato falls into the very trap he set out to destroy;[152] that is, that he betrays the dialectic.[153] In the light of such an admission his claim that Plato is the only one who saw the real issue "steadily and whole" is hardly persuasive.[154]

Vernant's studies of myth in ancient Greece provide further corroboration of the thesis set out here, for he, like Havelock, provides a persuasive argument regarding the mechanism of change that pushed

152. Havelock, *Preface to Plato*, pp. 268–69.

153. Ibid., p. 271.

154. Ibid., p. 267. Indeed, a comparison of Plato's ontology with that implicit in archaic and primitive modes of thought, which is essentially dualistic, reveals remarkable similarities. Eliade, in *Cosmos and History*, maintains that in the archaic frame of mind (the "archaic mentality") neither acts nor objects/things have any intrinsic value but only acquire value by participating in a reality that transcends them (p. 4, *et passim*). He then proceeds to claim, and I think quite rightly so, that "it could be said that this 'primitive' ontology has a Platonic structure; and [that] in that case Plato could be regarded as the outstanding philosopher of 'primitive mentality', that is, the thinker who succeeded in giving philosophic currency and validity to the modes of life and behavior of archaic humanity" (p. 34). Plato, according to Eliade, therefore provides theoretical justification of this archaic vision through "dialectical means"; I see it only as an attempt to coopt reason for such "ulterior purpose" and that it failed.

The same theme is sounded by Eliade in chapter six of his *Myth and Reality*, although with more ambiguity. Eliade seems to suggest that Presocratic philosophy, even where vestiges of mythopoeic thought are present, is still a break with that mode of thought: "It was in seeking the source, the principle, the *arche*, that philosophical speculation for a short time coincided with cosmogony; but it was no longer cosmogonic myth, it was ontological problem" (p. 111). Greek religion, therefore, is "'demythicized" – a process that, paradoxically, flowers in Socrates and Plato (p. 112). However, Eliade also notes that even philosophical thought can be used to fulfill the function of myth, and he maintains that Plato is still a partisan of the archaic mode of thought (pp. 111–12). He goes on to suggest that mythological themes still "'survive" (p. 112) in Aristotle. If his choice of the word survive is deliberate, as a contrast to Plato's "'partisanship," I am in agreement. If Eliade means that Aristotle is indistinguishable from Plato in this regard I would disagree – but that is a matter for discussion elsewhere or another time. (Similar themes are sounded in his *Australian Religions*, pp. 50, 58–59). Schlagel presents a similar view of Plato in his *From Myth to the Modern Mind*, vol. 1; see especially chapter 12, "Plato's Mythical Cosmology." Schlagel's general thesis about Greek philosophy is similar to that which I present in this chapter. Unfortunately, his work came to my attention too late for consideration. Although our positions are very much alike, our different intentions have led to significant differences in our respective treatments of the problem of the emergence of the modern mind.

Greek thinking out of the poetic fold. Like the other scholars reviewed here, he maintains, despite differences in the detailed interpretations, that between the eighth and the fourth centuries BCE various tensions in the mental universe of the Greeks emerged and led to a clear separation of *mythos* from *logos* – a separation that did not exist prior to that period. Those tensions emerged, he suggests, with the invention of writing which represents not only a different mode of expression of thought from that of the oral tradition and its poetic composition but also a wholly new form of thought. Similarly, of course, the operation of reading presupposes a different attitude of mind that has a direct bearing on myths and their reception. According to Vernant, "oral narration stimulates its public to an affective communion with the dramatic actions recounted in the story."[155] Writing and prose composition, on the other hand, allow for a stricter ordering of conceptual material and more rigorous analysis and call for more rigorous reasoning compared with the persuasive techniques of rhetorical argument. Consequently, by foregoing drama, the *logos* acts on the mind at a different level. Indeed, so different are these ways of thought that Vernant speaks easily of the movement "from myth to history and philosophy." Thus, in the final analysis, the Greek tradition itself, especially in Plato and Aristotle condemns mythical thinking: "There is now such a gap between mythos and logos that communication between the two breaks down; dialogue becomes impossible since the break is complete. Even when they appear to have the same object, to be directed towards the same end, the two types of discourse remain mutually impenetrable. *From now on to choose one of the two types of language is in effect to dismiss the other.*"[156]

In an earlier work (although only recently translated), Vernant also connects the emergence of Greek thought to peculiar social and politi-

---

155. Vernant, *Myth and Society*, p. 189.
156. Ibid., p. 193; emphasis added. In his essay "The Formation of Positivist Thought in Archaic Greece," he characterizes the contrast as follows: "Mythical logic rests on this ambiguity. Myth operates on two levels at once: Thus the same phenomenon – for example, the separation of water from earth is understood simultaneously, both as a natural fact in the visible world and a divine birth at the beginning of time." What is new in the Milesians "is that these powers are strictly defined and conceived in abstract terms: they are limited to producing a definite physical effect, and this effect is a general abstract quality" (p. 348).

cal developments in early Greek culture.[157] Of the greatest significance, he insists, is the destruction of a peculiar kind of oriental kingship with the crumbling of Mycenaean power. In the ensuing period (1100–900 BCE) there emerges the institution of the city-state and with it, the birth of rational thought. In the city-state Greek political life aimed to become the subject of *public debate* between citizens defined as equals – whose plural rights presented problems of equilibrium. This requires openness and makes for critical thought – it constituted a kind of secularization of political thought; a rejection of authority that allowed for the give-and-take of debate. "The advent of the *polis*," Vernant argues then, "constitutes a decisive event in the history of Greek thought."[158] Of just how original this innovation was, the Greeks were quite unaware. Vernant concludes: "The advent of the *polis*, the birth of philosophy – the two sequences of phenomena are so closely linked that the origin of rational thought must be seen as bound up with the social and mental structure peculiar to the Greek city."[159] The evolution of rational thought, therefore, may have been gradual, but its distinctness from the nonrational thought that precedes it is nevertheless obvious.

Finally, a comment on George Thomson's *The First Philosophers: Studies in Ancient Greek Society*. Thomson attempts to account for the Milesian revolution of thought in terms of the social relations brought about by new means of commodity production and the circulation of money. Although space does not allow examination of his argument here, the thesis certainly warrants further investigation.

THE BIRTH OF THE MODERN MIND.

There are still some scholars who are not persuaded that the Milesians entered into a new mode of mental existence opposed to the mythic mode already in place. I shall bring this chapter to a conclusion in examining the force of at least one such opponent, namely G. S. Kirk. His main arguments are to be found in his *Myth: Its Meaning and Function in Ancient and Other Cultures* and in his later *The Nature of*

157. Vernant, *The Origins of Greek Thought*. See also on this count Cornford's "Mystery Religions and Pre-Socratic Philosophy" and Thomson, *Aeschylus and Athens*.
158. Ibid., p. 49.
159. Ibid., p. 130.

Greek Myths. In the former volume he maintains that the enormously complex formation of myths, and in particular of Greek myths, has not been understood, and that further examination will show the emergence of the earliest Ionian philosophers to be not quite so simple and cataclysmic as is often thought.[160] According to Kirk, there may rather have been a mythical stage of thought in the far distant past but only at a time when the term Greek had almost no meaning. And even then, given our present ignorance of myth in the second millenium BCE in Greece, we would do well, he argues, "to omit from it the element of mythopoeic thought as an exclusive mode of conceptualizing and discovery."[161] Greek thought, therefore, has been a combination of myth and fable mixed with literal statement and intermittent logic for many generations preceding the emergence of Ionian philosophy and is not to be found exclusively either in the Milesians or, say, in Hesiod before them. Furthermore, Kirk maintains, such a mixed form of thought is retained by the Ionians as well,[162] and therefore that "direct statement, or *logos*, only gradually replaced *mythos*, and then with heavy travail, in the course of the fifth and fourth centuries B.C."[163]

The ambiguity in Kirk's conclusions is obvious: mythical explanations do seem at some point to give way to rational ones, and conceptual language seems to gain ascendency over nonconceptual language or symbolic language. One can agree with Kirk that this is not, in all probability, a matter of an innate rationality amongst Greeks that made them immune to the fantasies of myth, but rather that it emerged

---

160. Kirk, *Myth*, p. 249. Otto, in *The Homeric Gods*, for example sees Homeric thought to represent such a shift of thought which, he insists, constitutes the source of all later Greek science as well as of the arts. "We can classify the world view of peoples according to the degree by which they are preoccupied and controlled by magic thinking. None has so completely overcome magic in its characteristic world of thought as has the Greek. In the Homeric world, magic possesses no importance, whether we look at gods or men, and the few cases where knowledge of magic is indicated only go to show how remote it had become. The gods do not practice enchantment even though at times they bring things to pass in a manner reminiscent of ancient magic. Their might, like their essence, is based not on magical *power*, but on the *being* of nature. 'Nature' is the great new word which the matured Greek spirit opposed to ancient magic. From here the path leads directly to the arts and to the sciences of the Greeks" (p. 37). See also p. 236 on the role of the Olympian gods in determining the direction of Greek thought.

161. Kirk, *Myth*, p. 241.

162. Ibid., p. 247.

163. Ibid., p. 249.

because of other factors, political and social (e.g., the rise of the city-state and its unique form of democracy, and the spread of literacy), without foregoing the dichotomy view of mind.

Kirk's rejection of a mythopoeic mode of thought is, however, set out even more forcefully in the later volume on Greek myths. He writes: "Deprived of support from dreams (not a form of thought) and primitive mentality (a chimera) 'mythical thinking' can be clearly seen for what it is: the unnatural offspring of a psychological anachronism, and epistemological confusion and a historical red herring."[164] Yet even here he recognizes that, for example, "the organic use of myths," as he puts it, must be given up before philosophy can even become a possibility.[165] Furthermore, he also admits that rational thinking involves a "special kind of *attitude*" that involves general terms and systematic structure.[166] Moreover, that attitude involved a rejection of the supernatural. He does, however, reject the idea that the acceptance of divine elements in myth should be associated with an exclusive kind of mythical thinking, even though it might be indicative of a kind of "religious thinking."[167] His own thinking here however, it seems to me, is quite confused. He recognizes that the supernatural element in myths is not merely a conventional matter, but one "drastically altering the limits of the possible," and therefore indicating "a degree of systematic irrationality,"[168] and yet still argues that it is not the polar opposite of rational thinking but *merely* a different logic. This obviously is to espouse a form of the dichotomy view he has been arguing against so vociferously. The ambiguity is obvious in the following passage: "Beside religious thinking one could set a kind that is better termed poetic, the common quality of both modes being that each, while applying reason to some parts of its subject matter, uses various looser metaphorical procedures for other parts. Myths in their primary forms

---

164. Kirk, *The Nature of Greek Myths*, p. 286. The relationship of myths to dreams has not been discussed here. However, I think the evidence presented in section three of this chapter shows Kirk's claim that mythical thinking is a chimera to be premature at best and probably false. Talk of mythical thinking, it has been argued above, is not an anachronism. That it is not an epistemological confusion has been given strong support in Gellner's analysis above and, lastly, the argument in this section suggests that it is not a historical red herring.

165. Ibid., p. 279.
166. Ibid., p. 289.
167. Ibid., p. 292.
168. Ibid., p. 292.

may be held to involve something like poetic thinking, which proceeds by emotional as well as logical stages to achieve a quasi-intellectual end by impressionistic or inconsequential means."[169] These modes of thought, however, had to be abandoned before philosophy could get off the ground, and the Ionians, he seems to admit, were the first to take this step by consciously rejecting "the tradition of mythical explanation."[170]

Given the weight of the argument and evidence set out here and given the weaknesses of the critics and their alternative accounts of the nature and significance of the Milesian experiment in thought, one is almost forced to conclude that the Milesian revolution, for the first time in history, provided humankind with a second mode of mental existence quite distinct from the prevalent mythopoeic structures of mind characteristic of the human race up to that time.

I want to be very clear about this. I am not claiming that no rational thought or nonmythical thought antedated the Presocratics. Indeed, there is little question, as I have admitted in the discussion of Levi-Strauss in the preceding chapter, that primitives are motivated by a need to construct conceptual frameworks to insure successful existence. But even Levi-Strauss, it was pointed out, was forced to draw a distinction between the concrete operational sciences of the primitive and the abstract theoretical sciences of the modern, and, I would argue, of the ancient Greek philosophers. The crucial difference between the two sciences is the autonomy of the latter and the subordinate character of the former. This difference is clearly documented throughout this chapter and it is sharply focused in H. J. Muller's account of the beginning of philosophy and science to which he refers as "The Birth of the Modern World."[171] "The singular originality and audacity of the Greeks," he writes, "can be appreciated only by contrast with the ancient East. There had been plenty of nonmythical thought in the East, as evidenced by all the empirical knowledge it had accumulated in agriculture, metallurgy, medicine, mathematics, and astronomy. . . . Yet all this industry only underlines the failure of the East to develop philosophy and science. Its learning simply fortified its essential irratio-

169. Ibid., p. 292.
170. Ibid., p. 295. It is interesting that in neither of these volumes does Kirk advert to his differences with Popper or to the response of Lloyd to his debate with Popper on precisely these questions.
171. Muller, The Loom of History, p. 97.

nality. From the beginning its thinkers were on the wrong track, and they never suspected it, never discovered a means of getting on another track. Magic remained their premise, myth their conclusion."[172] The essential Oriental failing here is not that of shortcomings of the civil law or abuses of monarchy, but rather an essential irrationality in the voluntarist framework within which their sciences were undertaken. Obedience to the king as representative of the gods remained a ruling principle that bred renunciation and resignation rather than critical searching for understanding and power (control). The intellectuals, that is, perceived their task to be to serve the gods. The primary principle is the (arbitrary) will of the gods, not the immutable principles of the transformation of substance(s) that can explain the world impersonally. Herschel Baker, in his *The Image of Man*, had already come to the same conclusion on this score. The Greeks, unlike their "oriental neighbours" bowed to no priest and submitted to no sacred book(s): "Their universe was to be philosophically understood, not religiously venerated and worshipped for its master,"[173] or relied upon, one might add, for grace.

This failing may be defined more abstractly as the inability of oriental culture to move out of a narrative and into a discursive mode of thought. Both cultures presume to explain the world but the former is *necessarily* incomplete and hence arbitrary and irrational. Finley's assessment of the matter cannot, I think, be disputed: "Myth is specific and concrete, explaining both natural and human phenomena by reference to particular supernatural events or actions, in themselves unaccountable. The Ionian revolution was simply this, that Thales and his successors asked generalized questions and proposed general, rational, 'impersonal' answers."[174]

172. Ibid., pp. 121–22. The "East" referred to here is not, of course, the civilizations of India and China referred to in n. 97 to chapter 1 but rather the "ancient near East."
173. Baker, *The Image of Man*, p. 4. There are some interesting questions involved here. Christianity, for example, seems to turn the tables on these developments (see pp. 140ff). See also on this score, Schneidau's *Sacred Discontent*. One might well consult as well, however, Havelock's *The Crucifixion of Intellectual Man*, pp. 33, 36, 106.
174. Finley, *The Ancient Greeks*, pp. 117–18. There are many other readings of the Presocratics that I have not been able to treat here. There is one, however, that is of particular relevance to my argument that must receive at least a passing comment, namely that of Heidegger. Heidegger's understanding of the Presocratics is eccentric, to say the least. His thinking, I would argue, is essentially religious/mythopoeic and his interpretation of the early Greek thinkers therefore also essentially a "religious" reading. I cannot here develop his understanding of the nature of thought but a few comments

in that regard should help account for not focussing attention on his reading of the Presocratics in this book.

In his *Discourse on Thinking*, Heidegger seems to present a "dichotomous" understanding of thinking, distinguishing calculative thought from meditative thought. Calculative thought corresponds to philosophic/scientific thought and is referred to as computation: "Calculative thinking races from one prospect to the next. Calculative thinking never stops, never collects itself. Calculative thinking is not meditative thinking, not thinking which contemplates the meaning which reigns in everything that is" (p. 46). Heidegger refuses to countenance the value of calculative thinking which he sees as a seventeenth-century revolution in thought, remaining unknown outside the West, and being, he asserts, "altogether alien to former ages and histories" (p. 50). The Presocratics, consequently, could not have achieved what has been described in this chapter.

It is the meditative kind of thinking that is Heidegger's special concern in all his later works. In *What is Called Thinking* he maintains that we can only come to know it "if we radically unlearn what thinking has been traditionally" (p. 8, see also p. 213). "Surely," he writes, "as long as we take the view that logic gives us any information about what thinking is, we shall never be able to think how much all poesy rests upon thinking back, recollection" (p. 11). And the attack on logic in his *Introduction to Metaphysics* is a sustained attempt to arrive at what he calls a radical and stricter thinking – "a thinking that is part and parcel with being" (p. 103). Meditative thinking, therefore, does not bring knowledge as do the sciences; does not produce any useable practical wisdom; solves no cosmic riddles; and does not endow one with the power to act (*What is Called Thinking*, p. 159). It becomes obvious in very short order, then, that for Heidegger, thinking is a "Way" to be embarked upon (p. 167) and not something to be spoken about – it is, in fact, a kind of divination (p. 207). That "religious quality" to thinking becomes even more apparent in Heidegger's "The End of Philosophy and the Task of Thinking" (in *On Time and Being*), in which a notion of poetic thinking and its peculiar meditative character begins to take shape.

With such an understanding of what thinking is Heidegger could have nothing but scorn for the attempt to delineate the nature of thought sketched in this chapter. "To search for influences and dependencies among thinkers," he writes, "is to misunderstand thinking. Every thinker is dependent – upon the address of Being" (*Early Greek Thinking*, p. 55). Thinking does not "originate" but is simply present when "Being presences" (p. 39–40). To understand thinking, then, is to enter upon the way of thinking which requires a patient waiting – even a whole lifetime of waiting (*Introduction to Metaphysics*, p. 172). Such meditative thinking, according to him, is to be found in the work of the earliest Greek philosophers.

This pastiche of passages is not meant to pass for an adequate description of Heidegger's notion of thinking. I have provided this sketch merely to reveal Heidegger's peculiar view of the Greeks and to show the radically different understanding of thinking from the one I have detected in the Presocratics. This description is accurate enough to show that what Heidegger understands to be thinking has far greater affinities with what I have described in the preceding chapter as mythopoeic thinking, but with a distinctly religious tone. (See on this score, for example, Macquarrie, *Martin Heidegger*; Williams, *Martin Heidegger's Philosophy of Religion*; Waterhouse, *A Heidegger Critique*; and Gadamer, "The Religious Dimension of Heidegger."

Heidegger's work on the Greeks, therefore, is in my opinion, more an eisegesis than

If this is overstating the case, it can at least be said that such a view of the significance of the Milesians and Presocratics more generally, is not at all implausible. Furthermore, the argument here also makes it quite evident that a logical chasm separates the two modes of thought, and that makes it impossible to inhabit both simultaneously with consistency.[175]

---

an exegesis. It is self-consciously concerned with undermining the power of scientific (calculative) thought. Though espousing a dichotomy view of thought similar to the one developed in chapter 2 above, Heidegger, on *a priori* grounds it seems, pronounces the bankruptcy of our present day scientific thought and therefore presumes that the thought upon which our present culture seems founded could not be scientific in character but rather mythopoeic. The argument of the present chapter, I think, shows the inadequacy of that conclusion. A contrary, i.e., sympathetic view of Heidegger's readings of the presocratics can be found in Seidel, *Martin Heidegger and the Presocratics*.

175. My position, which I attempt to elaborate in chapter four, stands in stark contrast to the Foucaultian stance adopted by Veyne in his *Did the Greeks Believe in Their Myths?*. Veyne talks of the emergence of "modalities of wavering belief" that permit simultaneous belief in "incompatible truths" (p. 56). That such coexistence of contradictory beliefs is possible is not in dispute here. What is in dispute is the further, and apparently contradictory, claim that since the beliefs are held simultaneously by many they cannot really be contradictory. Veyne, like Foucault, denies that it is possible to evade what Gellner (see chapter one) refers to as "the enchanted vision" that conflates the descriptive and explanatory function of language with its evaluative and identificatory function although, paradoxically, his own account of Greek beliefs is presented as if it were a neutral description of the ancient Greeks. The distinction between meaning and knowledge as different goals to which intellectual activity is directed, to which I draw attention in this book, shows a clear need for considerable refinement of the very ambiguous notion of truth used by Veyne – refinement that will seriously undermine his critique of interpretations of Greek thought that preserve a radical difference between its myth and its science.

IV

Theology and the Religion of Ancient Greece

RELIGION AND THEOLOGY: THE QUESTION OF CONTINUITY

AS THE DISCUSSION of the previous chapter amply illustrates, it is impossible to talk of the emergence of philosophical/scientific thought and its early development without making constant reference to Greek religion and theology. Indeed, that fact has often been invoked as justification for a religio-theological reading of the philosophers that makes of them but religious reformers, and for denying, therefore, any radical distinction between the structure of their thought and that which it succeeds. I do not here wish to dispute the claim that one can justifiably speak about a Presocratic theology or, more generally, Greek theology, but I shall argue that the so-called theology of the Presocratic philosophers is for the most part, not only not concerned with the reformation of traditional Greek religion or with its elaboration, but rather, in providing an account of the gods, winds up undermining it, even if only indirectly.

The persistence of religion and (mythopoeic) religious thought, despite the emergence of a mode of thought that in some senses supersedes it, should not be altogether surprising. It would simply be naive, as suggested earlier, to suppose that any new cultural development could, at a single stroke, wholly free itself from all traditional ideas and concepts. Philosophical/scientific thought did not spring forth fully formed like Athena from the brow of Zeus; earlier modes of thought lived on side by side with later intellectual developments; and the vocabularies of the two often overlapped. Although having formulated a new – if not, indeed, revolutionary – problematic, the new breed of thinkers did not have ready to hand an adequate technical vocabulary with which to tackle it. They could but borrow a terminology from the structures of thought from which they were emerging – stretching and shaping it to new aims and purposes. That some of the categories borrowed are religious, does not necessarily indicate a continuation of the original religious interest, even though a superficial reading may suggest as much. Reference to divinity in the hylozoist explanations of the universe by the Milesians, for example, may on first sight suggest the beginning of a form of theology, the intention of which is to elaborate on and advance the knowledge of the gods in the poets. On the other hand, however, the concept of divinity (*theos*) may have been the only available category whereby the "physicists" could, with any appropriate degree of adequacy, characterize that one substance from which the ever-changing, ephemeral world of day-to-day existence derives. "*Physis*" as "ensouled" matter can quite reasonably be read as the beginning of the development of the modern concept of nature, especially in light of the subsequent developments of Presocratic thought in Democritus and Leucippus. "*Theos*," it has been pointed out, is used predominantly as a predicate and is used in literature as "an ultimate principle that remains indispensable for speculation."[1] Its meaning is not wholly restricted to the religious meaning it has in the poets, but rather is used to ascribe, by analogy, a variety of attributes to the elementary substance the philosophers proposed as the source and origin of the world. James Adam, for example, argues that even though a traditional religious vocabulary may be used by the philosophers, "such subjects as the moral being and attributes of God lie outside the range of their inquiries."[2]

Unfortunately Adam's support for this claim is not wholly unambiguous for he also rejects M. Bovet's suggestion (in *Le dieu de platon*) that "the idea of God had, properly speaking, no place in any philosophical

1. Burkert, *Greek Religion*, p. 272. This point is made explicitly with respect to the concept of mind in Anaxagoras, for example, by Gershenson and Greenberg in their *Anaxagoras and the Birth of Physics*. They write: "In applying this name to a cosmic entity Anaxagoras was making use of a method frequently resorted to by scientists, and fundamental in human thought: the method of analogy" (p. 21). "Mind embodies the idea of natural law. It does not possess caprice or will or the ability to make decisions. Instead, it was meant to be the source of all changes in the Universe, as well as the source of all static order. Anaxagoras' theory of a cosmic Mind was the expression of the conviction that all of nature behaves according to strict law . . . ." (p. 23). His concept of Mind, as they point out, is that which accounts for ordered, rational behaviour (p. 23 *et passim*).

2. Adam, *The Religious Teachers of Greece*, p. 184.

system anterior to that of Plato."[3] In doing so, he implies that the
Presocratics were rightly credited with certain theological or quasi-
theological ideas and beliefs that foreshadow later reformational theological developments and therefore constitute the beginning of a feud
"between philosophy on the one hand, and the old Homeric and
Hesiodic religious ideas on the other. . . . "[4] He writes: "it is important
to observe that Greek philosophy contained from the first some elements which were bound to bring it into conflict with Greek polytheism, and which were at the same time capable of developing into a
more comprehensive and profound theology than anything that the
so-called 'Bible of the Greeks' provided."[5] Such a theological reading
of the Presocratics, both ancient and modern, is not uncommon as will
be seen below, but it is not justified. That the Milesians and other
Presocratics were not, in all likelihood, hostile to religion and therefore
did not intend their cosmologies as critiques of religion, hardly licences
such a theological reading of their work, even though they may make
use of certain religious/theological concepts. Such a reading has no
more justification than that which recognizes a hostility to religion in
the fact that the philosophers focused their attention on matters other
than "the moral being and attributes of the gods." The early philosophers are rather content with their existence as citizens in a cultic state,
intent neither on reforming the intellectual framework of the cult nor
with bringing about its demise. Their intentions were wholly other
than those of religion and so, in a sense, incommensurable with it.[6]
Consequently they would neither be under ideological pressure to
avoid the use of concepts and categories used in a mythical/religious
context, nor compelled necessarily to use them with their traditional
meanings and connotations.

Ascription of divinity to nature, then, is not an explicit theology,
although it is quite possible that such uses of *"theos"* were later capable
of being explicitly developed into a comprehensive theology. Indeed,
Xenophanes developed just such a theology that stands in tension
with the thought about the gods to be found in Homer and Hesiod.
However, that he did so, it must be stressed again, does not constitute
solid grounds for assuming that the Ionians in general saw themselves

3. Ibid., p. 190.
4. Ibid., p. 18.
5. Ibid., p. 190.
6. See in this regard note 4 to chapter 1.

as reforming theologians, bent on supplanting the polytheistic religious thought of Homer and Hesiod with a more sound, rational monotheism. In fact, it is possible to read the early Ionian *"physikoi"* as atheists in the modern sense of the term, as A. W. H. Adkins points out, in that they proposed cosmologies that made possible explanation without invoking divine causation.[7] Nor does such a reading contravene the claims I made above concerning the status of the early philosophers within their society, for, given the undogmatic character of Greek religion, there was no requirement laid upon any citizen explicitly to affirm belief in the gods. Since Greek religion was primarily a matter of cult rather than belief, it would have been entirely possible for a citizen to reject the whole of Greek mythology without being an atheist in the contemporary religious sense. As Adkins puts it, "For the Greek and his gods . . . the criterion was not belief but cult practice, the touchstone whether or no a man offered sacrifice."[8] Consequently we can conclude that, though some Presocratic philosophers, such as Xenophanes, for example, were directly concerned with religious issues and developed theological responses to them, there were others who, even though using a religious vocabulary and adverting to religious matters, were not religiously concerned, or, at most, were concerned to explain rather than to explicate such matters.

It is precisely this indifference to the religious issues implicit in the philosophers' project, as I shall hope to show in this chapter, that reveals the "theology of the Presocratics" to be all of a piece with their philosophy and therefore to harbour an intention rather different from that of the religious thought of the poets and playwrights. To seek to understand the world naturalistically, characterizes their so-called theology as it does their philosophy, and both have significant negative implications for religion. Even J. V. Muir who holds that the Milesians believed in a single, nonanthropomorphic, immortal divinity that was all-powerful and all-embracing, and that they were concerned to determine the nature of the relationship between "It" and "the way things were," argues as much. "The determination to search for certain causes only in nature – to establish a category of events to which only natural explanations are appropriate," he writes, "is a procedure which throws into serious question the credentials of a religion in which a god or divine presence may be held responsible for everything that

7. In his "Greek Religion."
8. Ibid., p. 424.

happens; divine intervention must henceforth be put in a special unnatural category."[9]

As I have noted earlier, clarity and precision as to what is meant by "theology" are not easily achieved. This makes it extremely difficult to determine whether or not a particular religious tradition even possesses a theology. Where "theology" is used simply to refer to beliefs – explicitly held or only implied in the cult and practice in which a people is immersed – every religion possesses a theology. However, where the word is used to refer to a self-conscious intellectual activity of a religious community, theology is a much less ubiquitous phenomenon. Furthermore, when used in this latter sense, there is still a great deal of ambiguity about what is meant, for the word can still denote a divergent range of intentionalities and activities. It might, for example, be used, as with Aristotle, to denote the systematization of the mythic repertoire of a people as in Hesiod's *Theogony*, if not, indeed, in Homer's even earlier organization of the mythic manifold of archaic Greece. It might also, however, be used to denote the work of tragedians like Aeschylus, who set about to refashion that mythic heritage; or, quite divergently, "theology" might also be used to designate the labours of later, clever thinkers who attempted, allegorically, to rationalize the mythic tradition by substituting a symbolic for the earlier reading of the community's story.

In none of these activities, however, does one find the thinkers involved concerned primarily with the requirements of "*logos*" – that is, with the requirements of the rationality of logical consistency and with a concern for an understanding (account) of the gods that is coherent and consistent with the logic of science and philosophy. Rather, all such activities still appear under the sway of mythical, intuitive thinking, governed by a "logic of feeling." If "theology," therefore, is not simply to be synonymous with "religious thought," it would seem that its use will have to be restricted to designating "rational discourse about" or "rational account of" the gods. However, even on that kind of account, "theology" might still refer to two divergent kinds of activities, namely, that which argues for the existence and nature of the gods from the natural world and that which is concerned to explain the gods, assuming their social *reality* but not their independent ontological *existence*.[10]

9. Muir, "Religion and the New Education," p. 206.
10. This distinction is borrowed from Smart; see especially his *The Phenomenon of Religion*.

That the Presocratics make reference to the gods – to divinity – is not in doubt. However, whether their discourse here constitutes a theology, and of whatever variety, is. And if it is theology, its character is not obviously of the natural theology kind. Indeed, I think it can be shown that where the Presocratic philosophers engage in a proreligious theological enterprise, they create a hybrid mode of thought that attempts to combine both mythic and rational/scientific components and is, in the final analysis, structurally assimilable to that of ordinary mythopoeic/religious thought. Where they undertake theology as an attempt to provide a purely rational/scientific understanding of the gods – on a par with their determination to understand the world rationally/scientifically – I shall show that they undermine belief in the gods and therefore are anything but theologians in the colloquial sense of the term. Before embarking on an assessment of the claims of those who detect a theology in Presocratic philosophical thought that ultimately blossoms in Plato, it will prove helpful to sketch, even though very briefly, an outline of the nature of Greek religion.

RELIGION IN ANCIENT GREECE

There is general agreement that obtaining an accurate account of Greek religion is well nigh impossible. Walter Burkert in his history of Greek religion writes: "An adequate account of Greek religion is nowadays an impossibility in more ways than one: the evidence is beyond the command of any one individual, methodology is hotly contested, and the subject itself is far from well defined."[11] In his survey of scholarship in this area he notes that, even though Greek religion has in some senses remained familiar to us, we are a long way yet from a true knowledge of it, from really understanding it.[12] This point is also made by E. R. Dodds in his attempt to determine "The Religion of the Ordinary Man in Classical Athens."[13] He writes: "The Homeric picture of the gods caught the imagination of the world, but it bears no close relation to the actual practice of religion as we know it in the Classical age. Homer ignored – it would seem deliberately – a whole body of ritual behaviour and religious or magical ideas which we have reason to think are very old, probably much older than

11. Burkert, *Greek Religion*, p. 7.
12. Ibid., p. 1.
13. The title of an article in his *The Ancient Concept of Progress and Other Essays on Greek Literature.*

Homer. He ignored them, but he did not succeed in killing them.
They lived on in the actions and thoughts of the people, and they keep
cropping up in later literature. . . . "[14] To accept the "soldier's creed"
of Homeric religion, therefore, is not to understand the religion of
Greece, but rather that of a fighting aristocracy. We are left with no
records of the beliefs and feelings of personal religious experience of
individuals, claims Dodds, and he insists that a study of the religious/
theological ideas and views of "great men" in Greece's history is not
the same as the study of Greek religion.[15]

As Adkins has pointed out, the problem with Greek religion is that
whatever it is, it is not some single entity upon which we can focus
attention. There is no orthodoxy, no canon, no unified priesthood,
and so on, that imposed even a superficial unity upon religious worship
in Greece.[16] He points out that "there never was anyone with the
authority or the superhuman intellectual power, needed to impose a
uniform pattern on the anarchic confusion of Greek belief and cult."[17]
Consequently, Adkins laments, it is neither possible to detect the
sources of the different aspects of Greek religious practice nor to trace
any single line of development within it. Greek religion, therefore, is
a large and complicated phenomenon in which new and advanced
beliefs evolved by later thinkers coexist with primitive practice and
belief, even when they cannot logically coexist, and no one "can hope
to impose order on it."[18] In his discussion of the gods, and in particular
of the Olympians, he does nevertheless allow for some order; Homer
and Hesiod give an Olympocentric order to the gods – but only to the
gods of the "upper world." He writes: "The gods who appear together
on Olympus in Homer and Hesiod were originally unrelated deities,
some deities of individual Greek states, others imported from abroad.
In cult practice, different states contrived to favour different Olympians: Athens worshipped all of them to some extent, but Athena – her
local deity – had first place in her affections. The bardic tradition must
have been one of the influences which led to the gradual assembly of

14. Ibid., pp. 143–44.
15. Ibid., p. 143. For similar comments see Easterling's "Greek Poetry and Greek
Religion."
16. See on this score as well Adam, *Religious Teachers of Greece*, p. 7 and Finley's
"Foreword" to Easterling and Muir, *Greek Religion and Society*.
17. Adkins, "Greek Religion," p. 385.
18. Ibid., p. 391. See here Burnet's comment that Greek religion "consisted entirely
of worship and not in theological affirmations," in his *Greek Philosophy,* p. 117.

these scattered deities into the divine household on Homer's Olympus and must have helped to perpetuate in literature at least the personality and certain attributes of the Olympians."[19]

It is this Olympocentrism, however, that seems to have constituted a kind of orthodoxy that has allowed some perception of development in Greek religion – at least more so in older scholarship. James Adam, for example, notes that Herodotus attributed to Homer and Hesiod something of the authority that other more unified religions possess in their focus upon the founders of their faith. Consequently, certain views of divinity and certain stories about the gods are so widely accepted that one might well be justified in designating them as orthodox, although in a restricted sense of the term.[20] It is only because that is so, he argues, that the feud between philosophy and religion in the late classical period can be understood. Indeed, he refers to it as "one of the most striking features in Greek religious development."[21] But Adam is nevertheless well aware of other "strains of piety" in the makeup of Greek religion.

What sense one makes of Greek religion, as Burkert points out, also depends upon the methodology employed in trying to understand it. The vast differences in style and approach between Nilsson and Otto, for example, produce radically different views (understandings) of religion. Nilsson's evolutionary *Religionswissenschaft* approach provides very much an "outsider's" understanding of Greek religious behaviour – reductionistic in that it attempts to explain it within a broader ecological, sociological, and anthropological framework. Otto, on the other hand, takes an "insider's" view in approaching an understanding of the Greek gods from a hermeneutic perspective. It is extremely unlikely that a synthesis of these two approaches is possible, since their differing presuppositions appear to be mutually exclusive.[22]

This does not prevent one, however, from sensitively describing religion – of making sense of it – where that sense does not automatically exclude seeking an explanation of the phenomenon. John Gould's essay, "On Making Sense of Greek Religion," by evading the question of the truth and/or falsity of Greek religious beliefs, attempts to avoid

19. Adkins, "Greek Religion," p. 391.
20. Adam, *Religious Teachers of Greece*, p. 7.
21. Ibid., p. 18.
22. The contrast between the two finds excellent treatment in McGinty's *Interpretation and Dionysos*.

both reductionistic and advocacy accounts of Greek religion.[23] Though recognizing the complexity of Greek religion he nevertheless argues that sense can be made of it and not only of its several aspects but also of it as a whole – as a system: "I want to consider," he writes, "the sense in which Greek religion is systematic (rather, that is, than a mere agglomeration of unconnected rituals and beliefs), and to explore the nature of the statement that it makes."[24] Myth and ritual are, Gould argues, modes of religious response to the experience of a chaotic world and function somewhat like a system of explanation. In making the notion of ambiguity a central aspect of the divine/human relationship, for example, the Greeks made their religion appear nonrational, paradoxical and even self-contradictory, but nevertheless something that could still underwrite human experience of conflict and contradiction in day-to-day living and so placed contradiction in human existence within a more fundamental *order*. The many gods form a "socialized company" and as such are a metaphor of human experience and therefore an explanation of it. As Gould puts it, "the model of the family provides a framework within which we can intuitively understand both unity and conflict as the working out of a complex web of loyalties, interests and obligations – conflict (inevitably) of ties, passions and personalities both within and outside the group, but also an ultimate unity, contained within the solidarity of the group and guaranteed in the person of Zeus the Father whose authority embodies the demand for an underlying unity, not chaos, in experience."[25]

Whether Gould's particular interpretation is right or not, need not be determined here. That some such systematic meaning characterizes Greek religion, seems not only a reasonable assumption but can be sketched out more fully. This does not, of course, mean that some one orthodox interpretation within a set of specified, attendant beliefs was required of everyone throughout the length and breadth of ancient Greece. That Greek religion had no revelation, no sacred books, no creed, no central ecclesiastical organisation and, hence, no grounds upon which, or authority whereby, to set down rules of belief or behaviour for the whole of the Greek world, is universally agreed.[26]

23. In Easterling and Muir, *Greek Religion and Society*.
24. Ibid., p. 14.
25. Ibid., pp. 24–25.
26. See here Finley's comments in his "Foreword," Easterling and Muir, *Greek Religion and Society*.

Yet it is also agreed that the toleration that situation permitted did not imply lack of concern for religious institutions or ceremonies. Indeed, in times of crisis very specific views of the gods and particular versions of the myths about the gods were upheld as sacrosanct.

Even in normal times the worshipper would hold, even if only vaguely, some beliefs about the gods and their nature which would have been derived from the myths. As Adkins points out: "Some myths form the framework within which most Greeks lived. No penalties attached to a refusal to believe in the truth of the Hesiodic or 'Orphic' cosmogonies; but the Greeks, save for the few who could comprehend the numerous competing cosmologies offered by their philosophers, had to accept one of these cosmogonies or nothing; *and they doubtless furnished an unquestioned background for most Greeks.*"[27] This background, moreover, as Adam put it, "is penetrated and quickened throughout all its parts by the multitudinous presence of the divine revealing itself not only in the uniform and regular sequence of natural phenomena, but also, from time to time, in those exceptional and arbitrary suspensions of natural law which later ages pronounce to be miraculous."[28] The Ionians' search for rational answers to their questions about the universe was obviously bound to clash with those implicit structures of belief – of "the inherited conglomerate" – that constituted Greek religion. Although this may be so on the overt level of existence, it is suspect at a deeper level, as the discussion here indicates. That they were not forced explicitly to avow any particular doctrinal truths or dogmas, does not mean either that they held no beliefs or that they did not take their beliefs seriously. This same point is made by E. R. Dodds in his rejection of Burnet's claim that Protagoras' statement of agnosticism would not have been seen as impious. Dodds writes: "As Diogenes of Oenoanda put it, to say that you have no means of knowing whether gods exist amounts in practice to saying that you know they do not exist; and 'worship' is hardly in the long run compatible with negation of what is worshipped."[29]

Ionian thought, even though in conflict with Greek polytheism, nevertheless contained elements capable of development into a more profound theological system. To raise the question as to whether or not that was their intent is both legitimate and reasonable. Indeed,

27. Adkins, "Greek Religion," p. 422; emphasis added.
28. Adam, *Religious Teachers of Greece*, p. 24.
29. Dodds, "The Sophistic Movement," p. 97.

with the thought of philosophers like Xenophanes, it is clear that such elements did exist in some cosmological systems and were extended beyond their original use. However, it is obvious as well, from what has been said above, that the opposite is also possible, especially in light of the culmination of this school of thought in the materialistic atomism of Leucippus and Democritus.[30] This is especially so in that the Ionians' search for rational answers to their cosmological questions soon extended to a similar quest regarding human society. Havelock argues in his *The Liberal Temper in Greek Politics* that Ionian science also included a theory of the origins of human society, technology, and civilization structured along naturalistic and evolutionary lines.[31] Dodds comes to the same conclusion, even though he is a little less sanguine about that Greek liberalism as it was taken up by the Sophists. "The concept of *physis* ('nature') with which the Ionian thinkers had operated," he writes, "was still the central concept, but it was extended to include human nature."[32] In the framework of thought of a Protagoras, he has no doubt that the gods have been eliminated from consideration.[33]

There is, as is to be expected, some dispute over the effect of the development of Ionian cosmological thinking on the religion of Greece and, indeed, dispute as to whether the philosopher-physicist intended any such effect. On the latter question I have already expressed my opinion above. Some comment on the former matter, however, may be of some assistance in the analysis of the various interpretations of the so-called "theology of the Presocratics" to follow.

The question here is a complex one, for we need to consider not only the relationship of the early Ionians to religion, but also what relation their thought bears to that of their successors, and especially so in respect of their influence on the Sophists.

It is obvious, as P. A. Meijer points out, that the early philosophers are not atheists and that atheism is really much more characteristic of

30. See here Kahn, *Anaximander and the Origins of Greek Cosmology:* "The final and most durable achievement of the Ionian study of nature was the atomist system of Leucippus and Democritus" (p. 206). See the argument to this effect in chapter 3.

31. Havelock, *The Liberal Temper in Greek Politics*, p. 5. On this score see also Meier, "The Emergence of Autonomous Intelligence Among the Greeks" and Humphreys, "Dynamics of the Greek Breakthrough."

32. Dodds, "The Sophistic Movement," p. 94.

33. Ibid., p. 97.

the later intellectuals of the sophistic movement.[34] He maintains that we know that at least some of the early philosophers were favourably inclined towards traditional religious thought and that some even made use of it in the construction of their own cosmologies.[35] This presents no problem for even the most materialistic of cosmologies, because the Greek gods are not creator gods and so do not stand in contradiction to a materialistic universe.[36] He concludes his general survey of Presocratic thought, therefore, by claiming that it neither is itself atheistic nor can be considered as having paved the way for atheism.[37] For him, for example, Anaxagoras' thought constitutes evidence for his claim, for he was "a very materialistically oriented thinker – even his *nous* is intellectual matter – [who] did not wish to be an atheist; such a thing did not so much as enter his horizon."[38]

Even though early philosophers may not have been interested in denying or disproving the existence of the gods, as Meijer puts it, this does not entail that their thought did not, understandably, have a corrosive effect on religion and on the beliefs quite unselfconsciously presupposed by traditional religious practice and devotion. As I have already pointed out above, the very determination to search for causes *only* in nature and to obtain *only* natural explanations for events, in itself constituted a project that is at odds with a traditional religious world-view which is characterized by a "double causation" – that is, a world-view in which all actions involve both human and divine activity. Adam was certainly aware of both that aspect of the traditional religious worldview and of the fact that philosophy therefore stood in revolutionary tension with it. Although he reads Anaxagoras' thought, somewhat in Meijer's fashion, as a religious development over against traditional polytheism, implicitly he leaves room in his description of

---

34. Meijer, "Philosophers, Intellectuals and Religion in Hellas."

35. Ibid., p. 220.

36. This does not mean, however, that the gods are not active in the world, which presents a very similar problem. The gods, that is, can interrupt the otherwise natural occurrences in the world. Adam, for example, refers to them as "exceptional and arbitrary suspensions of natural law which later ages pronounce to be miraculous" (*Religious Teachers of Greece*, p. 24). Muir similarly refers to such divine interventions as requiring "a special unnatural category" ("Religion and the New Education," p. 206). Gagarin, in another respect, refers to the action of the gods on human behaviour as producing "an 'illogical' sense of double motivation" (*Aeschylean Drama*, p. 20; see especially his first chapter, "The Early Greek World View").

37. Meijer, "Philosophers, Intellectuals and Religion in Hellas," p. 228.

38. Ibid., p. 226. The Greek original has been transliterated here.

Anaxagoras as a kind of Descartes or Newton, as the following passage shows, for him to be read also as a Laplace: "Anaxagoras occupies, in fact, the position of a tolerably orthodox man of science of the present day, who holds that without the postulate of an omnipotent and omniscient Deity the origin and continuance of the cosmos are alike inexplicable, and who, having once affirmed this principle, thenceforward pursues his scientific inquiries without any theological bias whatsoever."[39] Furthermore, Adam notes that Democritus did in fact do without such a postulate. Even Democritus was not simply atheistic although, as Adam points out, he believed in the gods but "degraded" them into daemons[40] – that is, he gave an explanation (logos, rationale) of them. This is the "spirit" he sees as having affected the rationalist movement of the Sophists.

It is of interest to take note as well of Charles H. Kahn's analysis of the thought of Heraclitus as a bridge between the overwhelmingly dominant Homeric culture – the popular culture of the poets and early sages – and the "scientific" culture of the Ionians that introduced a disturbingly new way of explaining the world. Though Heraclitus is himself still in the class of sages, he appears to have recognized in the Ionian physicists a mode of thought which traditional religious thought could not ignore. Indeed, he chose to write prose, so Kahn suggests, "because that was the new scientific language of his day and the traditional idiom of aphoristic wisdom."[41] However, Kahn also points out that, "whereas the general tendency of Ionian prose is towards directness and clarity of expression, the distinctive trait of Heraclitus' own style is more than Delphic delight in paradox, enigma and equivocation."[42] It is a device to bring that very scientific prose to self-awareness. It is clear, therefore, that Heraclitus affirms an affinity with the new scientific tradition but offers not to extend it but to reinterpret it. According to Kahn his "aim is not to improve the Milesian cosmology by altering a particular doctrine but to reinterpret its total meaning

39. Adam, *Religious Teachers of Greece*, p. 263. Adam is well aware that he stands in disagreement here with the interpretation offered by Bovet in his *Le Dieu de Platon*. Adkins, in "Greek Religion," it seems, also disagrees: "The cosmologies of Ionians like Anaxagoras made possible explanation without invoking divine causation, and some Ionians may have been atheists in the modern sense of the word" (pp. 423–24).

40. Adam, *Religious Teachers of Greece*, p. 220.

41. Kahn, *The Art and Thought of Heraclitus*. p. 97.

42. Ibid., p. 97.

by a radical shift in perspective."[43] Hence Kahn's judgment that "the attitude of Heraclitus to such science will turn out to be profoundly ambivalent. His own philosophic vision is inspired by the new scientific study of the world, but is directed towards a truth of an entirely different kind."[44] It is a complete reinterpretation, in light of traditional religion, of what all scientific knowledge is about and so constitutes a response to the challenge implicit in the new cognitive goals of science.[45]

Burkert seems to suggest much the same sentiments, arguing that, even though Milesian thought was anything but impious, it nevertheless constituted a movement, "which reflection on gods and things divine could not ignore or disregard in the long run."[46] He sees a kind of continuity of development in the post-enlightenment religious thought with that of Homer and Hesiod, but claims that the latter lost much in the battle with science, in that it could no longer be shown that the divinity cares for humankind. "Here a wound was opened in practical religion which would never close again."[47] Furthermore, Burkert recognizes that in this clash there was a complete "collapse of the authority of the poets and the myths administered by them," although claiming, quite rightly, that this did not bring an end to religion.[48] Plato's thought, especially in such works as the *Phaedo* and *Timaeus*, for example, shows the continuing struggle against science – the latter especially designed to counteract its materialistic tendencies.

Meijer certainly does not deny that atheism is characteristic of late (Sophistic) intellectuals, but rather claims to find its origin in a wholly different source, namely, in the rationalizing methods of the myth-historiographers. That tradition, however, emerges from a growing insight into the *nomos-physis* antithesis which scholars like E. R. Dodds and Eric Havelock see as an extension of the new mode of thinking first introduced by the Milesians. But this debate need not be pursued further here. There is need however, to touch on one or two further

43. Ibid., p. 23.
44. Ibid., p. 97.
45. Although, as Kahn points out in *The Art and Thought of Heraclitus*, it may also be "an implicit correction to the wisdom of Homer, Hesiod and Archilous" (p. 103). There is a striking "family resemblance" between the Heraclitean project in regard to the religion/science question and that of modern apologists influenced by Wittgenstein.
46. Burkert, *Greek Religion*, p. 310.
47. Ibid., p. 311.
48. Ibid., p. 311.

significant aspects of Greek religion that have not yet been given direct attention. Besides the Olympian strand of Greek religion and the influence that philosophic religious thought has had upon it, we must recognize at least two other strands – the Chthonic and Orphic traditions – that comprise parts of the complex whole, the former being for the most part considerably older than the others. Full understanding requires a thorough knowledge of the history and comparative study not only of the connection between Greece and the eastern Mediterranean area more generally, but also of the prehistoric foundations of the whole region down to the Minoan-Mycenaean age. Thus Walter Burkert writes: "Although the many broken lines of tradition and the innumerable catastrophes of early times cannot be lightly overlooked, forces of continuity have always reasserted themselves, and probably nowhere as much as in the sphere of religion."[49] There is no time here to try to disentangle this complex web of Chthonic, Orphic, Olympian, and philosophic strands of belief and behaviour, although it is important to be aware of the fact that there is neither a single source of Greek religion nor a simple single line in its historical development.[50]

THEOLOGY IN ANCIENT GREECE

Opinion as to the meaning and significance of the "god-related-talk" or theology to be found in the Presocratics and their successors is not, as one might by now have guessed, uniform, and not surprisingly so, given the fact that a sense of theological conviction was entirely foreign to them, as Havelock points out; it did not occur to the Greeks, until the time of Aristotle, to make the divine a topic of analytic discourse.[51] And yet, as Dodds points out, there was a considerable amount of *speculation* about the gods in Greek literature.[52] Whether or not that speculation about deity and divinity constitutes a development, or even a critique, of the religion of their society and so the central concern of

49. Ibid., p. 15. See also Farnell, *Greece and Babylon* and Gordon, *The Common Background of Greek and Hebrew Civilizations*. In an even broader sense see Levy's *The Gate of Horn* and, more recently, Marshack, *The Roots of Civilizations*. My differences with the last two mentioned authors has already been expressed in n. 36 to chapter 2.

50. This has, of course, been the essence of the argument of chapter 3. On this score, however, one might well refer to Hadas, *The Greek Ideal and Its Survival*, especially chapter 4, "The Supernatural."

51. Havelock, *The Crucifixion of Intellectual Man*, pp. 185–86.

52. In his "The Religion of the Ordinary Man in Classical Athens," pp. 141ff.

the cosmological systems of the philosophers, or rather is simply a vestige of the matrix from which those systems emerged, is not wholly clear. There is no doubt but that in some instances the central concern had been with a proper understanding of the gods or divinity. Whether that is so for the Milesians, however, is a much more difficult question. In a sense, the question is really one as to whether this apparently new philosophic/scientific mode of thought that emerges with them finds its true development in the atomism of Leucippus and Democritus, as I have argued in the preceding chapter, or rather in the later philosophy of Plato. However, a substantive body of scholarship exists that attempts to establish the contrary case; that reads the theological content of Presocratic thought as indicating generally a primary interest in the metaphysical and theological concerns that are implicit in the traditional religious outlook and practice of Greece, one which was brought to reflective awareness, and hence fulfilment, in Plato. It is to an examination and assessment of some of that scholarship that the remainder of this chapter is devoted. This analysis will reveal that where the theological element of early Greek philosophy is intentional – that is, not merely an indication of traditional piety or the use of a familiar model for a new cosmological idea – it can be read in one of two ways: as an *extension* of traditional religious thought (whether as development or critique makes little difference, since the one involves the other), that shares its essentially mythopoeic structure, or as a rational explanation of religion along with all else in the universe that is at odds not only with traditional religious thought in Greece but with religious thought *per se.*

In his Gifford lectures, *The Theology of the Early Greek Philosophers*, Werner Jaeger maintains that theology is a specific creation of the Greek mind. Although he admits a fracture in the development of that theology in that the very creation of the word as first used by Plato springs "from the conflict between the mythical tradition and the natural (rational) approach to the problem of God,"[53] he does not consider the fracture a serious matter – that is, as forcing upon one the necessity to see here any radical change in modes of thought. He acknowledges that the later Greek philosophers, including Plato and Aristotle, distinguished the thought of the nonphilosophers such as Hesiod and Pherecydes as mythical/theological in contrast to the thought of the Milesians, with the implication that philosophical

53. Jaeger, *The Theology of the Early Greek Philosophers*, p. 4.

thought appears to begin where religious thought comes to an end. Jaeger nevertheless sees a direct continuity here and not mere pious vestiges of religious thought inconsistently retained by the Presocratics. In this he seems to take up a position much like that espoused by Adam in his Gifford lectures, *The Religious Teachers of Greece*, some thirty or so years earlier, to which I have already made ample reference. One cannot, Jaeger argues, "think of pure thought as something hermetically sealed and isolated, essentially opposed to religion and shut off from it with as sharp a cleavage as that with which modern science sometimes cuts itself off from the Christian faith."[54] The speculations of the Milesians and their successors are therefore but the birth and growth of a peculiar religion of the intellect that will eventually replace the earlier theology of the poets. For Jaeger, therefore, Milesian thought does not represent a radical departure of thought – a revolution in thinking – that radically distinguishes the Milesian philosophers from their predecessors. He writes: "From the very beginning we have stressed the fact that there is no unbridgeable gulf between early Greek poetry and the rational sphere of philosophy. The rationalizations of reality began even in the mythical world of Homer and Hesiod, and there is still a germ of productive mythic power in the Milesians' fundamentally rational explanation of nature."[55]

There is something fundamentally suspect about this claim, however, for its ambiguity, of which Jaeger seems unaware, seems to hide alternative readings of Jaeger's data. One is left in doubt as to whether the fact that the beginning of the rationalization is to be found already in Homer and Hesiod also makes their thought rational instead of mythic. Or, on the other hand, is it implied that, because the rational explanations of nature proposed by the Milesians still contained a germ of mythopoeic power, they were not any more rational than the "explanations" of the poets. It is difficult to see how Jaeger's claim can avoid either of these implications. However, if both are true, it seems that we are forced to conclude that there really is no radical distinction between mythic and philosophic/scientific thinking. I do not wish to dispute here the historical validity of Jaeger's claim, but rather shall try to clarify its philosophical significance. That a "germ of productive mythopoeic power" is still present in Milesian philosophical thought does not imply that it is an "essential" or necessary aspect of it; and

54. Ibid., p. 91.
55. Ibid., p. 133.

Jaeger has not shown that it is either necessary or essential. That it then constitutes an inconsistency in their thought is obvious, but there is no necessity to assume their thought to be without flaw. It is not impossible, that is, that someone can hold, though inconsistently, within the same explanatory framework, elements of thought that are *logically* incompatible. Indeed, it is, unfortunately, an all too common occurrence.[56]

In his discussion of the hellenization of Christianity in his *Early Christianity and Greek Paideia* Jaeger seems to recognize that what may be historically so is not necessarily logically so. He maintains that "If we want to attain a genuine understanding of this historical phenomenon [of hellenization], we must not expect to find our own one-sided purism, be it humanistic or theological, confirmed in early Greek Christian thought. What we find in history is mostly the precise opposite of that clearcut logical consistency on which we insist in our theories. In reality the Greek cultural ideals and Christian faith did mix, however anxious we may be to keep each of them immaculate."[57] But the fact that they did mix does not mean that they are logically mixable, so to speak, and that seems to be just what Jaeger is implying in the tone of the passage just quoted. What results from such mixing also needs to be looked at more closely: does one still have true Christianity after the process? This is not obviously so, given that it is *subordinated* to the common denominator that allows for the mixing to occur which is supplied by "the higher vantage point of the Greek idea of paideia or education. . . ."[58] This, in fact, seems to clash with Jaeger's earlier claim that it is philosophical speculation that is used by the Christian faith to support a positive religion of revelation and not a religion of abstract rational inquiry.[59] That would seem to *subordinate* Greek philosophy to Christian revelation. The impression is not allowed to stand, however, for according to Jaeger the true character of the hellenization process shows itself in the apologetic theology of Origen, where "it is not only an abstract dogmatic system separate from his exegesis, but penetrates his whole understanding of the religion of

---

56. This may not, of course, be unfortunate from an other than a logical or epistemic point of view, but that is not a matter that is of concern in this work. Some discussion of the matter can be found in Munz, *Our Knowledge of the Growth of Knowledge.*

57. Jaeger, *Early Christianity*, p. 39.

58. Ibid., p. 62.

59. Ibid., p. 47.

Jesus and the Apostles, *transforming it into theology in the Greek manner.*[60]
Theology "in the Greek manner," however, seems to be a kind of
hybrid thought that mixes the rational with the mythic as if capable of
forming, as it were, a stable conglomerate.[61]

Not only does Jaeger's thinking reflect much of that of James Adam,
as I noted above, but he also seems to espouse that of another Gifford
lecturer who applied himself to the question of the theology of the
Greek philosophers, namely, Edward Caird, whose lectures were published as *The Evolution of Theology in the Greek Philosophers.* Caird,
although distinguishing theology from religion, saw it as a necessary
and nondistorting adjunct to religion in, as he puts it, "a time that has
outgrown simple faith and begun to feel the necessity for understanding what it believes."[62] Caird is well aware that religion is not necessarily
concerned with cognitive justification and that for the most part it has
done without it. Nevertheless, though religion does not primarily
concern itself with rational justification for its existence and nature,
that does not constitute grounds, Caird maintains, for claiming that it
cannot or ought not to be justified. Caird is also aware, however, that
such an argument to justify religion in a sense transcends religion and

60. Ibid., p. 49, emphasis added.

61. As will become clear, Hatch did not seem to read the influence of Greek thought
on Christianity in quite so sanguine a fashion in his *The Influence of Greek Ideas.* Many of
those elements in Christian theology, he insisted, were extraneous to the first form of
Christianity (p. 332) and were likely to be abandoned (p. 252). While dominant, they
do not seem to have provided it with anything particularly valuable (p. 349). Further
discussion of Hatch will follow below.

62. Caird, *The Evolution of Theology,* Vol. 1; p. 3. This is the position taken up by John
Watson in his Gifford Lectures of 1910–12, *The Interpretation of Religious Experience;* see
especially the first lecture, "Development of Greek Religion and Theology." Watson
writes: "it is sometimes held that religion is entirely independent of theology, and, in
fact, is the enemy of theology; and we are asked to abandon all efforts to imprison it
within the iron framework of theological abstractions" (p. 4). Watson thinks such a view
rests on a false idea of both religion and theology. However, his definition of theology
that identifies it with religious beliefs held explicitly or implicitly, rather than with a
systematic and rational analysis and exposition of religion, is not the theology under
discussion here.

A contemporary argument in a similar vein is to be found in another set of Gifford
Lectures (for 1982): see Clark's *From Athens to Jerusalem:* "Philosophy is not the enemy
of faith: if we permit it, it will lead us to that place from which we see that love which
moves the sun and other stars" (p. 95). The mark of reason, claims Clark, is to recognize
that not all things can be proved by reason. He is unaware, however, that such things
are not then the objects of knowledge in the sense of knowledge established in the
Milesian revolution in thought.

could be seen, therefore, to be its nemesis. But he thinks this dilemma can be overcome in an evolutionary perspective that is able to see faith and reason as "two factors or stages of one life."[63] Consequently, even though on the surface faith and reason (i.e., Greek religion and Milesian philosophy) appear to clash, there is a deeper unity, for it is simply absurd even to think that reason, which we hold dear, could possibly be detrimental to something so important in our lives as religion. Caird's argument here really amounts to little more than intuitive, moral/religious grounds for assuming a complementarity between reason and religion – the necessity for an unquestioned assumption of an underlying unity of faith and reason because society "wishes" to retain both.[64] He writes: "We must, therefore, maintain that though reason may accidentally become opposed to faith, its ultimate and healthy action must preserve for us or restore to us, all that is valuable in faith. Or, if it necessarily comes into collision with faith at a certain stage of development, at a further stage this antagonism must disappear, or be reduced within narrower limits."[65] This hardly resolves the issue, however; it but substitutes the rhetoric of a "complementarity thesis" for the needed argument. For Caird personally, it is obvious, religion – and therefore Christianity – contains a rational kernel of truth that will naturally, even if only gradually, grow into a coherent structure with the truths that spring from independent reason.

Caird notices, then, a certain apparent enmity, so to speak, between faith and reason, recognizing that a reason that accepts the reign of law and so espouses a positivist science seems to preclude any rational justification of religion. Nor does he think that it is reasonable to try to forge a synthesis of the two by allowing for exceptions to the laws

63. Caird, *The Evolution of Theology*, vol. 1, p. 18.
64. Such arguments, especially when elaborated so as to account for the relations between science and religion, have been referred to as "compatibility systems" (see, for example, Smart, *The Science of Religion*, pp. 82–83). I have discussed the issue in my "Science and Religion," though the views expressed there have since been radically altered. I have expressed that altered position in "Is Science Really an Implicit Religion?" Concerning those who come to contrary conclusions Caird wrote in *The Evolution of Theology*: "they are either the objections of those who would separate philosophy from life or the objections of those who would separate life from philosophy" (p. 24), dismissing both possibilities *a priori* as counterintuitive, if not simply absurd. The substance of chapter 6 will show good grounds for such a position, however, and consequently, though perhaps reluctantly, for foregoing the comfort of Caird's assumption of harmony between philosophy (science) and religion.
65. Caird, *The Evolution of Theology*, vol. 1, p. 19.

of nature that permit supernatural agency a purchase on the world. In his earlier set of Gifford lectures on *The Evolution of Religion* he writes: "I do not think that we can admit *in general* the mode of thinking represented by the Enlightenment of the last century, and by the Positivism of the present day, and then say that, here and there, whether in a few or in many instances, the objective connexion of nature is interrupted by agencies that are outside of the system of nature."[66] To seek to establish such special exceptions, he sees as tantamount to a rejection of reason – not of forging a connection between reason and religion. To try to place the supernaturalism of religion alongside a naturalistic understanding of reason in this fashion, is to force a choice between the two. Rather than making room for miracles within a naturalistic world, he argues that one must come to see the universe itself as miraculous. After Carlyle, he refers to this as a "Natural Supernaturalism" that supplants a view of the world as a mechanical system with a view of the world as an organism. "The idealist must be prepared to show," he insists, "that the mechanical or external view of the world to which Positivism tends is an essentially imperfect view, a view which, no doubt, has its uses, and represents certain aspects of the truth, but which can never be taken as a final account of anything, not even inorganic matter."[67] In this sense he sees the positivist/scientific and the idealist ways of thinking not as strict alternatives but as stages of development in which the latter corrects the former.[68] It is this doctrine of Caird's that seems, from the description of James Adam's position above, to have influenced Adam considerably. And not only Adam, but Jaeger as well.

In his Aquinas lecture, *Humanism and Theology*, delivered some years after the Gifford lectures (although published before them), Jaeger finds this apparent antinomy of faith and reason reflected "in the most striking manner in the succession and mutual struggle of the cultural ideals of ancient Greece."[69] The "reason" he finds problematic is that of modern humanism, which in adopting an agnostic philosophy, leaves no room for faith. Such a position stands opposed to classical humanism, denying "emphatically the possibility of that rational approach to the realm of the invisible which we call philosophy in the

---

66. Caird, *The Evolution of Religion*, vol. 1, p. 318.
67. Ibid., p. 320.
68. Caird seems to have inverted the stages in his second set of Gifford lectures, *The Evolution of Theology*.
69. Jaeger, *Humanism and Theology*, p. 42.

sense of Plato and Aristotle, or of St. Thomas."[70] The ancient world similarly saw the *paideia* of the sophists pitted against that of Socrates, Plato, and Aristotle. The latter, moreover, recovers the essence of traditional Greek religion – "the kernel of reality which religion in its mythical stage had symbolized in mythical form"[71] – whereas the former is but a symbol of the decline of Greek civilization in its rejection of the belief in something higher than humanity. But it recovers this belief, not simply by returning to the modes of intellection in the mythical age, but rationally – by means of *reason* (logos).[72] Jaeger, consequently, sees theology as a hybrid rational-mythical mode of intellection; a mode of thought that both transcends the mythical mode of thought and yet does not. I can do no better to clarify the nature of this new mode of thought, that is both rational *and* mythopoeic, *and yet neither*, than to quote Jaeger *in extenso*:

The historical development of the Greek mind seems to move in a circle, for Plato has arrived again at the same point at which the Greek way had started. The world of Plato like that of Homer may be described as at once anthropomorphic and theocentric. Man and human life are in the foreground and in that sense it is anthropocentric; but God is in the center of the human world. In spite of this analogy with Homer the relation of man to the superhuman in Plato's philosophy is no longer the Homeric one. It is based on the intrinsic experience of the soul and its forces, most of all on the force of reason which is the golden link that connects the philosopher with God. Thus the circle of which we spoke is not a real circle after all, but the development resembles a spiral which ascends and thereby arrives at a higher point perpendicularly above its point of departure. The insight into the nature of this development of the philosophical mind of the Greeks is enlightening in the highest degree. For the return of the human mind to its point of departure and the new synthesis of all the elements which had emancipated themselves from their original unity during the earlier stages of that process seems to indicate an inherent structural law of the mind which requires God as the center of its world, the cosmos both without and within.[73]

Jaeger's continuity thesis is, it seems, based on an assumption that Greek philosophy differs radically from oriental religion as well as from

70. Ibid., p. 37.
71. Ibid., p. 45.
72. Ibid., p. 46.
73. Ibid., pp. 53–54.

Greek religion. There is already a rationalization in Greek religion not to be found in other religious traditions, which allows for what he refers to in the concluding chapter of his Gifford lectures as the "rehabilitation of popular religion."[74] Though acknowledging that beginning of the process of rationalization in Homer and Hesiod in the preceding chapter, I am nevertheless not persuaded of his position, for it constitutes not only a historical claim of connectedness between earlier and later communities of thought, which I should not wish to deny, but also a philosophical claim that the two modes of thought are, if not much the same, at least complementary, a thesis I find unpersuasive. I shall not submit his formulation of the continuity thesis to criticism at great length, for it is taken up in a more recent, sustained defence of Plato's theology to which I shall give careful attention below. However, two extended comments can be usefully made here: the one concerning the origins of Greek religion and the other the influence of Greek theology. Their significance will become apparent as the discussion unfolds.

It is of some importance to the issues under discussion to recognize that the Hebrew civilization which, at least superficially, differs radically from the Greek, is a parallel structure, as Cyrus Gordon, among others, has pointed out, built upon the same east Mediterranean foundation.[75] "Just as the Christian and Roman West grew out of the Hellenistic synthesis," he tells us, "early Israel and Mycenean Greece sprang from the Amarna synthesis."[76] There was a broad exposure of Greece to Mesopotamian culture in law, literature, and science which, according to Gordon, accounts for much of the accomplishment of

74. Jaeger, *The Theology of the Early Greek Philosophers*, see pp. 16, 178.

75. See Gordon, *The Common Background*, and Farnell, *Greece and Babylon*. This is the central concern of Bernal's *Black Athena*, although he there looks specifically at Egyptian and Semitic roles in the formation of Greece in the middle and late Bronze Age. Only volume 1, *The Fabrication of Ancient Greece 1785-1985*, has as yet been published; "Greece, European or Levantine? The Egyptians and West Semitic Components of Greek Civilization" and "Solving the Riddle of the Sphinx and Other Studies in Egypto-Greek Mythology" are forthcoming. It would be premature to attempt an assessment of his general argument which is only available in a synoptic form in the introduction to the first of the three volumes. On this topic see also the recent essay by Burkert, "Oriental and Greek Mythology," as well as Olela's "The African Foundations of Greek Philosophy." Keita's "The African Philosophical Tradition" also discusses African influence on Western philosophy – ancient, medieval and contemporary. Keita, moreover, relies on the earlier work of Diop in *The African Origin of Civilization*.

76. Gordon, *The Common Background*, p. 214.

what is peculiarly Greek. Gordon does not mean to suggest that Asia Minor produced philosophers like the Greeks – or even epic poets like Homer. Nevertheless, "the Greeks did not produce perfection from a vacuum."[77]

To read the archaeological evidence that established a continuity between the intellectual heritage of Asia Minor and that of Greece as a simple development without any radical or revolutionary changes, however, would be quite misleading. As one scholar has put it, "[t]he Greeks learned how to compute eclipses from the Babylonians; but they were the first to *explain* them."[78] Nor does Gordon suggest as much; he is aware of "the miracle of Greece," even though he does not think it occurred overnight. There is a gulf between Hebrews and Greeks that must be acknowledged despite the historical links. Thus he insists only that "the gulf separating classical Israel (of the great prophets) from classical Greece (of the scientists and philosophers) must not be read back into the heroic age when both peoples formed part of the same international complex."[79] That a kind of development exists – as Jaeger quite rightly argues – between Homeric and Milesian thought, does not require one to see complementarity between the two; the possibility of a gulf between them is not only possible but is, as I have argued in chapter three, quite plausible. Though neither the Homeric tradition nor the scientific tradition that emerges from within it is internally simple or uniform in development, the gulf between the two is discernable – especially in the light of the later developments of "physical thought." Charles H. Kahn summarizes the situation superbly in the introduction to his work on Heraclitus: "Despite a wide range of mythic and poetic antecedents, the Ionian conception of the

77. Ibid., p. 252.
78. Kahn, *The Art and Thought of Heraclitus*, p. 16. I think the evidence presented in chapter 3 supports Kahn's claim and that the continuity thesis found in Levy, *The Gate of Horn*, and Marshack, *The Roots of Civilization*, is inconsistent with the evidence. The same applies, to two more recent works on the history of science. Gregory, in *Mind in Science*, has no doubt that science emerges by a process of demarcation from myth (pp. 34, 43) and that much of this was achieved by the Presocratics. He does, however, think that the philosophers minimized the contribution of technology to abstract thinking and scientific explanation (see pp. 2, 558). Olson, on the other hand, in *Science Deified and Science Defied*, sees Anaximander quite differently (p. 77) and sees Ionian science, although undermining traditional Greek religion, as productive of a new theology (e.g., Xenophanes, p. 82). This seems an unbalanced judgment and one inconsistent with other comments on science and 'scientism' in ancient Greece (p. 62).
79. Gordon, *The Common Background*, p. 18.

world as *kosmos* was something new, and its novelty is identical with
the emergence of western science and philosophy as such. What we
find in sixth century Miletus is a scientific revolution in Kuhn's sense,
the creation of a new paradigm of theoretical explanation, with the
peculiar distinction that this world view is the first one to be recognizably scientific, so that the innovation in this case is not so much a
revolution *within* science as a revolution *into* science for the first time.
The Milesian cosmologies are scientific, in the sense in which, for
example, the world picture of Hesiod is not, because the new view of
the *kosmos* is connected both with a geometric model and with empirical
observation in such a way that the model can be progressively refined
and corrected to provide a better explanation for a wider range of
empirical data."[80]

My second comment concerns Jaeger's sanguine perception of the
influence of Greek philosophy-theology on Christianity; seeing here a
similar continuity and complementarity. Obviously, perceptions of that
influence vary widely, although I shall refer here only to Edwin Hatch's
treatment of the topic.[81] Hatch determines that that influence constituted a "change in the centre of gravity" in the Christian faith,[82] and

80. Kahn, *The Art and Thought of Heraclitus*, p. 16. See also his *Anaximander and the
Origins of Greek Cosmology*: "If these philosophers had been able to take for granted a
coherent, ready-made cosmology, then they would not have been the first after all. On
the other hand, once the Milesians had worked out a consistent cosmic scheme, it
naturally exerted a powerful influence on the poets and on the educated public in
general. Hence, when we find traces of such a scheme in Euripides or in the Potidaea
epitaph of 432 – or in the updated Orphic poems – we must recognize this as evidence
for the diffusion of Ionian cosmology, not for its pre-existence in the popular imagination" (pp. xii–xiii); "What Anaximander and his fellows brought into being is nothing
less than science and the natural philosophy of antiquity" (p. 119); "The final and most
durable achievement of the Ionian study of nature was the atomist system of Leucippus
and Democritus" (p. 206). See also pp. 209–210. Kahn also notes that Plato attempted
to counteract many of the tendencies of Ionian science by reinterpreting the meaning
of its achievements (p. 206).

81. Hatch, *The Influence of Greek Ideas and Usages Upon the Christian Church*. This book
was republished by Harper and Row in 1957 as *The Influence of Greek Ideas on Christianity*.
References here are to the original edition.

82. Ibid., p. 2. See here also Uffenheimer, "Myth and Reality in Ancient Israel."
Uffenheimer writes: "It is the central contention of this study that the essential factor
molding the spiritual world of the Bible, the Apocrypha, Rabbinic literature and emergent Christianity was mythical thought and expression" (p. 135; see also pp. 150–51
and 166–67).

he contrasts Palestinian with Greek thought.[83] Earliest Christianity, that is, did not reflect the philosophy of Greece, though it did not take long for it to be conquered by that philosophy. Hatch notes: "The earliest forms of Christianity were not only outside the sphere of Greek philosophy, but they also appealed, on the one hand, mainly to the classes which philosophy did not reach, and, on the other hand, to a standard which philosophy did not recognize. . . . "[84] The "unelaborated faith of Jesus Christ," his research suggests, was swamped by compromise, in which that "original orthodoxy" became a heresy, although he stops short of saying that the faith had been destroyed.[85] It was not the speculations of the philosophers that clashed with this faith, but rather the new habit of mind that embraced the *tendency* to speculate, a tendency which had come to pervade society in those first centuries of the Christian era. It is not necessary here to flesh out fully the various elements of Hatch's argument. A brief review will do.

Hatch leaves the reader in no doubt that the connection between religion and philosophy – in particular, Christianity and Hellenistic philosophy – was not one of simple development from unelaborated faith to elaborated faith, but rather that philosophy had become both handmaid and rival to theology.[86] His assessment of that development differs vastly from Jaeger's. He adamantly maintains, for example, that Christianity has won no great victories since its transformation by philosophy and sees the continuing dominance of philosophy within Christianity as grounds for despair, though hinting that he thinks such continued dominance is unlikely.[87] His conclusion, which I shall quote here, indicates how deep a suspicion he holds of philosophy as contrary to the religious spirit – especially with respect to any continuation of its influence.

It is an argument for the divine life of Christianity that it has been able to assimilate so much that was at first alien to it. It is an argument for the truth of much of that which has been assimilated, that it has been strong enough to oust many of the earlier elements. But the question which forces itself upon

83. Hatch, *The Influence of Greek Ideas and Usages Upon the Christian Church*, p. 123.
84. Ibid., p. 124.
85. Ibid., p. 132.
86. Ibid., p. 284.
87. Ibid., p. 349.

our attention as the phenomena pass before us in review, is the question of the relation of these Greek elements in Christianity to the nature of Christianity itself.

It is possible to argue that what was absent from the early form cannot be essential, and that the Sermon on the Mount is not an outlying part of the Gospel, but its sum. It is possible to argue, on the other hand, that the tree of life, which was planted by the hand of God Himself in the soul of human society, was intended from the first to grow by assimilating to itself whatever elements it found there. It is possible to maintain that Christianity was intended to be a development, and that its successive growths are for the time at which they exist integral and essential. It is possible to hold that it is the duty of each succeeding age at once to accept the developments of the past, and to do its part in bringing on the developments of the future.[88]

There is another, and interesting, interpretation of "the theology of the Greek philosophers" that I shall briefly review before proceeding with my assessment of the discontinuity of the mythopoeic thought of Homer and the theological thought that emerges together with the rise of a philosophic/scientific mode of thought. That interpretation is put forward by Richard Kroner in *Speculation in Pre-Christian Philosophy*, the first of a three-volume work on "Speculation and Revelation in the History of Philosophy."[89] Kroner's view differs radically not only from the analysis to follow, but also from the view proposed by Jaeger. Ancient philosophy, he insists, is the rival of ancient religion,[90] although he is in essential agreement with Jaeger that there is a religious intentionality in the thought of the early Greek philosophers.[91]

88. Ibid., p. 350–351.

89. Kroner, *Speculation in Pre-Christian Philosophy*. The other two volumes are *Speculation and Revelation in the Age of Christian Philosophy* and *Speculation and Revelation in Modern Philosophy*. The same thesis is carried in his Gifford lectures, *The Primacy of Faith*, *Culture and Faith*, and the essays in his *Between Faith and Thought*.

90. Kroner, *Speculation in Pre-Christian Philosophy*, p. 49.

91. Kroner does not, of course, stand alone. Zuurdeeg, in *Man Before Chaos*, sees philosophy existentially rather than intellectually rooted – in "a cry for an eternal truth" rather than in a search for knowledge (p. 15). Weil's earlier work, *Intimations of Christianity*, argues a similar but much more specific thesis. More recently similar claims have been put forward by W. C. Smith and Huston Smith. W. C. Smith ("Philosophia, as One of the Religious Traditions of Humankind") argues, for example, "that the Greek tradition in Western civilization . . . is best understood when considered within the generic context of the various – other – religious traditions of humankind" (p. 254). He

Indeed, as even a cursory reading of Kroner will show, that intentionality will eventually prove to be the only ground on which the "seemingly

---

admits that superficially, the philosophical tradition does not seem religious, but that if understood in respect of "what it has meant to persons who have lived their lives in terms of it" (p. 267), it can only be so understood. It is immediately obvious, however, that his view is formulated on the basis of an undifferentiated and very unhistorical view of the emergence and development of philosophy. He writes: "I am concerned not specifically with what Plato or Aristotle said, nor with the plays of Sophocles, nor the art of Praxiteles; but with the movement of the human spirit that over the centuries in Western life since, these things inspired, nurtured and were felt to express" (p. 267), as if the legacy of Greece were as clear and unambiguous as all that.

Were he to pay attention to the historically differentiated understandings in the development of philosophy and of the nature of reason, his argument would be considerably more difficult to construct. However, his adoption of a functionalist definition of religion (p. 264) would still allow him to come to similar conclusions since, by that definition, everyone, it appears, has to be religious – even the apparently unreligious or irreligious who belong to what he refers to as the tradition of Western Science (p. 275): "For those who accept a religious awareness of transcendence, I would urge that *philosophia* has made available on earth one of the major ways by which that transcendence has entered human history, or men have touched the hem of the garment of transcendent truth. For those, on the other hand, whose sympathies are on the other side of the Western duality, I would argue that man's religious systems can be more truly apprehended when discerned as comparable phenomena to that very loyalty to and pursuit of truth and understanding in which they themselves are involved" (p. 278). This claim suggests little more than a radical misunderstanding of what "science's pursuit of truth" is all about. Huston Smith ("Western Philosophy as a Great Religion") develops W. C. Smith's ideas along different lines, that is, seeing western philosophy as a western version of *jñana yoga* (p. 26), although he restricts his analysis primarily to "the gnostic strand of Greek-originated philosophy" (p. 30). On that ground he is much less vulnerable than is W. C. Smith in his more general claims.

Eric Voegelin's concern with "Order and History" in his discussion of Greek thought (in *The World of the Polis* and *Plato and Aristotle*) seems to provide a similar account of the ultimately religious character of Greek thought. As he puts it in the latter volume, "Plato's philosophy . . . is not a philosophy but the symbolic form in which a Dionysiac soul expresses its ascent to God" (p. 70). He refers to Plato's thought as a "leap in being" "toward the transcendent source of order" (p. 92). As I shall show below, his analysis does apply to Socrates and Plato but not to the prime movers, so to speak, of the Ionian revolution in thought against which those two react. (On this score see especially *Plato and Aristotle*, p. 188–90, also his restatement of matters in *The Ecumenic Age*, pp. 244ff., in which he sounds much like Zuurdeeg.)

Altizer, in his *Oriental Mysticism and Biblical Eschatology*, seems to hold a view not unlike those already mentioned here, although he restricts it to the Socratic/Platonic vision in its essential oneness with the achievement of Homer and the "Olympian Conquest." He does, however, see the dawn of rationalism in Ionia as "some sort of reformation" of religion (p. 17) but it is also seen as hostile to religion (pp. 36–37). Aristotle, furthermore,

impossible chasm" that exists between Greek philosophy and biblical religion is bridged, although this is not wholly accurate, for Kroner also seems to maintain that the chasm is real and absolute and so can never be bridged.[92] He argues that that religious intention is to be seen in the attempt by the philosophers to reconcile religion and science, but for them the reconciliation is possible only on the "higher plane" of science. Unlike Jaeger, Kroner sees this as amounting to a complete abolition of the traditional religion.[93] For Kroner, religion, even the philosophic religion of the Greek cosmologists, is a matter of revelation and personal relationship – even though not to the same extent as is biblical religion – whereas philosophy and science attempt to transcend precisely those conditions. He writes: "Speculation can never be a substitute for religion. Even on the lowest level of superstition and

---

is seen as sacrificing faith to preserve what I have attributed to the Ionians – that is, an understanding of the world (p. 44).

92. Kroner, *Speculation in Pre-Christian Philosophy*, see especially pp. 19–21, 60. Biblical revelation, says Kroner, is more averse to speculation than any other religion. In *Speculation and Revelation in the Age of Christian Philosophy* he does suggest a continuity between the two in asserting that some exertion of the abstracting mind is required for apprehending even the biblical God and that the bible is a spiritually rational book. But the phrase "spiritually rational" is then defined as a 'living and personifying rationality' which itself stands in contrast to speculative philosophy as adopted by the Greek philosophers (see pp. 19–20, 159). The chasm is still there, and is increased in the repeated emphasis on the role of faith and revelation: "Philosophic speculation has no right and is unable to criticize the Christian faith, because this faith fills the gap of knowledge that speculation leaves hollow: it pronounces a truth that lies forever outside the region of reason. No wonder, therefore, that this truth offends reason; no wonder that it is impossible to affirm by means of reason what faith announces" (p. 57). So runs the description of the conflict of revelation with philosophy in this volume. And the same holds for *Speculation and Revelation in Modern Philosophy* (see especially p. 115).

This position had already been developed in his Gifford lectures, *The Primacy of Faith*, and his *Culture and Faith*. In the former he writes: "the Scripture gives reasons for belief in God, and provides us with a kind of knowledge. But this knowledge is neither scientific nor philosophic, strictly speaking; it is not conceptual and not rational. Rather it is imaginative" (pp. 3–4). These varieties of knowledge, moreover, "do not dwell in peace together" (p. 4). In the latter book he protests against William Temple's assumption "that human and divine, secular and sacred views can be united without any break or leap from the one to the other sphere . . . ." (p. 7). And in both books he argues against the use of theology as a hybrid knowledge that bridges the chasm between religious and scientific knowledge. In the latter he writes: "There is a chasm between such a knowledge for the sake of salvation and mathematics or physics, a chasm which sacred theology cannot and should not try to bridge" (p. 7). A more detailed account of his argument cannot be provided here.

93. Kroner, *Speculation in Pre-Christian Philosophy*, p. 52.

idolatry, religion implies a personal relationship between man and the gods. Speculation, on the contrary, implies an impersonal comprehension or vision and an understanding of critical analysis."[94]

Though denying a strict continuity, Kroner nevertheless admits that at least Greek philosophy and religion have something in common. He distinguishes Greek speculative philosophy sharply from modern philosophy. The former is aesthetic while the latter is scientific and so, obviously, for Kroner, more like religion. Of early Greek philosophy he writes: "Speculation, the daughter of poetical and mythological fancy and of methodical thinking, is the outcome of a synthesis between an intuitive and an analytical, an imaginative and critical activity. More correctly it is an analytical operation that thinks out an underlying intuition."[95] Early philosophical thinking, therefore, even though in opposition to religious thought, transcends the opposition of a narrow naturalism. However, later philosophy – such as the speculative cosmological thought of a Democritus – increasingly anticipates the blatant positivism of the modern sciences and is seen by Kroner as the bankruptcy of philosophy. "The adventurers and discoverers had their day," he writes, "[and] nothing new seemed to remain." He continues: "The turn to physics and to accurate observation of the empirical world, the turn to what we would today call 'positivism,' was the result of speculative disenchantment and disappointment."[96]

For Kroner, then, the later developments of the Presocratic philosophy in the direction of a scientific naturalism was blasphemous and discontinuous with its initial impulse. Its original religious matrix, according to Kroner, however, is not wholly jettisoned and is, furthermore, restored in Plato's speculative thought that reestablishes the original link between philosophy and religion.

If the philosophy from Thales to Democritus can be seen as a progressive development in thought, as I have suggested in chapter three, it could then well be argued that it stands as a great hiatus between that which precedes and follows it. For not only does Milesian thought ultimately disenchant – in the Weberian sense of that term – the world, it is itself followed by a deliberate effort in Plato's thought to reenchant the world. The argument that there is a continuity between archaic Greek religion and Greek philosophy/theology, as promoted by Jaeger,

94. Ibid., p. 65.
95. Ibid., p. 56.
96. Ibid., pp. 127, 129.

can be sustained only if one ignores "the Milesian revolution in thought" and looks to the philosophy of Plato and beyond. Kroner's argument is dimly aware of this fact but fails explicitly to recognize it, expressing its continuity/discontinuity thesis vaguely and with ambiguity. Such a claim finds support, moreover, from a broader social-cultural analysis of Greek culture at the time of the Sophistic movement that reveals a profound crisis which was, ultimately, fatal to Greek rationalism – that new mode of thought given birth in the Milesian experiment – though it is not an analysis that can be undertaken here. Plato's thought is therefore, a "reactionary rationalism" – that is, an ideological use of reason – that attempts to recapture or reconstruct what he considered to be the basic social schemes of Greek life; or, in E. R. Dodds' words, to stabilise "the inherited conglomerate" of the poets *and* the physicists.[97] This can most easily be shown to be so by means of close and careful analysis and assessment of Michel Despland's recent defence of Plato's philosophy of religion. Before proceeding to that task, however, it might be helpful to summarize the argument to this point. I shall do this very much with an eye to Friedrich Solmsen's view of the development of Greek theology from the Milesians to Plato.

MEANING/KNOWLEDGE: THE ESSENCE OF DISCONTINUITY

The existence of theology or "talk of the gods" in the Presocratic philosophers does not undermine the discontinuity thesis I have set out in the preceding chapter. The evidence for a direct continuation of "Homeric religion," or the Greek religious tradition more broadly conceived, is ambiguous in the extreme. I do not mean to suggest, however, that no continuity whatsoever exists between Presocratic theology and the religious thought that antedates it. Not even the Greek world was wholly mythopoeic one day and entirely philosophic-scientific the next. And I certainly do not mean to argue that the philosophers intended to undermine the gods – to divest the universe of them. Given the very close connection between the gods and the city-state, to question their existence would have been tantamount to an act of treason. It is not only likely that the majority of ordinary citizens continued to "believe in" (i.e., worship) the gods but that the philosophers, as well, remained "believers." Indeed, as a number of

97. See Dodds, *The Greeks and the Irrational*, p. 207.

scholars have pointed out,[98] some philosophers were more than likely intent upon more firmly establishing the gods, whose positions had appeared somewhat vulnerable in light of the alternative philosophic/ scientific explanations of the world and all that takes place in it. Friedrich Solmsen claims, for example, that some philosophers attempted to provide a theoretical foundation for such belief and so can be said to have had a theology in the ordinary sense of that term – that is, in the sense of a reasoned set of convictions concerning the nature and activities of the deity. "A new conception of the gods and their status," he writes, "had also taken shape in the physical philosophy of the Presocratics."[99] However, it is necessary to bear in mind that such theology – such critical and reflective "talk of the gods" – is a striking novelty, if not a revolutionary development in itself. Moreover, it is not always clear that the new reflection on the gods is at all a central interest in the philosophical system developed. The gods are also "aspects" of the world and so could – and often did – become the objects of explanation. "Theology" in that case is, like "biology" or "geology," a cognitive matter and not a religious one. And if that were to be the case, such thought could have a disruptive effect on religion, whether or not the philosopher concerned intended to undermine belief in the gods.

That not only the philosophy but also the theology of the Greek philosophers is something radically new, seems also to be recognized by Solmsen. In that such reasoned discussion about the gods is part and parcel of the physical systems of the philosophers, as he readily admits is the case, the philosophers appear to attempt a reestablishment of the gods by employing the same "tools" – the very methods, techniques of investigation, and arguments – that led to the gods' being disestablished in the first place. Solmsen recognizes, moreover, that the gods, "suitably cleaned up" by such theoretically reconstructive work, could not but be identified with the causality or necessity that characterizes physics, and so they become wholly ensconced in nature. They seemed to disappear in a humanism that emerged from such an understanding of the universe that was able to emancipate itself from

98. For example, Meijer, "Philosophers, Intellectuals and Religion in Hellas," and Solmsen, *Plato's Theology*.

99. Solmsen, *Plato's Theology*, p. 40, emphasis added. I have just pointed out, however, that not all hold such a view – see, for example, the reference to Havelock in n. 51, as well as Meijer's work referred to in n. 98.

the authority of tradition; that is, from the hold of the mythopoeic mind. It is this to which I adverted in chapter one when I referred to the irony of (Greek) theology in assessing Gregory Vlastos' claim regarding philosophy's greatest contribution to religion. In traditional religious thought, cosmology is of subsidiary importance to, and can only be understood in the light of, knowledge of the gods, since the world derives its structure and significance by their (will and) action.[100] In post-Milesian "talk of the gods," however, the gods are a part of the cosmos, and theology is seen as an element of cosmology, its concern being to provide an explanation for this particular element of the universe and not the whole.

In summary, then, I would agree that Solmsen is right to claim that "unlike modern science, early Greek physics had never committed itself to methodological axioms which exclude the divine cause *ab initio*,"[101] but I would also maintain that he is less justified in inferring that those axioms are not inhospitable to divinity. Presocratic theology appears to constitute a kind of knowledge of the world that is indistinguishable from that provided for us by their physics. And that is also how Plato appears to have read it, for he turns against Presocratic thought as a whole – its philosophy and theology – in his own theological argumentation in the *Phaedo* and the *Laws*.

For Plato, as Solmsen agrees, physical necessity alone cannot explain the cosmos and the place of humankind in it – that is, it cannot provide an understanding of the universe that guarantees significance to humankind. As Solmsen puts it, "[i]t was, in all probability, more essential for Plato to invest the Universe with qualities which guarantee its metaphysical worth than to solve the problem of its origin."[102] Plato seems to have perceived something fundamentally detrimental for *meaning* and *significance* (of our human existence) in the philosophic quest for *knowledge* that derives from thinking wholly emancipated from the authority of tradition (myth).[103] Plato does not seem to reject this new intellectual approach in "coming to terms" with the universe, but he certainly felt that it needed to be kept under strict control. And

100. This may, of course, require further elaboration and work in light of Dihle's recent conclusions about the role will plays in classical culture: see his *The Theory of the Will*. I have already commented on the problem of the relation of the gods to the world (n. 36) which is sufficient for the claims being made here.

101. Solmsen, *Plato's Theology*, p. 54.

102. Ibid., p. 109.

103. Some comment on this contrast can be found in chapter 2. I shall pay further attention to it in the final chapter.

the strictness of that control creates sufficient grounds for doubts as to his acceptance of the new mode of thought. In his own system he attempts to combine both intellect and piety in the discussion of religion (the gods) and so adopts an attitude to religion that, as Solmsen puts it, is both archaic and hellenistic.[104] Solmsen admits that this appears paradoxical but concludes his study of Plato's theology with the claim that "[by] presenting the nature of the divine principle in a new light Plato transformed 'physics' and created a new hierarchy of values."[105]

This transformation of the physics of the Presocratics may well, however, be read as a distortion of it, for it is a subtle *apologia* for the religion of the past. And in making a bid for its revival there is involved a rejection of the intellect (mode of thought) as it had come to be embodied in the philosophy/science of the Presocratics. The revival of poetic religion in Plato's work involves an integration of reason and myth in which, as I shall shortly point out, only myth can survive intact. Plato's natural theology will be seen to be contaminated with a nostalgic piety that requires more than reason and evidence alone can deliver. Reason in his theology is not the reason of the Presocratics, emancipated as it is from myth, but rather something destructive of their type of reasoning in that it makes of it little more than a myth-retrieving activity.[106] Though some prefer to see such "rationally controlled mythmaking" as a creative exercise that combines rational thinking with the mythic imagination, it is, in the final analysis, simply the subordination of reason to myth. In denying reason the independence from myth that makes it what it is in the thought of the philosophers, Plato effectively destroys it. Plato's "god-talk," therefore, appears as a form of poetic theology that replaces a theology he saw as destructive of the very thing upon which it focused its attention. An analysis and critique of Michel Despland's recent work on Plato's philosophy of religion will substantiate that claim.[107]

PLATO'S REACTIONARY RATIONALISM

Despland's work on Plato is a complex and ambitious undertaking. His primary aim, however, is to provide an introduction to the art of

104. Solmsen, *Plato's Theology*, p. 170.
105. Ibid., p. 177.
106. I have borrowed this idea from Budick, *Poetry of Civilization*.
107. Despland, *The Education of Desire*.

doing philosophy of religion by showing it to be a process of discerning meaning and making it publicly available. The nature of that art is established in his conclusion to the story of its first emergence in the thought of Plato. Proving the claim that Plato "fathered" this art is a further major goal of this work and is the burden of the argument of its first nine chapters. And in an "Un-Platonic Postscript," that might more aptly have been titled "An Un-Platonic Platonic Postscript," he adumbrates a philosophy of religion that transcends Plato in substance (i.e., doctrine) but affirms in its entirety the framework Plato established. Despland sees Plato's work as a "hermeneutic of recovery"[108] that saved Greece from a terrible fate at the hands of the Milesian Enlightenment and, consequently, sees his own proposal as a similar hermeneutic that, in recovering the Christian religious tradition, will save a declining and decadent western civilization. Though he insists this "philosophy of religion" is an intellectual and rational activity, I will show it to be, whether in Plato or Despland, a mythical activity that attempts to "turn back the clock" and return to the comfortable world of *meaning* structured by past myths, but so abruptly shattered by the emergence of scientific *knowledge*.

Despland begins his analysis of Plato's philosophy of religion with an account of the ambiguities of the place of religion in Athenian life as he sees it displayed in the *Euthyphro*. Those ambiguities, he maintains, are clearly seen in the contrasts between Socrates and Euthyphro on questions of religious import. Although Despland does clearly establish that religion, as we think of it today, did not really exist in Plato's Athens, the meeting between Socrates and Euthyphro nevertheless suggests enough of a sense of the meeting between philosophy and religion. Religion for the first time becomes the focus of philosophical attention in this meeting which, therefore, constitutes the beginning of the philosophy of religion.

Despland is well aware that philosophical thought about the gods antedates the encounter between Socrates and Euthyphro. Presocratic thinkers like Xenophanes, for example, concerned themselves with "truths about God" that could be attested to by reason. Despland

---

108. The phrase is borrowed from P. Ricoeur's talk of interpretation as a "recollection of meaning" in the introduction to his "interpretation" of Freud (*Freud and Philosophy*, pp. 28ff.). One must understand that for Ricoeur such a hermeneutic exercise is a faith, even if a faith that has undergone criticism; it is still a naiveté, although a second naiveté, for it is the contrary of suspicion. That is surely how both Plato and Despland interpret their respective traditions. On this matter see Ricoeur's earlier *Symbolism of Evil*.

insists, however, that their thought constitutes a philosophical theology rather than philosophy of religion; the object of their attention is not religion but rather God and the gods.

Despland notes that such a philosophical theology is not the only Presocratic intellectual tradition; there is also a more secular philosophical tradition of thought concerned with understanding (i.e., knowing) the physical or natural world and achieving that understanding/knowledge nontheologically. He recognizes that religion receives some attention from this school of thought, but points out that it does so only, as he puts it, as a "derivative" phenomenon.[109]

It is the clash between these two traditions, according to Despland, that is represented in the meeting of Euthyphro and Socrates. Euthyphro represents a philosophical theology that attempts, quite unthinkingly, to hold fast to tradition – to religion – whereas Socrates, strange as it may seem to some, represents the scepticism of materialistic naturalism and therefore the rejection of tradition. Plato, he argues, sees in this encounter a crisis in the transmission of "the paradigms of culture"[110] – a clash between the simple reassertion of tradition in the face of the "modern enlightenment" and the loss of the tradition that gave birth to and sustained (Greek/Athenian) society. The "modern enlightenment" brought much of value that Plato did not wish to reject, but he also saw it as destructive of society in that it gave birth to a ruthless individualism[111] – an impulsive assertion of the self in contempt of everything else. Socrates, being wedded overmuch to some of its forms, namely questioning, is part of that problem although, as Despland puts it, even Socrates recognized "that the liberty of philosophical speech had gone too far. . . . "[112] "Plato and Socrates," he writes, "shared the notion that those forces which ruined myths and dissolved the society that gets its order from them must be checked and that a norm must be found for these new rational forces."[113] Plato's concern, therefore, is with piety – with the behaviour/action of persons in community – with orthopraxy rather than orthodoxy. (His philosophy of religion is, then, also a political philosophy, as Despland himself recognizes later in the text.) The enlightenment, in undermining

109. Despland, *The Education of Desire*, p. 33.
110. Ibid., p. 57.
111. Ibid., p. 41.
112. Ibid., p. 34.
113. Ibid., p. 55.

myth, destroys the means of transmitting "the paradigms of culture." The attempt to reinstate the old paradigm – à la Euthyphro – is naive, for it fails to recognize the force of the enlightenment critique. Plato, according to Despland, saw the problem quite clearly: "how can a philosopher strive to maintain – or renew – a widespread sense of piety, that inner sense of restraint or obligation without which there is no moderation and no health in the human handling of human affairs."[114] His response implies the existence of a mode of thought that neither rejects the enlightenment nor is seduced by it; a mode of thought that rethinks the religious tradition. As Despland has it, "Plato proposed to overcome the weakness of the enlightenment by way of increased enlightenment."[115] And that "increased enlightenment" is achieved by Plato, Despland declares, in a twofold manner: (1) in the development of the doctrine of the Forms which is a direct correlate of philosophical practice as understood by and exemplified in Socrates, and (2) in reconceiving the relationship of philosophic thought to religion.[116]

The theory of Forms constitutes a critique of those who seek a scientific explanation for everything – that is, a critique of that Presocratic tradition of thought that undermined the credibility of the Homeric pantheon. The theory implies that the mind is not, contrary to much in the scientific tradition, a product of matter but rather the ruler of it. Philosophy, therefore, is more than reasoning/explaining – it is a contemplative activity seeking a disinterested vision of the truth. Plato maintains that the religious tradition defended by Euthyphro and the philosophic/scientific tradition represented by Socrates both achieved such a vision of the truth, but only in part. Plato's mode of thought is a challenge to the authority of the religious tradition and to science. Philosophic thought and the philosopher transcend both the poet and the scientist while incorporating the best of both. Only in this fashion can destructive individualism be stemmed and the restraint that makes possible community, which had traditionally been provided by religion, be restored. The task of the philosopher, therefore, is one of "educating desire."[117]

In discussing Plato's relationship to traditional religion, Despland

114. Ibid., p. 57.
115. Ibid., p. 55.
116. Ibid., the first part of the development is discussed in chapters 4 and 5, while the second is treated in chapters 6 through 9.
117. Ibid., p. 84.

points out how it aided the soul in the achievement of purity by properly orienting people who were victims of their lower appetites. Plato, he goes on to argue, tries to recapture that power of religion (for restraining or constraining desire) by means of a theology publicly taught. Only with right belief can desire be properly educated: "His means are a theology: a set of stories, a set of beliefs and a set of laws."[118] Despland refers to this complex of beliefs of Plato as his "philosophic faith" – a faith that is simply "a rearticulation of the meaning of Greek religion."[119] And that rearticulation will reverse the worst effects of the materialistic speculations of the Ionians by reinstating myth which alone can bring about a shared consensus so essential to society. As Despland writes: "Myth is indispensable in providing living human beings with reality bearings in a changing cosmos and conflictual social world."[120]

Despland's conclusions summarize his views as to Plato's achievements and what in them is of lasting value. There is in Plato neither simple acceptance nor rejection of either traditional Greek religion or the Presocratic scientific tradition. Plato is seen as a critic of religion but less so than of the Presocratic enlightenment. Religion for him is a cultural force that counteracts worse forms of decay in society. As Despland puts it, "Plato's philosophy of religion strives to interpret the fears and hopes expressed in the Greek religious practice of his day and tries to set in motion a healing process."[121] He wants, paradoxically, consciously to change religion and yet remain schooled by it. Only religion, for Plato, can prevent the degeneration of society; only religion can provide a normative theory of culture and civilization. Despland admits that this means that an element of coercion characterizes Plato's understanding as to how human nature can become good – that knowledge alone is not enough for that work of transformation. Indeed, Plato fights the development of critical knowledge – the modern enlightenment – as a process of decay. The restraint of religion (transmuted by this philosophic faith) also requires "deception" as well as coercion – hence the role of myth in Plato's thought. Despland writes: "Public piety lives in human hearts thanks to the unexamined grasp of some myths."[122]

118. Ibid., p. 171.
119. Ibid., p. 170.
120. Ibid., p. 179.
121. Ibid., p. 203.
122. Ibid., p. 123. There is an irony in Despland's claim here that I think entirely escapes him.

Plato's rehabilitated mythical religion, therefore, is a mode of philosophic thought that, according to Despland, *transcends* the pure *logos* of the Presocratics (which, though lucid, can never say things fully) and the pure *mythos* of Homeric society (which, though obscure, and inexact conveys a fullness of meaning). It is a "new mode of thought" that "weaves together *logos* and *mythos*" – the former emancipating one from dead copies of a lost truth, and the latter continuing it.[123]

Despland's 'Postscript' provides the reader with a further set of conclusions. "None of us today can be Platonists," he insists.[124] There are obvious failures, he argues: Plato's need to infuse reason with an authoritarian bent; his limited reliance on reason; his lack of a principle of individuality and subjective freedom. A case can be made for philosophy of religion, however, but only from within a different – a better – myth. This Despland finds to have been provided by the rise and spread of Christianity. That "event" brought about a shift in worldview that set aside Plato's metaphysics, thereby changing the whole cultural context, as he puts it, for emerging human self-awareness. It provided a new understanding and *practice* of love over against Plato's religion of cosmic love, and it also brought a deep egalitarian thrust to society. Philosophy of religion in this new context is still a search for progress in the education of desire, but adds to it education of the will, overcoming the failure that elicited from Plato the infusion of coercion into the political philosophy that accompanies his religious philosophy. Despland writes: "That Plato had to devise means of coercion means that he failed to create the new powerful myth that would elicit the voluntary moves towards a new restructured order. The Christians did have such new myths."[125]

Philosophy of religion for Despland, then, is a thinking about human living. It is not the scientific desire for certain knowledge or the acquiring of a technology for direct, practical decision making. It will not, however, scorn science or technology. It involves – as did Plato's philosophy of religion – a transcending of these activities, while retaining what is of value in them through a hermeneutical appropriation of them that involves a learning from the prephilosophical expressions of human wisdom from which science and technology themselves have emerged. That prephilosophical wisdom – the functional equivalent

123. Ibid., p. 226.
124. Ibid., p. 225.
125. Ibid., p. 254.

of Plato's myth – represents what cannot be controlled or anticipated and therefore constitutes a limit to reason. Structurally, therefore, Despland's philosophy of religion parallels Plato's. The difference between them is to be found in the "controlling myths" – the prephilosophical expressions of human wisdom. Christianity constitutes a new myth – a new prephilosophical wisdom – that addresses not only the problem of human desire but also the question of the human will. In the new myth humankind is essentially unfinished and therefore open to change and development, allowing the Necessity of Plato's philosophy of religion to be transcended by the Openness of hope to be found in that philosophy of religion that directs its "corrective (transposing) attention" to the Christian myths.

The plurality of aims and intentions in Despland's work precludes provision of a full and adequate critique here. The nature of his argument and the wide-ranging character of the evidence he adduces in its favour make this task even more difficult. He is thoroughly familiar with the voluminous secondary literature as well and always takes into consideration the complex cultural context in which Plato operated. To criticize his views – with any degree of credibility – would require an opportunity to show how all the evidence he marshals can be rearranged so as to support an entirely different understanding of the nature of Plato's enterprise. Whereas Despland sees Plato in some sense as the father of a philosophy of religion that provided a genuine understanding of the world and therefore also provided meaning for the society of his day, I see him rather as a reactionary religious thinker attempting to recapture a meaningfulness that once characterized Athenian culture, but that had long since been undermined, if not entirely washed away. The construction of a fully argued alternative view is not necessary here. I shall rather simply raise some questions as to the general philosophical framework that shapes Despland's reading of Plato, and draw attention to its fatal weaknesses.

Despland's argument is carried on in a kind of Hegelian mode that makes it virtually impossible for him to recognize contradictions in Plato's enterprise, should they exist. Traditional Greek religion as thesis, it appears, finds its antithesis in Presocratic science, and Plato, seeing the strengths and weaknesses of each, transcends them both, while still weaving together what is of value in each into a new synthesis that Despland refers to as Plato's "philosophic faith." Despland's understanding of Plato has a kind of dialectical structure to it as well. He finds both strengths and weaknesses in Plato's philosophy of religion. His rearticulation or transposition of traditional Greek religion had its value – and apparently still does – but finds an antithesis in the new Christian myth. The philosophic rearticulation of that new myth (in Christian "theology"), therefore, seems to fill the role of synthesis.

The Platonic synthesis that Despland sees is, I think, spurious and is the result of pressing historical facts into a procrustean bed. Despland simply does not do justice to the Presocratic tradition of philosophy – particularly to the secular, scientific Ionian tradition. To read the "modern enlightenment," as he refers to this line of intellectual development in ancient Greece, essentially as the foundation for an individualism that is, in turn, the source of contempt for virtually everything of value in and to Athenian society, is grossly misleading. To recognize that philosophical speech and scientific intention may indeed have eroded the power of traditional religious thought, is hardly grounds for concluding, as Despland seems to, in company with Socrates and Plato, that philosophic speech has "gone too far." To assume that norms to harness this new emergent power of rationality are necessary and must necessarily come from the prephilosophical wisdom in one's culture, is to make of that reason a handmaiden, so to speak, to Greek/ Athenian religion. That some in society may have abused this new tool, in employing it for their own self-aggrandizement, is hardly sufficient grounds for claiming that one must limit its use in coming to understand our universe. Furthermore, it ought to be noted that, although Despland talks of the need to harness the power of rationality, he also, problematically, talks of the need to recognize its (natural) limitations. But that appears paradoxical at best, if not contradictory, and in need of explication. The talk of Plato overcoming the weakness of the enlightenment "by way of increased enlightenment" is similarly confusing, if not meaningless, without further explication. These almost deliberate ambiguities – and Despland indulges in others – are, indications of a failure to recognize the real force of the enlightenment critique of Homeric Greece and the emancipation of thought from the authority and power of tradition. Religion and philosophy in ancient Greece are incompatible modes of thought and the (Socratic/)Platonic response to the Ionians an indication of that culture's "failure of nerve," rather than an example of affecting a Hegelian style *Aufhebung* (synthesis). Eric Havelock captures the contrast succinctly in his discussion of "the liberal temper of Greek politics": "The Greeks, so far as we know, were the first people to realize that the religious-metaphysical and the biological-historical furnished alternative explanations of the nature of man and man's culture. Hebrew thought had embraced the first alternative exclusively; the older tradition in Greece itself was similar. It received, as we shall see, classic exposition in Hesiod, and was than revived, some two and a half centuries later, in a sophisticated form by Platonism."[126] Havelock here points to the essentially mythical character of Plato's thinking – a matter borne out in the remarkable similarities of Plato's ontology with the dualism implicit in archaic and primitive modes of thought and its contrast to the ontology of Presocratic thought. M. Eliade, for example, when pointing out that in the archaic frame of mind neither acts nor objects/things have any intrinsic value but only acquire value by participating in a reality that transcends them, argues that Plato simply makes explicit what the archaic mentality holds implicitly. According to Eliade, "it could be said that this primitive ontology has a Platonic structure; and [that] in that case Plato could be regarded as the outstanding philosopher of 'primitive mentality,' that is, the thinker who succeeded in giving philosophic currency and validity to the modes of life and behavior of archaic humanity."[127]

Despland's claim that Plato is the "father" of philosophy of religion simply confirms that Eliaden insight, despite the questionable nature of his argument in support of it. Such a claim can only hold true, if one assumes that philosophical scrutiny implies an assumption of the truth of the so-called prephilosophical wisdom contained in one's tradition, and that the only task for philosophy is its rearticulation in a new key. Understanding religious phenomena (or the phenomenon of religion) does not in itself involve any such assumption, so what counts or can count as philosophy of religion will be considerably broadened. (Indeed, if it is not, it is difficult to avoid having to conclude that Plato's philosophy of religion is really only a religious philosophy under another guise.) Since a number of Presocratic thinkers do pay attention to religious phenomena (as Despland admits, they do theology), it seems reasonable to refer to them as philosophers of religion. If approaching their subject matter in a naturalistic vein precludes calling them philosophers of religion, one must be religious – i.e., prephilosophically wise. It also needs to be noted here that to recognize, as Despland does, that Plato's philosophy of religion is a transposition

---

126. Havelock, *The Liberal Temper in Greek Politics*, pp. 30–31.

127. Eliade, *Cosmos and History*, p. 34. This sentiment, it seems to me, is echoed in Altizer's treatment of Plato as well in his *Oriental Mysticism and Biblical Eschatology*.

of religion to a new key that makes use of the new rationality by subordinating it to a principle other than its own, is to fail to recognize Ionian science/philosophy as a new mode of thought wholly independent of – and therefore transcending – religion. Presocratic scientific/ philosophic thinking is not rearticulated in Plato's thought: it is not transposed or even transmuted, in that its central principle is not kept intact, but rather wholly destroyed in being subordinated to the central truth of religion – of prephilosophical wisdom. One needs, therefore, in this regard, to see the essentially religious (mythic) rather than rational character of Plato's philosophy – to see that his philosophy is, in effect, a "philosophic faith" that is structurally indistinguishable from religion itself. This seems obvious in that Plato's philosophic faith finds its expression in a philosophical "theology" and in myths and stories. Despland does seem to recognize much of this, but does not draw the conclusion I would draw, namely, that Plato essentially sides with Euthyphro, although he appears less naive than Euthyprho. Despland seems to see Plato as having passed through the enlightenment, while yet returning to traditional preenlightenment insights, and therefore having transcended naiveté while yet remaining naive.[128]

Despland's general understanding of science and rationality are problematic in the extreme. He is blinded by what he calls the richness (i.e., the ambiguity) of myth. That richness calls for a hermeneutic activity, he maintains, as opposed to a reasoning or scientific activity. Reasoned analysis and the concern for scientific results are seen as shallowness rather than as signs of a clearly delimited and focused cognitive act. Despland seems to think that depth and profundity require clarity *and* opacity – "clarities surrounded by opacities."[129] "The invitation to the practice of philosophy," he writes, "is both a summons to keep talking as accurately as possible and a call to vague mythic adventure."[130] Ambiguity must *not* be removed.[131] Like Plato, he calls for a "proper integration of mythical language into philosophi-

---

128. This is the naiveté that, because it is the contrary of suspicion, constitutes faith. See n. 108. I suspect that Ricoeur's understanding of the two naivetés lies behind Despland's thinking here, but in my opinion neither of these scholars shows the specific differences that distinguish the two naivetés, which makes their claims based on the distinction suspect.

129. Despland, *The Education of Desire*, p. 199.

130. Ibid., p. 198.

131. Ibid., p. 207.

cal discourse,"[132] which is but to call for the reinstatement of myth *simpliciter*, for in weaving clarity together with ambiguity (unclarity) the result can only be ambiguity. And it is an ambiguity that has dark implications. As Despland himself recognizes, Plato's philosophy of religion also constituted a political philosophy (and perhaps also a philosophy of history, although I can only advert to that matter here). His philosophy of religion is concerned not only with the act of discerning the truth, but also with making it publicly available. He is also aware that "the education of desire" within the Platonic scheme required an infusion of the coercive power of an authoritarian state. It is unfortunate, however, that he refers to this merely as a weakness in Plato's system, for it is indicative of a massive failure of vision that clearly shows Plato's philosophy deficient. Despland suggests in the postscript that the philosophy of the Christian religion does not share this Platonic weakness, but he does not, I think, show how "the education of the will" that complements "the education of desire" in this new philosophy of religion evades it.

It should be noted that Despland's synthesis, his transcending of Plato's philosophic faith, is not entirely like Plato's synthesis. The tension here is not one between myth and rationality, but rather one between two myths, for Despland has accepted Plato's restricted understanding of rationality. It is important to see Plato's philosophy of religion as a philosophy of Greek religion (constituted by an *Aufhebung* of *mythos* and *logos*). According to Despland, our philosophy of religion today must be a philosophy of the Christian religion and should, one would assume, be an *Aufhebung* of *mythos* and *logos*, although the myth involved now would be quite different. In each case, however, *mythos* represents a prephilosophical wisdom. What we do not know, however, is how the Christian myth comes to replace (not merely transpose or even transmute) the Greek myth so central for Plato. It cannot be by reason or argument, but neither is it clear in what sense the replacement is a dialectical one. Despland's proposal, therefore, is doubly mythical and puts him foursquare into the Platonic camp. And it would appear that for both Plato and Despland reason must be sacrificed to religion.

132. Ibid., p. 224.

V

Theology and the Christian Religion

"THEOLOGY" IN REVIEW

I SUGGESTED in chapter one that a wide gap exists between Christian theology and the ordinary religious thinking of the Christian devotee. Having then argued the case for the existence of (at least two) distinct and radically different modes of thought, and having shown the historical emergence of a philosophic/scientific thinking from a preexisting mythopoeic matrix of thought, which it transcends, I proceeded to argue that, when Greek theology emerged, it undermined rather than complemented traditional Greek religion. In light of those arguments I shall now return to the question of theology and the Christian religion, for I think that here, too, it can be shown that theology does not so much complement the Christian faith as undermine it. This chapter therefore picks up the theme of chapter one in the sense that it tries to provide both argument and evidence for what appeared there to be merely a suggestive analysis of the use of the concept of theology. As in the preceding chapter, where it was shown that theological and religious thinking in ancient Greece were both (paradoxical as it may sound) incommensurable and incompatible, so I shall attempt to show here that Christianity embodies a similar problematic structure – not perhaps from its inception, but certainly within a very short period of time following its emergence as a distinct sect of the mainstream Hebrew tradition.

My first task will be to show that Christian thinking is, or at least was, mythopoeic. I shall tackle that problem by showing that Hebrew thought – as, indeed, the thought of the ancient Near East more generally – is mythopoeic, since Christianity is, quite obviously, in alignment with it. (I shall, for convenience, refer to this pattern of thinking in the discussion to follow as "biblical thinking.") I hope then to be able show that that particular form of mythopoeic thought underwent a twofold process of hellenization – the first stage of that process involving a restructuring of its thought patterns, making theology a distinct possibility, and the second actually bringing such a theology to birth. The tension between it and the matrix of biblical thought from which it originally emerged will become clear in the course of the argument.

It may be helpful to the structuring of that argument to recall here the tentative definition of theology for which I argued in chapter one. I there argued that not all forms of theology are detrimental to or in conflict with religion; that not all theology is incompatible or incommensurable with religion, but only the theology that emerges as an academic/scientific discipline is so. "Theology," I showed there, always requires qualification as poetic or (theopoetic), and I argued that the force of such qualification distinguished such "theologies" – structurally indistinguishable from each other – from "academic theology." The latter alone attempts to be scientific in the sense that the other sciences seek a natural (nonrevelational) knowledge about the world. Such "theologies," therefore, are really not theology at all but rather peculiar varieties of religious thinking – rationalized religious thinking disguised as theology. As I have also tried to show in the preceding chapter, "theology" is taken to be a hybrid mode of thought that, so it is claimed, dialectically synthesizes the structural incompatibilities of *mythos* and *logos*, but in fact simply subordinates the latter to the former. It uses reason (*logos*) to explicate "the Faith" (*mythos* or prephilosophical wisdom), all the while maintaining that "the Faith" (*mythos*) is not – at least not fully – rationally explicable, and that it therefore transcends reason and theology. This hybrid kind of thinking seems to constitute a theology only in the sense that it attempts to create plausible arguments for beliefs which people either hold or are expected to hold on other than rational grounds – by faith. It is of psychological importance perhaps, and especially so in a period when cognitive issues are of special concern to a particular society, but it is not itself acceptable as of genuine cognitive value. Recognizing this will help make sense of that strange and rapid hellenization of the essentially nonrational, religious faith of the Christian community. It will also help to make sense of the continuing tension within that community between faith and reason and for the essential emergence of academic theology and its subsequent corrosive effects on "the Faith."

It is not obviously not possible to deal with the question of the nature and role of theology in the Christian religion within the space of a chapter of a book. But then neither, fortunately, is it necessary to do so in order to establish with some degree of plausibility the claims I have just adumbrated. I shall give attention, therefore, only to what is necessary, namely, the question as to the nature of Christian thought in the earliest stages of the existence of that community; the rapid hellenization of that mode of thought during the early centuries of the development and growth of that community (emphasizing the essentially superficial character of what appear to be fundamental structural changes); and, finally, the emergence of academic theology as an aspect of Christianity in the Middle Ages.

THE NATURE OF EARLY CHRISTIAN THOUGHT

As the very brief discussion of the ancient Near East in chapter four has shown, there is general agreement that a radical distinction in modes of thought characterizes Greek and Semitic cultures and, consequently, Greek and Christian thought. Cyrus Gordon, though clearly recognizing a common Near Eastern background, so to speak, for both Greece and Israel in the Heroic age, nevertheless points to something he calls "the miracle of Greece," which created a gulf that separates the classical Israel of the prophets from the classical Greece of the philosophers and scientists. And Edwin Hatch, as I also noted, clearly indicates a stark contrast between Greek thinking and what he calls Palestinian thinking, which characterizes early Christian thought – or, perhaps better, Judeo-Christian thought. For Hatch the former is analytical, philosophical, and metaphysical whereas the latter is pragmatic and practical in the sense of being concerned with ethics and behaviour. And the latter, he insists, recognizes an authority *outside itself* that the former, as autonomous, could not.

That apparent difference between Greek philosophy and Christian thought was made popular about mid-century by Thorleif Boman in his treatment of the topic in his *Hebrew Thought Compared with Greek*. Boman argues that Hebrew (biblical) thinking diverges widely from the form of thought found among the Greeks. He holds that view, moreover, even though he argues that Hebrew thought had transcended the prelogical phase of thought spoken of by Lévy-Bruhl. "It can surely be regarded as generally recognized," he writes, "that Hebrew thinking is dynamic and Greek thinking static. . . . "[1] The former is vigorous, passionate, and even explosive, while the latter is peaceful, moderate, and harmonious. As with anthropologists in the examination of primitive cultures, so Boman finds important differences between Hebrew and Greek notions of time, space, causality, and other similar concepts and categories. The concepts in the former linguistic context are subjective, while in the latter they are objective; the Hebrew concepts are personal and the Greek impersonal. In the final analysis, therefore, Boman concludes that Hebrew thought is a "kind of" prelogical thought; it is prelogical, "to the extent that it stands closer to natural life than the subtle, lifeless, unimaginative and almost fossilized abstractions of our highly scientific thinking. . . . "[2] Greek mental life is far more advanced in that respect because, according to Boman, it is clearly "logical knowing," whereas Hebraic thinking constitutes a "deep psychological understanding."

Although Boman's argument has come under severe criticism, his central claim with respect to the argument of this book remains virtually untouched. Criticism has been directed not at his dichotomy thesis but rather at the method or approach he has taken to substantiate the thesis. Such is the nature of James Barr's critique, for example, in his *The Semantics of Biblical Language*. It is not the validity of the claim that Hebrew and Greek modes of thought differ drastically that draws Barr's criticism, but rather the argument that that contrast rests on differences between the two languages. He attacks, that is, the attempt to correlate a way of thought with a particular type of grammatical phenomenon. Thus he writes: "The idea that the grammatical structure of a language reflects the thought structure of those speaking it, and that it correspondingly reflects the differences from the thought of those speaking a language with a different grammatical structure, has very great difficulties."[3] William Foxwell Albright similarly maintained that "Boman's approach is completely wrong"[4] without, however, rejecting the dichotomy thesis for which Boman was arguing. He maintains that "Boman took a concept 'to be,' which is somewhat

1. Boman, *Hebrew Thought*, p. 19.
2. Ibid., p. 195.
3. Barr, *The Semantics of Biblical Language*, p. 39.
4. Albright, "The Place of the Old Testament in the History of Thought," p. 89.

differently expressed in Hebrew and Greek, and arbitrarily assumed that the differences were characteristic of different ways of thinking. If he had looked through his dictionaries carefully, he would have found that exactly the same ideas can be expressed, though in somewhat different ways. *The hypothesis of different forms of logic and different mentalities based on differences of language is erroneous.*"[5]

Neither Barr nor Albright, however, attack Boman's dichotomy thesis but rather, in varying degrees, give it support. Barr notes, for example, how extremely commonplace that distinction has become in modern theological discussion and sets out both to summarize the nature of the contrast and to account for its growing popularity.[6] Although he warns against over-dramatizing the distinction, he nevertheless recognizes it as not unreasonable. William Albright goes considerably further on this score than does Barr and, given his prodigious work in the field of Near Eastern studies, it will be of benefit to take a close look at his position.

Albright first set out his position on this matter in his 1940 book, *From the Stone Age To Christianity: Monotheism and the Historical Process*, in the context of a general discussion of methods and approaches necessary for coming to an understanding of the ancient Near East. He there makes use of Lévy-Bruhl's terminology (in effect, adopting his dichotomy thesis) in structuring a system of classification for history on the basis of the varieties of human mental achievement. That mental development begins, he suggests, at an unknown time in the stone age with a kind of "prelogical, corporative thinking," *à la* Lévy-Bruhl, and reaches its pinnacle in the development of "logical thinking" (following Lévy-Bruhl again) with the Greeks in the fifth century BCE. Unlike Lévy-Bruhl, however, Albright detects an intervening stage of thought between these two in the thought-life of the ancient Near East from the time of the third millennium BCE and on. Societies in this region prior to that time were prelogical and corporative in their mental life, but thereafter progressively exchanged prelogical patterns of thought for what he calls an "empirico-logical" style of thought. That new style of thought, however, is none too clearly delineated by Albright, either here or in his subsequent discussions of these matters. He suggests that such thought is logical in that it draws its sanctions from experience rather than from formal canons of thinking as with the philosophi-

5. Ibid., p. 89; emphasis added.
6. Barr, *Semantics*, pp. 8–14.

cal Greeks. Thus, in being logical, it is distinct from prelogical thought, and in being based on experience – which is not, it seems, restricted to simply empirical experience despite the rubric "empirico-logical" – rather than on formal and abstract canons of thought, it is distinct from that logical mode of modern thought to which Lévy-Bruhl referred. Not a great deal is provided by way of descriptive account of this new type of thinking Albright thought he could discern. He tells us, however, that within it the individual begins to receive formal recognition, indicating, therefore, that it is no longer corporative thinking. This is seen in the fact that personal responsibility begins for the first time to emerge in ethical teaching.[7] Nevertheless, this mode of thought remains contented with empirical knowledge – presumably with respect to the nature of the relationships and obligations of human persons to one another (Albright is none too clear here) – and it does not, as with the Greek philosophers, seek for a theoretical understanding of the facts learned.[8] Such a search for laws and theories lay beyond the realm of empirico-logical thinking, just as it lay beyond the prelogical thought of primitives. As Albright notes: "The prophets were not interested, so far as we can tell, in how the world had come into existence or how the forces of nature operated; it was quite enough for them to know that God controlled them. They had a real moral interest in knowing why God did certain things, but the idea that any of God's actions were subject to general physical laws which man might discover by observation and reasoning were totally foreign to them, as it was to all pre-philosophical thought."[9]

Albright's acceptance of the Lévy-Bruhlian thesis, however, was *not* uncritical.[10] Even in his first use of Lévy-Bruhl's thought in interpreting the ancient Near East he maintained that Lévy-Bruhl exaggerated the differences between the savage and the modern mind. He also insisted that Lévy-Bruhl underestimated the degree to which many so-called modern minds still operated in a prelogical and primitive fashion.[11] In a later book, *Archaeology and the Religion of Israel*, he further modified his use of Lévy-Bruhl by substituting the word "protological" for "pre-logical," insisting that even this primitive stage of thought

---

7. Albright, *From the Stone Age to Christianity*, p. 84.
8. Ibid., p. 258.
9. Ibid., p. 251.
10. I say this despite Rogerson's claim to the contrary in his *Anthropology and the Old Testament*, p. 35, n. 59.
11. Albright, *From the Stone Age to Christianity*, p. 124.

could not be without a logic of its own.[12] Nevertheless, he still acknowledged here his indebtedness and commitment to Lévy-Bruhl's position as late as 1968 in the preface to the fifth edition of that work, claiming that there has been practically no valid criticism of his approach over the intervening years.[13] The nature of that indebtedness to Lévy-Bruhl is seen much more fully in the first chapter of this book – "Archaeology and the Ancient Near Eastern Mind" – than anywhere else in his writing. Albright's work here shows, moreover, to what extent archaeology can contribute to the history of the workings of the human mind and the extent to which it provides hard empirical evidence for Lévy-Bruhl's understanding of the nature of primitive thought.[14]

Albright attempts in this work to give a fuller description of the three modes of thought that he detects in the evolution of the human mind, namely, the protological, the empirico-logical, and the logical. The first is still described in essentially Lévy-Bruhlian terms[15] but is now taken to overlap in a sense with the later empirico-logical stage of thought. Primitive minds, Albright now argues, behave in their everyday practical activities in much the same fashion as do modern or empirico-logical minds. "Empirico-logical thought," he insists, "is as old as *Homo sapiens* and goes back in simple forms to the animal world."[16] Primitives or savages learned via experience to do a great many things correctly and in all ordinary matters were governed by an empirical logic that really governs all animal life.[17] However, primitives entered the zone of the protological, so to speak, as soon as they left

12. Albright, *Archaeology and the Religion of Israel*, preface to the third edition; p. 18.
13. There has, of course, been criticism since, as I have already pointed out in n. 10. Nevertheless Rogerson does acknowledge (*Anthropology and the Old Testament*) that Lévy-Bruhl's "theoretical position is still tenable" and may yet give lead, as it did in Albright's work, for further 'Old Testament' research (p. 59). This is considerably more than he allowed for in his earlier work; on this see n. 56.
14. Albright, *Archaeology*, writes: "the gap between savage mentality and the mind of modern man is too great to be easily bridged by direct observation, and the attempt to fill the gap by studying the ideas of half-savage peoples of today is nearly always vitiated by the fact that these peoples have been strongly influenced by highly developed civilizations, virtually all of which reflect a post-Hellenic stage of progress" (p. 4). A more recent work on the place of archaeology in determining the nature and development of the human mind is Marshack's *The Roots of Civilization*. Also of considerable interest is Fairservice's *The Threshold of Civilization*.
15. Albright, *Archaeology*, p. 27.
16. Ibid., p. 29.
17. Though influenced to some degree by Lévi-Strauss's work, Albright nevertheless remains attached to the Lévy-Bruhlian dichotomy.

the world of everyday activity, dominated as it is by sensation, for only in that fashion could they rise above the limitations of their daily routine. The empirico-logical stage, consequently, emerges when what Albright calls "the logic of experience" is extended by human communities into those areas of life not directly under the sway of the senses. That began, according to Albright, in the third millennium BCE, and achieves its fullest level of development in the Old Testament (Hebrew Bible) where "survivals from the early proto-logical stage are very few and far between. . . . "[18] In a later essay on "The Place of the Old Testament in the History of Thought" he writes: "I place the Old Testament, from the standpoint of the history of ways of thinking, between the proto-logical thought of the pagan world (which includes non-metaphysical Greco-Roman and Indic polytheism) and Greek systematic reasoning."[19]

Like persons/communities at the proto-logical stage of thought, those at Albright's empirico-logical stage are interested in the basic problems of humanity, but they do not try to resolve those problems from a vantage-point, so to speak, beyond experience but rather on the basis of their experience(s). They do not, however, make use of logical reasoning or abstract generalization – activities to be found at the next stage of thought. That next stage of thought, he quite arbitrarily maintains, takes no interest whatever in those basic problems of humanity.[20] Thus he argues that "[t]he Old Testament exhibits everywhere the logic born of experience, empirical logic,"[21] and insists that this logic is as logical as any formal logic to be found in Greek philosophy and differs from it only in that it is implicit rather than explicit. (This, in fact, is a point that he comes to criticize in the views of others as I shall show later.) But it is not at all clear why that same judgment does not apply to the "kind of logic" he has himself suggested is implicit in the proto-logical thinking of the primitive mind (and especially so at the level of everyday activity.) It appears, that Albright is here involved in special pleading with regard to empirico-logical thought for which he sees some contemporary value no longer accruing to proto-logical or mythical thought. Furthermore, there is a good deal of ambiguity over the character of the experience that makes

18. Albright, *Archaeology*, p. 23.
19. Albright, "The Place of the Old Testament," p. 84; see also pp. 86–87.
20. Ibid., p. 91.
21. Ibid., p. 92.

empirico-logical thought what it is for Albright. There is ample suggestion in addition to the word empirical in the rubric itself to suggest
that experience means "empirical experience" or "sensory experience." And yet in his talk of Hebrew thought as empirico-logical (in
the other-than-everyday level; that is, at the level of "the basic problems
of humanity"), it appears that "experience" means something much
wider; more like "experiential." For all we know from Albright's discussion is that empirico-logical Hebrew thinking responds to the basic
problems of human existence neither mythically, as do proto-logical
thinkers, nor in a generalized, theoretical manner, as would logical
thinkers, if they in fact were to show concern for such problems.

That rather confusing picture is made even more confusing, moreover, in Albright's reference, later in that same essay, to experiential
logic and in his suggestion that it constitutes an intuitive discovery,
where by "intuitive" he means "a subconscious interpretation of empirical information received and registered by the human brain."[22] The
intuitive discovery – that is, the argument implicit in experiential
logic – shows "that the incongruities of polytheism flouted the empirically recognized unity of nature," which brought about "a transformation which was to revolutionize man's relation to man."[23] But the
argument is hardly logically/rationally persuasive and even less so in
that, having confused empirico-logical thinking with intuitive discovery, he maintains that, even if the process of subconscious interpretation in such intuition is not understood, he, being a theist, is happy to
accept the role of divine providence in the process.[24] In the final
analysis, his so-called argument on behalf of an empirico-logical stage
in the development of the human mind seems grossly over-extended,
suggesting that the differences between the modes of thought of the
primitive mind and the ancient Near Eastern mind after the third
millennium BCE is but one of degree rather than one of kind. That, in
any event, is a claim that, as I shall argue below, has much to recom-
mend it. If successful, of course, Albright's archaeological evidence
with regard to the development of the human mind will stand even
more forcefully in support of the Lévy-Bruhlian hypothesis as set out
in chapter two.

It ought to be noted here that, though Albright detects three stages

22. Ibid., p. 99, n. 35.
23. Ibid., pp. 99–100.
24. Ibid., p. 99, n. 35.

in the evolution of human thought, he does not seem to hold a consistent view of the nature of the evolutionary development from stage to stage. The proto-logical stage of development is never really outgrown, in that thinking at such a level still takes place in some modern minds, but, where it does so, it seems in Albright's estimation a sign of failure. But the same assessment does not hold for the next level of thought. "Whatever happens," he writes in the essay on the nature of the Near Eastern mind, "man will never outgrow the empirical logic of Israel or the Aristotelian logic of Greece. Future progress must conserve all the essential elements of both."[25] As a radically distinct type of thought, then, empirico-logical thinking transcends (and abrogates) the preceding stage of logical thought. This asymmetry in his analysis is overcome, however, when it is seen that, even though Near Eastern thought after the third millennium BCE is different from primitive mythopoeic thought, it is so only in degree. As a variant form of mythopoeic – proto-logical – thinking, I shall show below, one can better understand the facts that he has unearthed about the ancient Near Eastern mind.

It is necessary here to return for a moment to Boman's thesis with which this discussion began. It is even less satisfactory than is suggested in the critiques by Barr and Albright – although I do not on that account wish to suggest that the dichotomy thesis ought to be abandoned. It is important, though, to see that Boman's argument is not only methodologically naive but also philosophically weak, for in seeing those problems clearly, a more adequate argument can be constructed from the evidence available.

Boman recognizes the tension that exists between the Hebrew and Greek modes of thought but, strangely, does not draw the conclusion that they are mutually exclusive, as one might have expected him to do. Rather, like Albright, he simply asserts, and quite categorically, that the Hebrew and Greek forms of thought are complementary: "the Greeks describe reality as being, the Hebrews as movement. Reality is however, both at the same time; this is logically impossible, and yet it is correct."[26]

25. Albright, *Archaeology*, p. 35. See also Machinist's similar view of the complex structure of thought in ancient Mesopotamia in his "On Self-Consciousness in Mesopotamia." Machinist sees a radical difference between Greek and Mesopotamian thought (p. 195) but does not see the latter as wholly without elements of abstract, analytical thinking (p. 196). For him all three modes of thought – mythopoeic, empirico-logical and philosophic/scientific – are to be found in Mesopotamian thinking (p. 199).

26. Boman, *Hebrew Thought Compared with Greek*, p. 208.

The logical impossibility to which Boman refers here is less stark than may first appear, for Boman does not mean by "philosophy" the philosophic/scientific thinking to which I have referred as emerging with the Milesians. For Boman, as for Nygren whom he follows in this respect,[27] Plato is the acme of Greek philosophical thought. And both Nygren and Boman recognize that that philosophy is essentially religious in nature,[28] which obviously implies some degree of comparability between Israelite and Greek (i.e., Platonic) thinking, for the latter too, as he puts it, "is religious through and through."[29] Indeed, because of this similarity he insists that there is a *necessary* relationship between Hebrew and Greek thinking: "both kinds of thinking are equally necessary if one means to be in touch with the whole of reality."[30]

Boman's rhetoric, however, is hardly persuasive. As I have already shown, his understanding of philosophy is naive at best; there is an almost complete failure to see that Plato's thought is a rejection of philosophic/scientific thinking – that it is an attempt, making use of reason, to recapture the essence of traditional Greek religion which is mythopoeic. And he fails, moreover, to see that for that very reason Plato's thought is either incoherent or but a disguised return to a religious mode of thought that transcends reason and philosophy. The combination of Hebrew and Platonic thinking, therefore, is not combining two radically different modes of thought, except insofar as Platonic thought to some degree transmits something of the nature of reason, since it uses a limited form of reason in "repackaging" traditional Greek religious thought. Plato's thought is itself a kind of hybrid of Greek traditional religious thought and philosophic/scientific thought as I have argued above (chapter 4).

The weaknesses in Boman's dichotomy thesis do not constitute a refutation of his claims, although they leave it stranded without either evidential or sound argumentative support. However, as the discussion of Albright has already shown, the claim that Hebrew thought differs radically from that of Greek philosophy as it emerged with the Milesians, does find support in a careful comparative analysis of the two. Albright maintains that his thesis in this regard has not come under persuasive critical attack. However, a very similar thesis, floated by a

27. Ibid., p. 18. See Nygren, *Eros and Agape.*
28. Boman, *Hebrew Thought Compared with Greek*, p. 18.
29. Ibid., p. 18.
30. Ibid., p. 204.

group of scholars at about the same time, in a volume entitled *Before Philosophy: The Intellectual Adventure of Ancient Man*, edited by H. and H. A. Frankfort, did come under sustained attack. Before resting easy with Albright's conclusions, therefore, it is necessary to restate the Frankforts' version of the dichotomy thesis and assess the weight of the criticisms raised against it.

The "Frankfort thesis," though the Frankforts explicitly rejected Lévy-Bruhl's terminology and attempted to distance themselves from his formulation of the dichotomy thesis, appears not to differ radically from Lévy-Bruhl's understanding of the nature of primitive thought. As a recent examination of their thesis indicates, their thought is probably dependent more upon E. Cassirer's understanding of the nature of mythic thought, as it is to be found in the second volume (*Mythical Thought*) of his multi-volume *The Philosophy of Symbolic Forms*, although significant differences between the Frankforts' thesis and Cassirer's understanding of the nature of mythic thought are clearly noted. For example, whereas the Frankforts see some emancipation of Hebrew thought from the mythopoeic, Cassirer simply sees development within the framework of mythical thought.[31] Nevertheless, even though the Frankforts see Hebrew thought as differing from the mythopoeic modes of thought that surround ancient Israel, they still maintain that it never entirely transcended the mythopoeic form.[32] For the

31. This is Rogerson's claim, for example, in chapter 7 ("The Old Testament versus Mythopoeic Thought") of his *Myth in Old Testament Interpretation*, pp. 86ff.

32. Other views on this matter are more ambiguous. Voegelin's argument regarding the nature of Hebrew thought in his *Israel and Revelation*, is a clear example. Voegelin distinguishes both Israel and Greece from the rest of the ancient Near Eastern patterns of thought which he describes as being "compact forms of (cosmological) myths." Israel and Greece are, by contrast, "differentiated forms of history and philosophy" (p. 13) and do not participate in that earlier form of "cosmological symbolization" (p. 27). Israel, he insists, "discovered" history as a new form of existence. However, "history" here does not mean what it is generally taken to mean in common usage. Voegelin distinguishes, that is, "pragmatic history" (essentially equivalent to "common usage") from "paradigmatic history" (p. 123; see also p. 163), which seems very much to have the quality of myth as that word has been used in this essay. Against historiographic assumptions of scholars like Wellhausen and others Voegelin writes: "Faced with the alternatives that either the compositors of the Biblical narratives have ruined the meaning of their sources or that the literary critics have ruined the meaning of the compositorial work, we prefer the second one" (p. 155). For Voegelin, then, history concerns meaning which in turn presupposes a divinely willed order in the world and society and hence revelation (pp. 164, 171, 409, *et passim*). The historiographic work of the Hebrews, therefore, "contains genuine myths, genuine history, and enactment of the myth that we find in the affair

Frankforts, therefore, as for Cassirer and Lévy-Bruhl – with whom Cassirer differs little as shown above (chapter 2) – mythopoeic thought, and therefore Hebrew thought, transcends the bounds of reason and therefore constitutes a radically different kind of thought from that represented by the Milesian philosophers.

The Frankforts' version of the dichotomy thesis came under heavy critical fire almost immediately upon its publication, and the criticisms made against it were not merely methodological but also substantive.

---

of the Deuteronomy. The three types of content are blended into a new type of story that is neither myth nor pragmatic history but the previously analyzed 'world-history' with its experiential nucleus in the historical present constituted by Moses and the Covenant, and its elaboration through speculations on the origins of being and the periods of world-history. The 'narrative' thus has absorbed variegated types of materials and transformed them according to its own principle of construction. It is a symbolic form *sui generis*. Hence, when now again we raise the question concerning the 'subject matter' of the narrative, we are forced to the conclusion that it has no 'subject matter', but a meaning which can be ascertained only by recourse to the experiential motivations of the form" (pp. 175–76; see also pp. 195, 355, 364). This new *sui generis* symbolic form does not, then, appear to have broken free of the myth.

Schneidau also sees a considerable difference between Hebrew thought and that of the rest of the ancient Near East in his *Sacred Discontent*. He admits that the Hebrews also have myth but claims that Hebrew society, as Western society in general after it, interprets – that is, attacks and undercuts – its own myths (p. 14). In the alienation produced by such an approach to their myths Schneidau detects the emergence of the notion of objectivity that comes to characterize western thought in general but which has generally been claimed to be a discovery of the Greeks. He writes: "the prophets, who antedate Plato by several hundred years, retain their priority in the Western development of knowledge by dissociation of self, and their alienation from culture is the archetype – and remains the precondition – of the 'objectivity' about which we are now dubious" (p. 21; see also p. 26). Nevertheless, he also claims that "[t]he traditional derivation of science from Ionian philosophy is not in question, of course; the aim is simply to emphasize the catalytic role of Biblical thought" (p. 28).

Schneidau's analysis in places overlaps that of Voegelin. However, he seems explicitly to accept a dichotomy thesis regarding primitive and modern thought (pp. 57, 73) that bears on the issue, even though he is not altogether convinced that the Hebrews can be assigned to one or the other side of the divide. Though Moses, according to Schneidau, refuses to go back to the gods of culture and nature and therefore abrogates the I-Thou relationship to the world (p. 65), he nevertheless argues that the talk of a will behind the events in the Old Testament extends 'Thou-ness' to history which parallels the personifying aspects of nature by mythological peoples (p. 185). On this matter see also Stone, "Eschatology, Remythologization and Cosmic *Aporia*," p. 245.

There is much in both Voegelin and Schneidau that complicates the picture of Hebrew thought developed in the Frankfort thesis, but not such that it requires its rejection. Hebrew thought, that is, is more mythopoeic than it is scientific thought, although it is not, to be sure, of the identical structure of the "compact myth."

A careful review of that critical literature will, however, reveal the essential soundness of their thesis and therefore strengthen the claim that Hebrew thought – and that of Christianity which is aligned with it – stands in conflict with the philosophic/scientific modes of thought characteristic of the Greeks (Milesians).

The most severe and sustained attack upon the Frankfort thesis was launched by Kramer in a lengthy review in the *Journal of Cuneiform Studies*.[33] He maintains there, for example, that the psychological analysis of the mind of ancient Near Eastern humankind is not grounded upon fact, and argues that, "[i]n the case of the Sumerians . . . there is good evidence to show that they had a group of thinkers who were quite capable of viewing nature with a detailed and reflective mind. . . ."[34] He maintains in fact that they "succeeded in working out a systematic metaphysics and theology."[35] He does so, however, recognizing that the source material here is essentially mythopoeic and does not, therefore, provide detached, speculative thought. Nevertheless, he claims that these sources, "in spite of their essentially mythopoeic character, presuppose the existence of such systems and reflect them at every turn."[36] His claim is therefore that there is in the extant literary sources an *implicit* philosophy and theology.[37] Fifteen years on, Kramer reiterates his opposition to the Frankfort thesis in his book *The Sumerians: Their History, Culture and Character*, although his position there is stated in an indirect and more subdued way. In the fourth chapter of that book – "Religion: Theology, Rite and Myth" – he refers to the "Sumerian thinker" and talks of the "logical" and "inferential" thought of the "Sumerian theologians" and of their "metaphysical inferences."[38]

Later studies of the ancient Near East do not bear out the harsh criticisms raised by Kramer as reference to the work of Gordon and Albright above already indicates. A. Leo Oppenheim in *Ancient Mesopotamia: Portrait of a Dead Civilization*, moreover, maintains that it is not possible to write a history of Mesopotamian religion because of the

33. Kramer, a review of "Frankfort, et al, *The Intellectual Adventure of Ancient Man.*
34. Ibid., p. 41.
35. Ibid., pp. 41, 47–48.
36. Ibid., pp. 42.
37. Not all reviews were as biting and harsh as this. See, for example, the review by Meek of the University of Toronto.
38. Kramer, *The Summerians*, pp. 114–115.

quality of its thought; because, as he puts it, there is a "problem of comprehension across the barriers of conceptual conditioning."[39] Of this conceptual barrier he writes, reminding us of the Lévy-Bruhl-like thesis in the work of the Frankforts and their colleagues: "It is open to serious doubt whether we will ever be able to cross the gap caused by the difference in 'dimension.' This conceptual barrier, in fact, is a more serious impediment [to the study of the ancient Near East] than the reason usually given, the lack of data and specific information. Even if more material were preserved, and that in an ideal distribution in content, period and locale, no real insight would be forthcoming – only more problems. Western man seems to be both unable and, ultimately, unwilling, to understand such religions except from the distorting angle of antiquarian interest and apologetic pretences."[40]

Oppenheim reinforces this Lévy-Bruhl-like position in his later article on the "Position of the Intellectual in Mesopotamian Society," in which he draws a sharp contrast between the intellectual in Mesopotamia and in Greece which he bases on the lack of polemic to be found in cuneiform literature.[41]

Certainly Thorkild Jacobsen, one of the authors in *Before Philosophy* criticized by Kramer, has not been moved by Kramer's arguments, as can be readily seen in the argument he structures in his more recent *The Treasures of Darkness: A History of Mesopotamian Religion*. At first glance one might presume, on the basis of the title, that Jacobsen is in agreement with Kramer rather than with Oppenheim. However, the first chapter, and Jacobsen's use there of Otto's phenomenology of religion as a framework for his analysis, soon dispel that first impression. Indeed, Jacobsen throughout his work reiterates the earlier claims made in *Before Philosophy* and remains unpersuaded by Kramer.

Although opinion differs as to whether or not a Lévy-Bruhl-like view of the thought of the ancient Near East is plausible, the weight of the available evidence suggests that it is. This does not mean that the work of the critics of such a view is of no significance or can simply be ignored, but only that when all is said and done, the critics' work does not justify a more rationalist interpretation of the ancient Near Eastern

39. Oppenheim, *Ancient Mesopotamia*, p. 172.
40. Ibid., pp. 182–183.
41. Oppenheim, "Position of the Intellectual in Mesopotamian Society"; see especially pp. 38ff. See also his "The Interpretation of Dreams in the Ancient Near East."

mind. The Hebrews, we must admit, do appear to differ radically from their neighbours, and the ancient Near Eastern mode of thought itself, similarly, seems to transcend in some respects the mythopoeic thought characteristic of more primitive communities. Those differences, however, seem more reasonably accounted for as developments which are within an essentially mythopoeic structure of thought, but which do not transcend the essence of that mode of thought. Sabatino Moscati's analysis of the question in his *The Face of the Ancient Orient* best sums up the conclusion to which one is driven by the available evidence and conflicting interpretations of it. He writes: "The description of the Oriental mentality as myth-making seems defensible as a generalization, provided we exclude Israelite and Zoroastrian thought, which in the religious sphere unmistakably reacts against myth. But even granted this exclusion, the myth-making character is not to be understood as eliminating rational thought but as including it in a higher unity. The Oriental is not unable to think rationally, but he feels no need to isolate reason as an independent faculty and theorize it as such."[42] Although Moscati seems here to be supporting Kramer's claims against Jacobsen and the Frankfort group, the support is illusory. Both Albright and the Frankforts recognize that Hebrew thought differs from other modes of thought of the ancient Near Eastern mind, but the former sees it as neither mythical nor logical and the latter see the Hebrews as having created a new myth of "the will of God" that replaced the older cosmogonical myths. Furthermore, it must be noted that the higher unity – of which the rational or logical element in the thinking of the ancient Near East recognized by Kramer or Moscati, or implicit in that which distinguishes Hebrew thought from that of her neighbours for the Frankforts and others,[43] or implicit in the empirical logic of Albright – is the unity not of reason but of myth. Whatever rational component is to be found in the mythopoeic mind – whether in a primitive or an ancient Near Eastern pattern – is therefore, *subordinated* (though unconsciously so) to the unity of the cultural myth which, to put it bluntly, makes the myth superior to reason and so ultimately denatures reason. (To claim, or even suggest, that the Oriental does not feel the need to isolate reason as an independent faculty is a curious kind of overstatement. Moscati talks as if the Oriental mind had given consideration to the possibility of a "Milesian move"

---

42. Moscati, *The Face of the Ancient Orient*, p. 330.
43. On this matter see n. 32.

and had consciously and deliberately rejected it. There is of course no evidence to support such an interpretation.) The reason that myth possesses in that unity of which Moscati speaks is precisely not that autonomous reason which in the thought of the Milesians is marked especially by its transcendence of the cultural myths of Greece. Reason functions in such a unity in the same limited fashion that Plato gives it in his, ultimately, mythical understanding of the world.

It must be noted here that all the while such argument about the nature of ancient Near Eastern thought was in the process of elaboration, an opposite point of view was also being vigorously defended. Duncan Black McDonald, for example, set out to vindicate what he referred to as "the Hebrew philosophic genius" – although, like many others in the field, he also identified Greek philosophy with Platonism,[44] even though he also refers to reason here as a form of independent thinking.[45] Despite the reference to independent thinking, however, he insists that the Hebrews subordinated reason to the authority of God.[46] "The Hebrews never had the slightest intention, however philosophical they might be," he writes, "of turning from Jehovah and giving themselves to pure Reason."[47] Nevertheless, they held certain fundamental ideas about God, life and the world that amounted to "a philosophy of becoming" similar in many respects to that espoused by Plato. But they did not consciously set out to structure such a "world-view" but rather held it implicitly – it formed an unconscious part of their knowledge, being implied by their daily round of existence and worship.

Although Albright was aware of McDonald's work, he was not persuaded by his argument. Following the lead of his colleague G. Boas, Albright pointed out that McDonald confuses implicitly held beliefs with logical analysis of them.[48] He admits that in its implicit beliefs Hebrew thought represents a very important prephilosophical stage of development, yet maintains that "none of the characteristics of Greek philosophy is found in the Hebrew Bible."[49] And elaborating on that point he writes: "There is no logical reasoning; there is no abstract generalization of the type familiar from Plato and subsequent

44. McDonald, *The Hebrew Philosophical Genius*, p. ix.
45. Ibid., p. 2.
46. Ibid., p. 32.
47. Ibid., p. 47.
48. Albright, "The Place of the Old Testament," p. 91.
49. Ibid., p. 91.

Greek philosophers; there is no systematic classification; there are no creeds . . . ; the Old Testament is not philosophical. . . . "[50] Given its prephilosophical character, however, Albright readily accounts for the hellenization of Jewish thought in Philo and such subsequent rationalist developments as are to be found in the likes of Maimonides and Spinoza.

A similar kind of argument for an implicit metaphysics of the Bible has been put forward subsequently by Claude Tresmontant in a series of separate works. In his *A Study of Hebrew Thought* he maintains that the idea of creation forms the basis for a Hebrew metaphysical system as a rival to that of the Greeks.[51] Christianity was not simply invaded by Greek philosophy, but rather the Greeks and Hebrews concerned themselves with similar questions about reality and produced alternative sets of answers. Hebrew thinkers, he insists, arrived at uniquely different valuations of reality, even though their doctrines, as he refers to their specific beliefs, often overlapped. Consequently, Tresmontant insists that a proper understanding of the scriptures requires the adoption of a body of doctrines or theses that can only be called metaphysical – although "adoption" here may be too strong a concept for their unconscious acquiescence in such a world-view. Tresmontant argues this claim in *The Origins of Christian Philosophy* and again in his *Christian Metaphysics*. However, as he admits in the last mentioned work, those necessary beliefs, doctrines, or positions found to be implicitly espoused in the scriptures are not, technically, philosophical nor do they constitute a philosophical system. "Biblical thought and after it Christian thought," he writes, "involve an original, metaphysical structure, even before this structure is described and formulated in a technical and explicit fashion."[52] This, of course, seems to make nonsense of the notion of philosophy which is generally understood to be

---

50. Ibid., p. 91. See the similar judgment of Sandmel in his "The Ancient Mind and Ours": "Philosophy could and did develop among the Greeks; it did not follow a similar course among the Hebrews" (p. 31). For Sandmel the ancient mind in general is radically different from the Western in general: "The ancient mind was elastic, ours is rigid. Theirs was essentially intuitive, creative; ours is self-consciously disciplined and restrained, prone to eclecticism; theirs was passionate, ours dispassionate; theirs was adventurous, ours is safe; they were artisans or artists; we, perhaps, are craftsmen; they were religious, and even superstitious; we are theological, and maybe even devoid of religion" (p. 44).

51. Tresmontant, *A Study of Hebrew Thought*, p. 14.

52. Ibid., p. 29.

the activity of consciously enquiring into the nature and structure of reality. However, Tresmontant also maintains that the scriptures quite consciously and explicitly express metaphysical doctrines – the doctrine of being, for example, in the book of Genesis. That interpretation has not garnered much support. Indeed, the criticism lodged against McDonald carries equal weight here against Tresmontant's theory of an implicit metaphysics in Hebrew thought. For Tresmontant, as for McDonald, "metaphysics" has lost its philosophical connotation – no longer referring to the conscious intellectual activity of individuals in search of knowledge of the ultimate structures (meaning) of the universe. Though it may include that, the word as used by Tresmontant also refers to the "unconscious holding" of presuppositions. But that makes virtually all thinking metaphysical, for all thinking involves implicit presuppositions – even the mythopoeic thought of primitive humanity. That kind of metaphysics is philosophically vacuous and therefore unable to bear the significance Tresmontant wishes it to carry.

Though Albright opposes the kind of position argued on behalf of Hebrew thought by the likes of McDonald and Tresmontant, he himself, nevertheless, seems at times to come close to espousing the same position, especially when he overemphasizes the empirico-logical character of the Old Testament (Hebrew Bible). On one occasion, for example, he writes: "The Old Testament exhibits everywhere the logic born of experience, empirical logic. As we have seen, it is just as 'logical' as any formal logic of the Greeks and their successors, but this logic is implicit; it emerges from experience and is not expressed in formal categories."[53] He argues that the seeds of formal syllogistic reasoning are already contained in Hebrew thought and are "merely waiting for a favourable climate in order to sprout."[54] Nevertheless, on the whole he interprets the ancient Near Eastern mind, including, with slight modification, the Hebrew mind, in Lévy-Bruhlian fashion, and his argument in that respect has found continuing support. J. W. Rogerson, for example, in a chapter on "Primitive Mentality" in his *Anthropology and the Old Testament* maintains that "Lévy-Bruhl's theoretical position is still tenable and to this extent he may give a lead for future Old Testament work."[55] Although he makes reference here primarily

53. Albright, "The Place of the Old Testament," pp. 92–93.
54. Ibid., p. 97.
55. Rogerson, *Anthropology and the Old Testament*, p. 59.

to Albright's work, he accepts it as essentially sound and as a portent of possible future developments – a significant conclusion, given that he had earlier written off any such possibility.[56] Given Christianity's alignment with Hebrew thought, it too, though I shall not argue the matter separately here, bears the same structure, and I shall refer here to both Hebrew and Christian thinking as "biblical thinking."[57]

CHRISTIAN THOUGHT TRANSFORMED?

The rapid hellenization of Christian thought to which I drew attention in the preceding chapter, it might well be argued, is a telling argument *against* a mythopoeic view of Hebrew, or more generally, biblical,

---

56. In his *Myth in Old Testament Interpretation*: "it is becoming clear that the notion of a primitive mentality different from that of moderns must be abandoned: (p. 180); "I would maintain that attempts to interpret ancient texts on the basis of theories of primitive mentality or mythopoeic thought must be abandoned" (p. 181).

57. On this matter see, for example, Snaith, *The Distinctive Ideas of the Old Testament*. For Snaith the ideas of the Old Testament are different and especially so from the ideas of the Greek thinkers (p. 9). He writes, "[t]he message of the New Testament is in the Hebrew tradition as against the Greek tradition" (p. 159). As he goes on to say, it is not Plato and the Academies that were 'our tutors to Christ' but rather Moses and the Prophets (p. 159). The following passage sharpens the point dramatically: "Traditional Christianity has sought to find a middle way, combining Zion and Greece into what is held to be a harmonious synthesis. The New Testament has been interpreted according to Plato and Aristotle, and the distinctive Old Testament ideas have been left out of account. Here is the cause of the modern neglect of the Old Testament. The 'righteousness' of Aristotle has been substituted for the 'righteousness' of the Old Testament. The *logos spermatikos* of the Stoics has largely transplanted the Holy Spirit. The wholly non-Biblical doctrine in the immortality of the human soul is accepted largely as a characteristic Christian doctrine. Plato is indeed, 'divine' and Aristotle 'the master of them that know' " (p. 9).

See here also Knight's discussion of the doctrine of the Trinity in his *A Biblical Approach to the Doctrine of the Trinity*, in which similar sentiments are expressed: "the whole Greek world of thought represented by the LXX translation of the Old Testament was inimical to the Hebraic approach, [i.e., to Hebraic thinking], what we now would call the biblical approach, to the claims of faith" (p. 3). For Knight, there is a "Hebraic thinking about God" that necessarily results in a radically different view of God among the Hebrews from that among the Greeks (e.g., pp. 1, 78). Knight, like Snaith, complains about the dominance of Greek patterns of thought that later distort Christian thought: "Much of this peculiar Hebraic way of thinking has been buried for centuries, and was indeed buried in the days of Origen and Athanasius and Arius and Augustine" (p. 6). Knight, it should be noted, rested his argument upon that of Hatch (see chapter 4, pp. 154–56 and below). Hatch, he insisted (p. 3) showed clearly that Greek thought profoundly modified the Christian habit of mind.

thinking. If, as Hatch has pointed out, the centre of gravity of the Christian faith changed so rapidly from ethics to belief and from practice to theory, so that within 150 years of the first contact between Christianity and philosophy the former should be nó less a philosophy than a religion,[58] then perhaps the only adequate explanation is that there is, beneath the level of superficial difference, a profound kinship between them. As Hatch puts it, "The explanation [for such influence] is to be found in the fact that, in spite of the apparent and superficial antagonism, between certain leading ideas of current philosophy and the leading ideas of Christianity there was a special and real kinship."[59] He goes on: "Christianity gave to the problems of philosophy a new solution which was cognate to the old, and to its doubts the certainty of a revelation."[60] From this perspective those who have argued that Judeo-Christian thought is ultimately philosophical and metaphysical rather than mythopoeic or empirico-logical should have another hearing. Perhaps, that is, McDonald and Tresmontant are closer to the truth than I have made them appear. One might even be tempted to suggest on the same grounds that Kramer's view of the nature of mind in the whole of the ancient Near East ought not to be written off quite so quickly.

Such reconsideration, however, would be unwarranted, for there is quite another – and more natural – way of interpreting this state of affairs. But before I can present that interpretation it will be necessary to clarify exactly what "the hellenization of Christianity" means. Given the distinction between Milesian philosophy and that of Plato that I have been at such pains to make clear in earlier chapters, the phrase is bound to be critically ambiguous. The contrast I have drawn between religion and philosophy involves philosophy of the Milesian variety only, for Plato's philosophizing is rather different – it is essentially a religious mode of thought. Platonism is only superficially distinguishable from the mythopoeic thought from which the Milesians and their successors broke free. For Christian thought to be heavily influenced, then, by Platonic thought and ideas would be considerably different from its coming under the influence of Greek philosophy of the Milesian variety. It is clear that on many occasions where the "hellenization" of Christianity or of Israelite religion is referred to, what is really meant

58. Hatch, *The Influence of Greek Ideas*, p. 125.
59. Ibid., p. 125.
60. Ibid., p. 126.

is the "Platonization" of that tradition – a process, that is, of thinking about the tradition in a Platonic way and of attempting to harmonize the tradition with the Platonic world-view. It is only because "Greek philosophy" is taken as symbolic for "Platonic thought" that Boman, for example, is able to argue that there is a peculiar relationship between Hebrew and Greek thinking. It is only for that reason that Boman is able to recognize a peculiar relationship between the two that permits the latter an overwhelming influence over the former, even though, at least in some respects, he sees the respective modes of thought of the two communities to be *logically* distinct types. Indeed, following Nygren, Boman accepts Plato as the acme of Greek philosophy and explicitly recognizes it to be an essentially religious mode of thought. Bearing in mind Walter Otto's work on the Homeric gods, he even proceeds to suggest that he might as well have used Homeric religion for his Hebrew/Greek contrast instead of Platonism. For Boman, then, "hellenization" quite clearly means "Platonization," for he is oblivious to the distinctive mode of philosophic/scientific thought that emerged with the Milesians.

In his treatment of the influence of Greek ideas on Christianity, Hatch also has chiefly the influence of Platonic thought in mind. After noting that "Christian philosophy" arose out of a kind of philosophical Judaism that combined apology with speculation, he writes: "The speculative part of it arose from some of its elements having found an especial affinity with some of the new developments of Pythagoreanism and Platonism."[61]

Given that "hellenization" really means "Platonization," at least in many crucial instances, the rapid transformation of Christianity that overwhelms Hatch is not as surprising as it might at first appear to be. Despite the affinity between these two essentially religious modes of thought, however, it must not be assumed that there were no important differences between Platonism and Christianity, for that is obviously not the case. Platonic thought is not simply a replay, so to speak, of the mythopoeic patterns of thought of traditional Greek religion. Plato provided traditional religion with a rational facade and so, at least inadvertently, injected some elements of Milesian "rationalism" into it. The Platonization (hellenization) of early Christianity, therefore, meant not only the absorption of Platonic (Greek) speculation, but also

61. Ibid., p. 129. See also pp. 121–122.

of the tendency to speculate, as Hatch points out.[62] Whatever elements of Milesian thinking "stuck" to Plato in his recovery of the Greek religious tradition were absorbed by Christian thinkers. The constraints with which Plato hedged in reason (i.e., reason of the Milesian variety) were naturally also present in the early philosophical reflection on the Christian faith.

There is not sufficient recognition of this peculiar character of the hellenization of Christianity in the early centuries of its existence; nor sufficient reflection upon its implications. Benjamin Nelson, however, is an exception. In an essay – "Civilizational Complexes and Intercivilizational Encounters" – in which he attempts to discern a series of patterns in the structures of consciousness that have emerged in the development of civilizations, he appears to understand clearly both what has occurred and what are the cultural/civilizational implications. He perceives, on the basis of the degree of collectivity or individualization to be found within a society, three basic types of consciousness that have emerged with the development of civilization. His "Consciousness-Type 1" and "Consciousness-Type 3" correspond relatively closely to what I have been referring to as mythopoeic and philosophic/scientific structures of thought.[63] Of particular interest, however, is his "Consciousness-Type 2," for not only does it appear to combine elements of the other two, but it takes that Platonized Christianity discussed and examined by Hatch as exemplary of it. That modified Christianity, he argues, is a faith-structure that implies a kind of *logos*, but a *logos* in which participation (i.e., a mythic form of existence) is still accessible.[64] And this, so it seems to me, also describes Plato's thought.

The hybrid thinking which characterizes Platonic philosophy is therefore a mythic form of existence with a hint of *logos* to distinguish it from purer modes of mythic existence. It involves a mode of thought that makes use of reason and analysis but only within strict and severe limits; the kind of use of reason within a broader mythic framework to which Moscati refers in his discussion of the ancient Near East. This, at least, seems to be what Nelson has in mind as characteristic of his "Consciousness-Type 2," as he makes clear in his essay on the natures of eastern and western science and civilizations, where he writes: "His-

62. Ibid., p. 133.
63. Nelson, "Civilizational Complexes," pp. 96–99.
64. Ibid., p. 94.

tory affords many illustrations of the limited institutionalization of universalism or rationality (or dialectic) within restricted spheres. We must not be surprised, therefore, if we find institutions apparently devoted to science or logic in many traditionalist societies. Here we need a distinction between a universalism of limited applications which is the base for an intellectual elite or a restricted meritocracy, and a societal commitment to encourage the expansion of the boundaries of participation to increase the awareness of communication and to develop skills in communication among those who have so far not truly entered into dialogue because of self-inhibition or the restraints imposed by others. . . . "[65] Thus, even though Nelson distinguishes three phases of consciousness, the second (or faith-consciousness) appears not to be a true form; it is either a variant of "Consciousness-Type 1" or that consciousness on its way to becoming "Consciousness-Type 3." He writes: "Faith-structures of consciousness are already a premonition of a next phase in the development of consciousness, the move toward rationalization of the contents of faith; that is, the systematic analysis of the contents of and evidences for the faith, the appearance of a science called theology."[66] I shall return shortly to this matter for further analysis, since the move to theology, Nelson quite rightly sees, is a move to a different kind of hellenization from that spoken of hitherto; a submission to the influence of ancient Greece, that is, the Greece represented by the Milesians, in which Nelson also detects a radical move away from "the tribal society" – "from particularism to universalism in spheres of science and philosophy."[67] He refers to this as a "comprehensive breakthrough in the moralities of thought and in the logic of decision which open out the possibilities of creative advance in the direction of wider universalities of discourse and participation in the confirmation of improved *rationales*."[68]

Nelson, moreover, sees a similar kind of breakthrough occurring in the twelfth century and refers to it as an "axial shift" and as a recapturing of the Greek heritage. For him the religious and ethical universalism in Christian thought that began to emerge in this century and is particularly evident in the emergence of theology as an academic discipline, is of tremendous importance in creating those conditions

65. Nelson, "Sciences and Civilizations," p. 185.
66. Nelson, "Civilizational Complexes," p. 94.
67. Ibid., p. 98.
68. Ibid., p. 99.

necessary for establishing modern philosophic/scientific thought. The twelfth century, according to Nelson, sees the crystallization of a new structure of consciousness that he refers to as a "rationalizing-and-rationalized structure of consciousness" which transcends the "faith-structure of consciousness" and "sacro-magical structure of consciousness."[69] This century "is the time," he writes, "when monastic theology gives ground to scholastic theology, and the time when new images and horizons of conscience, self, person, society, the cosmos, action, justice, forms of rule, institutions of law and learning take on a cast that have ever since been distinctive and primary features of the Western European world."[70]

Nelson presses this interpretation of the significance of the revolutionary intellectual developments of the twelfth and thirteenth centuries even further in his "*Eros, Logos, Nomos, Polis*: Shifting Balances of the Structures of Existence," showing them to be "the seedbeds of the control structures of Western social and cultural organization."[71] Paradigmatic of the revolution in thought for Nelson, as for my discussion of the nature of theology in chapter one, is the battle between Abelard and Bernard over the theology question. For Nelson, the victor in that encounter was Abelard, and with him came the move from a "faith-structure of consciousness" to a "rationalized-structure of consciousness." Abelard is a major architect of the structure of the rational consciousness of modernity – the cause of the axial shift implicit in his need to know what he believed. Nelson summarizes that axial transformation as follows: "The early scholastic writers, including Anselm, said that they believed in order to know. *Credo ut intelligam; fides quaerens intellectum*: such were their telling expressions. Those who apply these expressions often enough, those whose faith seeks understanding, find themselves imperceptibly shifting on their axes; they discover themselves passing from *wanting to know in order to believe to wanting to know for the sake of knowing*. . . . "[72] The revolutionary character of the Milesian experiment in thought is clearly evident in the emergence of scholastic (academic) theology from the matrix of the monastic religious thinking of the day.

---

69. Nelson, "Sciences and Civilizations," p. 184.
70. Ibid., p. 184. It is important to take note here with Nelson that even though the mode of thought referred to emerged in the West it is, nevertheless, universal.
71. Nelson, "*Eros, Logos, Nomos, Polis*," p. 217.
72. Ibid., p. 219.

Such a view of the significance of the twelfth century and of the meaning and significance of the academic theology that emerges in the intellectual struggles of that period is not, however, widely shared. But that view is not only more coherent than its rivals, it also makes more sense of a whole range of questions both historical and philosophical. The remainder of this chapter will therefore be devoted to its defence.

AN AXIAL SHIFT IN CHRISTIAN THOUGHT

In chapter one I made some reference to G. R. Evans' account of the marriage of secular and Christian learning in her *Old Arts and New Theology: The Beginning of Theology as an Academic Discipline* and suggested that her account of the beginnings of that discipline revealed the emergence of a mode of thought ultimately hostile to the traditional (religious) Christian faith. Evans, however, despite recognizing an underlying conflict of purpose that produces substantial differences between traditional monastic theology (represented by Bernard of Clairvaux) and the new discipline (represented by Peter Abelard), seems to think they are, ultimately, reconcilable. I do not. The contrasts she draws out for the reader between the two sides of the debate, however, seem to belie her assessment. She points out, for example, that there is a strong element of devotion and mystical piety in the monastic study of the bible which is, if at all, far less in evidence in the use of the rational methods of interpretation applied to the scriptures by the "new school theologians."[73] What was assumed indispensable to the *lectio divina* of the monastic community was seen as a mere adjunct to the subject in the cathedral schools.

The use of the arts in bringing some orderliness and rational method of treatment of matters scriptural and dogmatic, Evans points out, also created a good deal of friction. Academic theology was concerned to create a subject matter that was teachable in the way that the subjects of the *trivium* and *quadrivium* were teachable, which it did by reducing it to a system of rules. That, moreover, allowed a rapid overall mastery of theology that stood in stark contrast with, and in opposition to, the tradition of a slow absorption of these matters in the monastic context. Consequently, as Evans noted, "[t]he study of the *artes* provided not

---

73. Evans, *Old Arts*, pp. 43–44. See also her *The Language and Logic of the Bible*

only a stimulus to orderliness but also a good deal of contradiction of purpose."[74]

That contradiction of purpose, she points out, is particularly obvious in the tension and conflict between Abelard and Bernard of Clairvaux. Bernard's objection is not so much with the way Abelard went about his theologizing as with specific errors into which he was supposedly led, in applying the techniques of the arts to scripture and dogma;[75] a rarefied distinction if not a specious one. For she also, paradoxically, maintains that Bernard objected to this method of doing theology as providing "a ready but specious facility in handling deep questions."[76] The following description by Evans is an admirable summary of the essence of the debate:

The old school of the study of the Bible had not required any extensive knowledge of the secular *artes* – nothing, in fact, beyond a little elementary grammar. But the new breed of academic theologians approached ancient mysteries with a new confidence, with the aid of techniques which were unfamiliar and even incomprehensible to traditional biblical scholarship. They assumed that the knowledge they had would serve as well in theology as it did in the liberal arts. Bernard accused Abelard of precisely this attempt to set himself up as a theologian when his expertise as a scholar lay in dialectic, and even the gentle Anselm, himself no enemy of dialectical method sensibly applied, accused the *dialectici haeretici* of approaching the study of the Bible without reverence and without respect for a proper procedure which was different from their own.[77]

It may be true, as Evans argues, that Bernard did not object to the use of the arts *if* kept to the role of "handmaid" to theology. But that kind of subordination of the arts to the purposes of *lectio divina* is precisely what is excluded by the nature of the arts as then rediscovered. Thus, it is no wonder that Evans must ultimately admit that a conflict between monastic and scholastic theology existed even where the arts – that is, reason and dialectic – were not abused,[78] and that Bernard is wholly opposed to Abelard because he sees a fundamental irreconcilability

74. Evans, *Old Arts*, p. 45.
75. Ibid., p. 44.
76. Ibid., p. 45.
77. Ibid., pp. 58–9.
78. Ibid., p. 59.

between the arts and theology.[79] The scriptures and commentaries on them by the Fathers, Bernard maintained, contain mysteries that are simply too profound for Abelard's type of treatment of them and can only be understood via the *lectio divina*.[80] It is not surprising, therefore, to find Evans, after an assessment of the respective intellectual qualities and abilities of Bernard and Abelard, exclaiming "that the two scholars are entirely at cross-purposes in their methods of approach."[81] Moreover, in a discussion of the same matter in her book on *The Mind of St. Bernard of Clairvaux* she writes: "These two methods of approach, those of Bernard and the *lectio divina*, and of some of the professional academics of the day, are so different as to run in opposite directions from entirely different starting points."[82] Contemplation was entirely divorced from abstract thought, and emotion was given little or no place at all in the new theological classroom. The theological enterprise had come to be subordinated to the laws of thought that applied to all other subjects in the curriculum. *Knowledge of God*, it seemed, had come to supplant all other traditional theological goals or, though Evans does not put the point so strongly, were reduced to epistemological ones. Furthermore, as Evans puts it, "[i]t was only those aspects of knowledge about God which lent themselves to the new technical procedures which become the subject-matter of academic theology."[83] Knowledge of God was now available to any educated person, regardless of their possession of spiritual gifts; a matter to which Bernard reacted sternly, according to Evans,[84] for it was perceived as leading the faithful astray. Thus Evans, though suggesting the essential continuity of the new theology with the old, the arts, and the new theology, and denying any claim that Bernard is but a bigoted opponent of Abelard, nevertheless insists that Bernard saw it as "no merely superficial threat to the security of orthodox faith in the minds of the faithful, but to strike at its very foundations with both subtlety and force."[85] Curiosity – making of theology a search for *knowledge* – is for Bernard both an abuse of reason and a threat to the Faith.

Jean Leclerq's earlier and masterful study of monastic culture in his

79. Ibid., p. 80.
80. Ibid., p. 22.
81. Ibid., p. 89.
82. Evans, *The Mind of St. Bernard*, p. 76.
83. Evans, *Old Arts and New Theology*, p. 105.
84. Evans, *The Mind of St. Bernard*, p. 129.
85. Ibid., p. 141; see also p. 166.

The Love of Learning and the Desire for God had already set the pattern
of interpretation that is found in Evans' study of the emergence of
theology as an academic discipline. For Leclerq, monastic and scholastic theology are complementary, with both groups pursuing, as he puts
it, "the intelligence of faith." Theology's task, according to Leclerq, is
to give form to the faith – a process or activity in which the truths of
the Christian revelation are "interpreted, developed and ordered into
a body of doctrine."[86] Thus, though there may be two theologies, they
"draw in common on Christian sources and both enlist the aid of
reason." "Scholastic theology," Leclerq continues, "has recourse more
frequently to the philosopher, monastic theology contents itself more
generally with the authority of the Scripture and the Fathers. But the
fundamental sources in both cases are the same. Theology is a method
for reflecting on the mysteries revealed in Christian origins."[87]

   Despite the emphasis on the unity of theology in this period, and of
the complementarity of its two modes and contexts, Leclerq is also
quite aware of the difference of method between them, referring, in
fact, to their different "modes of expression and processes of
thought."[88] He summarizes the difference as follows:

Littera sordescit, logica sola placet: the entire conflict [between monastic and
scholastic theology] is rooted in this antithesis. The new style results from the
predominance accorded certain disciplines: the accent is no longer placed on
grammar, the *littera*, but on logic. Just as they are no longer satisfied with the
auctoritas of Holy Scripture and the Fathers, and invoke that of the philosophers, so clarity is what is sought in everything. Hence the fundamental
difference between scholastic style and monastic style. The monks speak in
images and comparisons borrowed from the Bible and which possess both a
richness and an obscurity in keeping with the mystery to be expressed. . . .
The Scholastics are concerned with achieving clarity; consequently they readily
make use of abstract terms, and they never hesitate to form new words, the
profanas vacum novitates which St. Bernard, for his part, avoids.[89]

Leclerq concludes, moreover, that "[a]s the monks' language differs
from that of the schools, so also do their thought processes differ from

86. Leclerq, *The Love of Learning*, p. 190.
87. Ibid., p. 225.
88. Ibid., p. 198.
89. Ibid., pp. 199–200.

those of scholasticism."[90] He enters a disclaimer at this point, however, insisting that the thought processes are not *essentially* different,[91] even as he, in acknowledging a contrast between the two theologies in the introduction to his study, denies that they are in constant opposition and affirms that they are interrelated.[92] Indeed, what he had earlier claimed to be the essential difference between the two – the emphasis on logic instead of grammar, and the move away from the authority of the Scriptures and the Fathers – he attributes in his conclusion wholly to the different environments in which "the same religious reflection was exercised."[93] But it is a disclaimer he feels compelled to make several times over, urging the reader not to oppose the two milieus of the two theologies too sharply;[94] to recognize that highlighting the monastic method does not discredit the scholastic approach;[95] that the two are complementary aspects of one theological enterprise;[96] and, finally, to see that the difference between the two is not fundamental.[97] The repeated warnings constitute an attempt to compensate, so to speak, for the profoundest of differences between the monastics and the new, emerging, scholastic communities that breaks through here and there in Leclerq's account.

Finally, Leclerq, in bringing his study to a close, maintains simply that the scholastics acquired a taste for certain intellectual activities useful to them in their pastoral life, whereas spiritual preoccupations predominated in the cloisters. But the difference is seen, even in his analysis, to be much more serious than that. Leclerq himself seems somehow to be vaguely aware of it. He recognizes, for example, that for the monastics, wisdom is far more than mere knowledge and that they had a profound anxiety that sacred doctrine would, in the hands of the scholastics, decline into being no more than "a mere liberal discipline."[98] Like Evans after him, however, Leclerq tries to argue that this is but a distrust of the abuse of logic and dialectic, but the matter can not be disposed of that simply, for the question of what

90. Ibid., p. 201.
91. Ibid., p. 201.
92. Ibid., p. 13.
93. Ibid., p. 251.
94. Ibid., p. 212.
95. Ibid., p. 218.
96. Ibid., p. 224.
97. Ibid., p. 251.
98. Ibid., p. 203.

constitutes the essential character of the new reason/logic is precisely
what is at stake here. The scholastics, as Leclerq acknowledges, were
aiming at *knowledge* – at impersonal and universal claims. Such a theology, moreover, as he himself notes, searches secular learning for more
objective modes of expression of religious reality. "Its purpose," he
writes, "is to organize Christian erudition by means of removing any
subjective material so as to make it purely scientific."[99] But Bernard
and the monastics saw this as a reduction of theology "to nothing more
than a rational science like any other,"[100] and therefore as a destruction
of the Faith. An indication of the implicit adoption of such a conclusion
by Leclerq is obvious in his description of the monastic style in liberal
studies: "The monastic humanists are not like those of the Renaissance,
torn between two cultures. They are not partially pagan. They are
wholly Christian, and in that sense, are in possession of the *sancta
simplicitas*."[101] In that the scholastics did not possess that same *sancta
simplicitas* they were, it would appear, at least partially, pagan. And it
seems to me that the monastics were clear-sighted enough to see that
that was so. Moreover, even Leclerq holds that true reverence for
God's mysteries requires an additional value to be "superimposed on
the scientific method,"[102] if they are to be understood. As he puts
it: "Theological research [with the scholastics] was approaching the
dangerous point at which it might escape the *limits set by faith*. In trying
to submit God's mysteries to reason, one *could be tempted* to forget their
transcendency and yield to *a kind of naturalism*. In the effort *to explain*
the realities of religion would they not reduce these realities to something which reason could understand?"[103] Yet to superimpose any
limit upon that reason espoused by the scholastics was precisely what
the scholastics saw, and rightly so, as destructive of it; it would make
of it something essentially other than what it really is. To submit to
such superimposition would therefore be tantamount to continuing
with the "prolongation of the patristic age" embodied in Bernard and
the monastic tradition.[104] Consequently, in the removal of all trace of
subjectivity and the adoption of a purely scientific method, the scholas-

99. Ibid., p. 225.
100. Ibid., p. 215.
101. Ibid., p. 151.
102. Ibid., p. 212.
103. Ibid., p. 208.
104. Ibid., p. 114.

tics were not only tempted to yield to naturalism but did so yield – although the fruits of their action would take some time to appear.

That the mode of thought embodied in monastic theology differs radically from that espoused by the scholastics, is also indicated, although only implicitly so, in Leclerq's discussion of the nature and sources of sacred learning in the monastic tradition. For example, although the monastics applied grammar to Scripture and the Fathers they did so in a way entirely their own. They had, as Leclerq states it, a procedure of "active reading" which was closely tied to the fundamental observances of the monastic life. It involved a meditation on the Scriptures that allowed for their slow "absorption" into one's life and permitted a learning that is beyond reason. It made prayer and humility necessary conditions for any religious knowledge. Such "active reading" involved the whole person. According to Leclerq, it is not simply a visual memory of the written words that are available for intellectual manipulation, but rather their "active reading," resulting in "a muscular memory of the words pronounced and an aural memory of the words heard."[105] The intellectual activity of the monastic tradition therefore seems to involve something of the mind-set of an oral/aural community rather than that of the literate communities referred to in chapter two. It is not that such monastic communities are not literate, but rather that they relate orally/aurally to the *texts* around which their intellectual activity is focused. Though Plato's thought has been acknowledged in this essay to be philosophic, it has also been referred to as a hybrid of philosophic and mythopoeic modes of thought of which the latter is predominant. In a similar way, though one can recognize the literate character of the monastic community, it too is a hybrid of literate and oral/aural components that might best be distinguished from both oral and literate communities by referring to it as a "textual community." I shall not here, however, elaborate on the peculiarities of such "textual communities."[106]

Before leaving examination of Leclerq's analysis of monastic culture, one further illuminating aspect of it must be noted. It is significant that that culture had three principal literary sources; besides Holy Scripture and the Patristic tradition, Leclerq notes, monastic scholars also made use of Classical Literature.[107] And they reshaped the

105. Ibid., p. 78.
106. On this matter, however, see Stock, *The Implications of Literacy*.
107. Leclerq, *The Love of Learning*, p. 76.

received materials in the light of their understanding of grammar, even though their application of grammar, especially to the Scriptures, was subordinated to the observances of the monastic life. In fact, it was their subordination of grammar to "higher rules," so to speak, that the monastics determined should be taken as exemplar for scholastic theology's use of logic and dialectic.[108]

Although the monastic scholars stood true to the Faith, they nevertheless seem to bear some responsibility for what they perceived as the apostasy of the scholastics, for they themselves had accepted, even if only in part, elements of a mode of thought in opposition to the Faith – that is, in accepting the applicability of grammar to the Scriptures and in adding classical literature to the traditional Christian sources of their thought. One might reasonably suggest that, just as Plato's hybrid thinking that gave traditional Greek religion a reprieve also carried within itself the seeds of the Milesian intellectual revolution, so, too, the monastic adoption of a grammatical methodology and acceptance of classical literature – even though tamed – carried within itself similar seeds of an intellectual revolution. (In this instance we know much more clearly than in the case of the Milesians that there was no intention of intellectual revolution on the part of these medieval thinkers.) Durkheim's historical analysis of the development of education in France leaves one in no doubt about this. The Church, in taking over the educational task in a crumbling Roman society, "impregnated" itself with a Roman civilization that was at odds with its own nature –

---

108. See here Chenu's "The Masters of the Theological 'Science' ": "Peter [of Blois] was berated for presenting the word of God as in a School and not as in a Monastic chapter. To be sure, the monks had cultivated and made magnificent use of the seven secular arts, but only after purging them of their arrogant ways and, according to the current image, *reducing them to handmaids*" (p. 304, emphasis added). Chenu's position opposes that which I have set out here. The new humanism of the twelfth century, even with its 'autonomy of reason, man, and nature' does not disrupt the unity of the Faith but rather shows that the Faith "provided several different abodes" for the devotee (p. 308). Or, again, he insists that "[t]he development of diverse trends should not be allowed to obscure the strong connections among these various strains of the *intellectus fidei* (p. 307). These claims, however, are not backed by argument, but rather are merely asserted. Indeed, the "danger" of dialectic – the incompatability of scholastic and monastic theology – seems implied in Chenu's "argument" for the permanent significance of monastic theology: "Men would take notice of this when the masters themselves would one day slip by their self-satisfaction into a decadent state, content, as professors, to be theorists about God instead of active theologians . . . content to construct their splendid systems without tending to their own vital roots in the scriptural, patristic and monastic soil" (pp. 308–09).

introducing into itself that of which it would not be able to rid itself later. Durkheim sheds a peculiar insight on the matter when he writes: "if the Church really did play this role it was at the cost of a contradiction against which it fought for centuries without ever achieving a resolution. For the fact was that in the literary and artistic monuments of antiquity there lived and breathed the very same pagan spirit which the Church had set itself the task of destroying, to say nothing of the more general fact that art, literature and science cannot but inspire profane ideas in the minds of the faithful and distract them from the only thought to which they should be giving their entire attention: the thought of their salvation."[109]

For Durkheim, then, monastic culture ultimately had only itself to blame for the deterioration of theology it claimed to perceive in the scholastics, for the monastics themselves had already introduced into Christianity elements – though superficially complementary to the Faith – that contradicted the Faith. And, since the cathedrals and their clergy stood in much closer relationship to the everyday world than did the monasteries, they were more exposed to secular interests and so more likely to succumb to those elements. The educational tasks of the Church – her schools – Durkheim therefore concludes, "carried within themselves the germ of that great struggle between the sacred and the profane."[110]

In light of this it is not at all surprising to find that Durkheim considered the Faith to be very much at stake in the Abelard/Bernard controversy. It was not at stake in the sense that the scholastics, any more than the monastics, were deliberately casting doubt or aspersion on the truth of the Christian religion, but rather because the very need to examine the Faith implied doubt. The need to *understand* the Faith, even without question as to whether it might be false, was, Durkheim points out, a remarkable innovation that both stirred the doubts and released the germs of that mode of thought first introduced by the

---

109. Durkheim, *The Evolution of Educational Thought*, p. 22.

110. Ibid., p. 26. Durkheim here reinforces my suggestion above that, though the "Platonization" (i.e., the first process of "hellenization") of Christian thought did not radically undermine the Christian faith, it certainly prepared for later developments (i.e., the second "hellenization" in the influence of Aristotle), that did. Kohanski argues for a similar deleterious effect of what he calls the Greek mode of thought on Christian thinking, though I find it difficult to extract the central structure of his argument. See his *The Greek Mode of Thought*, p. 113 *et passim*. See also the comments of Feuer in his *The Scientific Intellectual*, pp. 89, 107–108.

Milesians. The very right to examine the Faith claimed by the scholastics, also implies a diminution of the Faith. I quote Durkheim once
more in bringing this comment on Leclerq to a conclusion: "the
moment one introduces reason, criticism and the spirit of reflectiveness
into a set of ideas which up to that time has appeared unchallengeable
it is the beginning of the end; the enemy has gained a foothold. If
reason is not given its fair share, then from the moment that it has
established a foothold somewhere it always ends up by casting down
the artificial barriers within which attempts have been made to contain
it. This was the achievement of scholasticism."[111]

THE PROBLEM WITH CHRISTIAN PHILOSOPHY

There has been much debate over the question of the possibility of a
Christian philosophy. And it is obvious from the discussions in chapters
three and four that where a form of Christian philosophy is argued
for, that philosophy must be quite different from the Milesian version
of philosophy, in that it rests on faith, revelation, and authority, which
preclude reason's autonomy. The philosophy required is an intellectual activity that is directed towards the good of creating a body of
knowledge which rationally explicates the Faith and which can, having
done that, serve, strange though it may be, as a grounding for faith.
Though experiencing a need for such reasoning, Christianity tamed
(curtailed) the power of reason as best it could by undermining any
confidence it might in attempting to explain faith and religion. Christian philosophy is therefore a kind of interpenetration of faith and
reason within a single system of thought – an indissoluble combination
(hybrid) of the two with the latter subordinate to the former.

111. Durkheim, *The Evolution of Educational Thought*, p. 75. Murray in his *Abelard and
St. Bernard*, holds a similar view of the controversy between these two, although, unlike
Durkheim, he does not see this dispute as indicative of the more fundamental conflict
between reason and faith. Murray sees the battle between the two to be a fundamental
difference of attitude (p. 7); "a matter of one temper of mind against another temper
of mind" (p. 71, see also p. 87), meaning by that a good deal more than a mere
psychological difference of temperament. He writes: "Bernard is antagonistic to Abelard
because he insists on making everything intelligible, because there is nothing that he
will not make a subject of dialectical discussion, because he has no reverence and looks
into the secret things of God . . . because to him faith is a matter of opinion and because
he has no use for authority . . . ." (p. 140). However, like Leclerq and Evans, he fails to
see the full implications of this "difference of mind" and insists that "their gifts were
complementary" (p. 162).

Such a combination, however, is, as I have attempted indirectly to show above, inherently unstable, since reason is what it is because of its inherent autonomy. It is unstable because it attempts to combine in one intellectual system elements that are logically exclusive of each other. It has also been argued that it is inherently unstable on religious grounds; the names of Tertullian and Kierkegaard are renowned in that respect. It seems to me that a religious argument of that kind needs to be seriously considered, for it is in a sense a reiteration of the argument I have here been constructing against theology; that is, of the notion of "rational religious thinking." However, rather than arguing the case for the radical distinction between *logos* and *mythos* (philosophy and religion; reason and faith; etc.) from the perspective of *logos*, assessment of the relation of the two is made from the basis of *mythos* or "mythic self-understanding"; from a mythopoeic perspective. I shall conclude this discussion, therefore, with a very brief review of a powerful form of that argument, as it is found in Lev Shestov's penetrating critique of Etienne Gilson's understanding of "Christian philosophy" to be found in the latter's Gifford lectures on *The Spirit of Medieval Philosophy*.[112]

For Shestov, the medieval philosophers, in attempting to bridge the gulf between the bible (i.e., the Faith) and Greek philosophy, unwittingly recapitulated the sin of Adam and Eve. "[T]he medieval philosophers who aspired to transform faith into knowledge," he exclaims, "were far from suspecting that they were committing once again the act of the first man."[113] They were being seduced by the promise of knowledge; hoping to transform the truths received without attendant proof from God into proven truths. Medieval thinkers, he argues, succumbed to the rationalism implicit in their classical training and therefore came to understand their task to be one of

112. I have decided not to enter into argument with either Tertullian or Kierkegaard for several reasons. Proper treatment of those two imposing figures would involve a lengthier discussion than can be afforded here, involving careful assessment of a voluminous secondary literature. Furthermore, their positions do not relate directly to more recent proposals regarding "Christian philosophy," as does that of Shestov and would necessitate further treatment of more contemporary authors. Moreover, Shestov's treatment recapitulates their stances succinctly and has the advantage that a treatment of his much less widely known view lends a freshness to what is really a very ancient debate. I have dealt elsewhere with Shestov, although not at much greater length, in "Being Faithful and Being Reasonable" and "Religion Transcending Science Transcending Religion. . . ."

113. Shestov, *Jerusalem and Athens*, p. 282.

grounding the *revealed* truth of God, which Gilson refers to as "created Truth," through rational argument. This, however, subverted the "created truths" for, as Shestov puts it, "the principles of the Hellenic philosophy and the technique of Hellenic thought held them in their power and bewitched their minds."[114] But such a grounding, he also insists, is not possible, for the God of the bible is a God who creates and destroys everything, even the eternal laws of the Greeks, and therefore is a God who has nothing in common with either the rational or the moral principles of ancient Greek wisdom. Espousal of Greek philosophy (and metaphysics) therefore means a rejection of the bible – a rejection by ignoring it or *subordinating it to rules outside itself*. He writes: "The principles for seeking truth that it had received from the Greeks demanded imperiously that it not accept any judgement without having first verified it according to the rules by which all truths are verified: the truths of revelation do not enjoy any special privilege in this respect."[115]

For medieval philosophy, then, the goal was clearly set out: it must at all costs defend the truths of faith by the same means that all other truths are defended by or else find itself in an unbearable intellectual situation. This is not really a bridge between the bible and Greek philosophy, but rather a transformation or transmutation of the bible in that it makes the Christian Faith – the created truths of God – another kind of human knowledge. For, according to Shestov, "the philosopher seeks and finds 'proofs,' convinced in advance that the proven truth has much more value than the truth that is not proven, indeed, that only the proven truth has any value at all. Faith is then only a 'substitute' for knowledge, an imperfect knowledge, a knowledge – in a way – on credit and which must sooner or later present the promised proofs if it wishes to justify the credit that has been accorded it."[116]

But faith, and especially the faith of the bible, he maintains, has

---

114. Ibid., p. 305. Shestov maintains that this was done first by Philo for Judaism: "Philo praised Holy Scripture to the skies but in praising it he delivered it into the hands of Greek philosophy" *Kierkegaard and the Existentialist Philosophy*, p. 42. Shestov argues in this volume that Hegel did the same to Christianity much later. This theme is repeatedly raised by Shestov as well in his *Potestas Clavium*, e.g., p. 99. The Catholics, he argues here, are obviously the most "hellenized" (pp. 48ff.), but so also, he insists, are the Protestants (pp. 101ff.).

115. Shestov, *Jerusalem and Athens*, pp. 299–300.

116. Ibid., p. 299.

nothing to do with knowledge (i.e., as conscious search). Not only is faith not knowledge – and here Shestov invokes the authority of the lives of Abraham and St. Paul[117] – but rather stands opposed to the search for knowledge as an affront to God.[118] The "knowledge" of the Greeks is "impersonal knowledge" – a recognition that all of life is subject to Necessity (of natural/physical law) and that it is therefore, "indifferent to everything, truth that we raise above the will of all living beings."[119] Biblical faith, quite to the contrary, extends the life of Possibility and thereby transcends the death that inevitably comes of/ from Necessity. This is a theme sounded tirelessly by Shestov in all his writing, the force of which can hardly be captured in so brief an account as this. To *trust* the possibilities that faith opens up, lacking all proofs as did Abraham, for example, is foolishness to philosophy and the search for knowledge – is contrary to reason. Indeed, in his book on Kierkegaard, he sees Abraham's transgression of the law of ethics as the very essence of the movement of faith, pointing out that the bible glorifies Abraham rather than seeing him as a disgrace.[120] Faith, therefore, is not "credit knowledge" but rather a mysterious and creative power, "an incomparable gift."[121] For the Greeks – that is, for rational thought in general – such obedience to God is "war"; it is to find oneself in that unfortunate condition described by Socrates in the *Phaedo* as being a *miselogos*. But to follow reason is to deny Possibility and to destroy the power of God. Consequently, it is impossible to "defend" the God of the bible through rational argument, for that would amount to a destruction of rational argumentation itself. "We must," Shestov therefore urges, "before everything else, tear out from our being all the postulates of our 'natural knowledge' and our 'natural

117. Ibid., p. 321. See also his *Kierkegaard*, p. 27.

118. The "affront;' here, according to Shestov, comes in the fact that knowledge provides the means (i.e., technology) whereby humankind becomes progressively more independent of "the gods." This seems to be the import of the Judeo-Christian scriptures, for example, in god's ambiguous relationship to the city, as has been pointed out by Ellul in his *The Meaning of the City*. A similar understanding of knowledge (as technology) that permits humankind an independence from "the gods," and so constitutes an affront to them, can be seen in the Prometheus myth. On this score see especially Eric Havelock's account of it in his *The Crucifixion of Intellectual Man*.

119. Shestov, *Jerusalem and Athens*, p. 307.

120. Shestov, *Kierkegaard*, pp. 76, 135.

121. Shestov, *Jerusalem and Athens*, p. 323. See also his *Kierkegaard*, p. 94 where faith is described as the loss of reason in order to find God.

morality.' "[122] Salvation must, as Plotinus had already recognized centuries earlier, be sought outside of reason.[123]

122. Shestov, *Jerusalem and Athens*, p. 288.

123. Many see such a recognition of the inadequacy of philosophy to salvation as
the point at which Christian revelation can be added to philosophy as its necessary
complement. Obviously it is precisely that kind of thesis against which Shestov sets
himself because he sees it as seductive and dangerous.

VI

The Nature of Religious Thought

THEOLOGY either is a science like the other sciences or it is not. And if it is, then it is expected of its practitioners that they will possess the same intellectual qualities and commitments that characterize scholars in the other sciences. The same "morality of knowledge" applies to them all. However, if theology is not a science, no such allegiance need characterize those who practise the art, so to speak, although it will then be an art misleadingly named.

The argument in the preceding chapters has shown, not that theology as a science is impossible, but only that as a science it is not, as should have been obvious, a religious activity. It has been shown, moreover, that a great deal of religious thought exists prior to the emergence, and in the absence, of such theology, just as thought about other aspects of the world and human existence in it antedates scientific thought about them. The evidence adduced shows that such religious and mythopoeic thought possesses a radically different character from the theological and scientific thought that emerges from within those structures. Not only do they differ, they are mutually exclusive. The intentions that characterize them give rise to structures that require contradictory assumptions and mutually exclusive intellectual operations. Religion's quest is not for knowledge, nor is mythopoeic thought more generally a self-consciously critical cognitive undertaking. Thought, religious and mythopoeic, is quite "un-self-consciously" directed towards structuring human existence in a world hospitable to its emergence but also a constant threat to its continued existence. Its goal is therefore meaning – an understanding of the world in which sense can be made of being there and, more particularly, of being there under the peculiar conditions in which the community that gives birth to such thought finds itself. It tells a story that constitutes a knowledge of existence both as it is and as it is desired to be.

Scientific thought, in contrast, is not concerned with meaning in that sense at all (though that is not to deny that the scientist as a member of society is not so concerned). Such thought, in fact, emerges as the result of the appearance of a new intention "to know for the sake of knowing." Thought now becomes differentiated in a peculiar way and gives rise to a set of beliefs that are wholly cognitive and therefore unconcerned with the social, moral, and political meaning of society. Not only are such beliefs not concerned with structuring a meaningful world picture that determines the obligations of its members, they require a "diplomatic immunity" from those beliefs that are part of a normative structure.

With the rise of philosophic/scientific thought, therefore, a differentiation in believing, so to speak, also emerges. Primitive thought certainly produces and operates with beliefs, but they function more as a social bond amongst the members of the group rather than merely to supply the group with knowledge. Scientific beliefs do not function in such a "catechismic" fashion but rather only "cognitively" (epistemically).[1] In drawing this distinction between kinds of belief, I do not mean to suggest that catechismic beliefs do not have a cognitive function as well, but only to point out that their cognitive function is blurred and of subordinate interest; the cognitive elements of such beliefs are not a conscious and critically reflective concern. Indeed, the value of catechismic beliefs does not seem to depend on their being true. Religious beliefs in a whole range of cultures, for example, that are generally known to be false are also known to be of value to those who believe them to be true. Their sociological function depends not upon their being true but rather upon their being believed to be so. On the everyday material-object level of existence beliefs in both primitive and modern cultures seem to operate in much the same fashion. Malinowski, Lévi-Strauss, and others have made much of the fact, claiming that, at least on the empirical level, primitive cultures are also scientific. But this does not need to be denied, even though one distinguishes mythopoeic from modern scientific cultures. That beliefs

---

1. The notion of "catechismic" beliefs is borrowed from Munz, *Our Knowledge of the Growth of Knowledge*, p. 74.

about certain aspects of the physical world constitute knowledge in both kinds of culture, is what one would expect in an evolutionary perspective on the development of the human animal. But it is not beliefs at this material-object level and the level of primitive inductive experience that operate catechismically. Moreover, the knowledge at the material-object level and the level of primitive inductive experience does not exist on its own; it is not a body of knowledge independent of the other beliefs held by such communities. It is, rather, an aspect of an undifferentiated thinking that embodies an apprehension of the world as a whole; it is therefore an amalgam of cognition and constructive (imaginative) interpretation – with the latter by far the predominating factor – that results in the production of a meaningful intellectual structure within which life can be sensibly lived.

Philosophic/scientific thinking introduces differentiation. With the introduction of the intention "to know for the sake of knowing" it gives birth to beliefs that operate purely cognitively; to beliefs that do not simultaneously constitute the framework of a social and moral order. Concepts now behave quite differently than when governed by normative considerations as they are in mythopoeic contexts. They operate in the new context merely as tools of explanation rather than as tools for engineering certain kinds of experience, for the generation of meaning, or for controlling behaviour. And, all of this amounts to the birth of a new mode of thought. Furthermore, the new mode of thought is incompatible with the mythopoeic mode from which it emerged. Similarly theology, when understood as a cognitive and scientific exercise, is incompatible with the religious thought from which it emerged. (By contrast those "theologies" that see themselves as religious activities were shown to have essentially the mythopoeic structure that characterize the religious thought antedating the emergence of academic theology.)

Given this account of the radical difference of intentions that characterizes these two modes of thought, it could be argued that they are incommensurable and therefore that they could be neither compatible nor incompatible with each other. Although this is true on the intentional level, it must nevertheless be remembered that religion and other mythopoeic structures of thought contain or, perhaps better, constitute the knowledge of those who live within those frameworks. And it is a knowledge which, with the exceptions already referred to, is often in conflict with modern scientific knowledge and wholly so when considered in methodological terms. There can be no objection to comparing the unintentional cognitive component of such structures of thought, therefore, by isolating such implicit cognitive claims from their richer mythopoeic (meaning) matrix, so long as one is aware that such abstraction in some sense distorts the overall world-view of which it is a part. But that "distortion" is only the product of an analytical exercise and is not taken to represent the actual mind of the primitive, cognitively speaking. To expect a comparison between the two modes of thought with respect to cognition without that procedure of abstraction would involve an even greater distortion in our understanding of the nature of modern scientific thought. Through that abstractive exercise, then, one can arrive at the cognitive understanding of the nature of the world in various primitive world pictures; that is, at what would constitute the only (scientific) knowledge of the world of which they were, within their limitations, capable. If religions are not quasi-scientific in this sense but rather symbolical structures of thought that reveal only "non-scientific" truths, then, of course, religions and science would be wholly incommensurable. Such a noncognitivist interpretation of traditional belief structures, however, is difficult to support. Religion and science are both cognitively significant enterprises, whether indirectly so, as in religion, or directly so, as in science. And they can therefore also be incompatible.

In bringing this study to a conclusion I intend to review two corroborating arguments for the thesis set out here, one from a "religious" and the other from a "scientific" perspective, and to show the convergence between the two. The first involves an elaboration of Shestov's critique of "Christian philosophy" with which the previous chapter concluded. On its own it might reasonably be rejected as but a caricature of religion. In the light of the discussion of some contemporary "theologies" in chapter 1 and the discussion of the character of Greek, Hebrew, and Christian religious thought in the chapters following, such a simple rejection, however, is not possible. The argument "from science" is that to be found in Gellner. He is well aware that even if science is consensual the theory of science is not. Nevertheless, he does provide a generally persuasive account of science as a distinct type of cognition that has, rather recently in the history of *homo sapiens*, radically transformed human existence; of science as a mode of thought that has ensured a sustained growth of knowledge unknown until its recent emergence.

THE ARGUMENT FROM RELIGION

Shestov, arguing from a Christian existentialist position, boldly proclaims the incompatibility of religious and scientific modes of thought. In his *Potestas Clavium* he describes the move from religious (mythopoeic) to rational thought as a "bewitchment" of the human mind, because it involves a loss of Freedom through an acknowledgement and acceptance of (scientific) Necessity. He maintains, therefore, that "the 'logic' of the religious man . . . is quite different from the logic of the scientist."[2] To know, according to Shestov, is to be subject to the laws of the universe which, in the final analysis, predict the death, and therefore the insignificance, of persons, and so ultimately of ourselves. To cry to the gods (God) for help against that fate is of course simply absurd in a world of science – it is against reason – and yet that is precisely what religion, and in particular the religion of the bible, is all about. Such help could only be possible in a world not fully accountable in terms of necessary and binding physical "laws." And, as Shestov puts it, "[t]he Ancient Greeks were already obviously afraid to leave the universe to the sole will of the gods for this would have been equivalent to admitting arbitrariness as the fundamental principle of life."[3] To accept the necessity of scientific laws, therefore, is the destruction of a peculiar religious mode of thought and existence; this is, as he states it in *Potestas Clavium*, a millennial struggle between Jewish and Greek genius.

In *Kierkegaard and the Existential Philosophy* Shestov presents the same argument but uses here the story of "the fall of man" as symbol of this change in the style of thinking. God had warned Adam and Eve not to eat of the tree of knowledge (of good and evil) lest they die, and Shestov sees that death symbolically in the Necessity which is the essence of our knowledge: "Knowledge enslaves human will, making it subordinate to eternal truths which by their very nature are hostile to everything that lives and so at all capable of demonstrating its independence and which cannot bear to have even God as their equal."[4] As in the former volume, so also here Shestov maintains that the knowledge sought by us in a bid for power to control our own lives

2. Shestov, *Potestas Clavium*, p. 3.
3. Ibid., p. 29.
4. Shestov, *Kierkegaard*, p. 264; see also p. 165.

independently of the gods (God), is an intellectual vision of inevitable destruction of all that has ever come to be. The principles of causality are, if they are to be of any value, inflexible, but as such they can only account for the universe as a relentless round of birthing and dying. Consequently he once again concludes that science – the philosophic vision – makes nonsense of the human cry for help that is the centre of religion for, "when love comes face to face with truth, it is love that must retreat."[5]

In both these volumes Shestov maintains that the belief in the eternal validity of the principles of knowledge means that even the gods (God) are (is) subject to them and that because of this, humankind is enchanted into believing that in the loss of the self in the impersonality of the law salvation is to be found.[6] What I have referred to above as the disenchantment of the universe by philosophy Shestov refers to as a "bewitchment" and an "enchantment" of the human mind by God.[7] Theology, the hellenized (i.e., Platonized) thinking of the fathers of the Church, is an element of that enchantment/bewitchment by God: "theology itself which, as I have already indicated, was even in the Middle Ages, at the time of its highest flowering and triumph, the servant of philosophy, (ancilla philosophiae), wanted absolutely to be above and beyond God. The entire potestas audendi of the philosophers and theologians expressed itself chiefly in the endeavour to subordinate God to man."[8]

Religious thought – that is, faith – is, however, quite opposed to this way of thinking; it is a religious philosophy, he argues in Athens and Jerusalem, that surmounts such knowledge, for faith is the deus ex machina that smashes Necessity.[9] "God's thunder," he writes, "is the answer to human wisdom, to our logic, to our truths. It breaks to bits not man, but the 'impossibilities' placed by human reason – which is at the same time human cowardice – between itself and the Creator."[10] Either one follows reason by which reality is revealed according to scientific laws or one follows the biblical revelation of God. The dichotomy of the two ways of thought is unmistakable in Shestov: "if reality is rational, if

5. Ibid., p. 235.
6. Shestov, Potestas Clavium, pp. 154, 158.
7. Shestov, Kierkegaard, p. 308.
8. Shestov, Potestas Clavium, p. 257.
9. Shestov, Athens and Jerusalem, pp. 70, 98. The contrast here to a recent book of similar title – Stephen R. L. Clark's From Athens to Jerusalem – is almost total.
10. Shestov, Kierkegaard, p. 185.

we can derive truth only from reality, then elementary consistency demands of us that we pass Biblical revelation through the filter of the truths obtained from reality. And conversely, if revelation receives the sanction of truth, it must bear the halter of reality. . . . [R]evealed Truth engulfs and destroys all the coercive truths obtained by man from the tree of knowledge of good and evil."[11] The task of thinking – that is, religious thinking – is not to attempt to justify the revelation of God, for that is but to submit to reason – rather, one is to dispel the power of reason through faith which is a renunciation of the tree of knowledge and a return to the tree of life.[12]

According to Shestov, then, religion (Christianity) transcends (and therefore abrogates) reason, because a proper understanding of biblical (religious) thinking precludes the philosophy of the Greeks and the modern philosophy and science to which it has given birth.

THE ARGUMENT FROM SCIENCE

As has already been intimated above, Gellner, a philosopher and social scientist of a radically different frame of mind to that of Shestov,

11. Ibid., p. 306.

12. Ibid; p. 295. Of relevance to this point is Shestov's critique of Plato in *Athens and Jerusalem*. Plato erred, he insists, in seeking proofs to convince others of "his" revelation: "But it is precisely because and inasmuch as Plato wished to make his revelation a truth that constrains, a truth obligatory for all . . . " (p. 109), that he leaves himself open to "the fall"; "Plato did not succeed in bringing back to men what he had found beyond the limits of all possible knowledge. When he tried to show men what he had seen, the thing changed itself mysteriously under his eyes into its contrary" (p. 116). I have, of course, argued that Plato also changed "reason" and made it the contrary of what it was with/for the Milesians and their successors. Shestov admits that the revelation of God has no justification but claims that the same holds for reason: each of them provide a framework for justifications to be provided (p. 164). For a somewhat similar interpetation, although not evaluation, see Wernham's *Two Russian Thinkers*, especially pp. 63ff.

Shestov's position here may appear extreme, but he hardly stands alone. Löweth, for example, in an essay on "Knowledge and Faith," writes: "If Jaspers complains that there is no real communication with theologians and that every conversation with them breaks off at particular points without any understanding having been reached, then the reply must be that one can hardly expect a believer, who believes he has found the truth in his Christian faith, to be open to the uncertainties of philosophy in unlimited communication" (pp. 209–10). James adopts a similar stance in his *Myth and Ritual*: "With the development of rational thought and empirical knowledge the control of nature by magico-religious techniques has been abandoned and has lost its former significance" (p. 307). For James this does not, ultimately, create difficulty for the religious believer, because myth can still reveal to the devotee something about that reality of which his/

has a surprisingly similar understanding of the nature and history of human thought. For Gellner, too, there are modes of thought, and modern-western-scientific thought is discontinuous with earlier forms of thinking; the modern mind, as he implies in the title of an essay ("The Savage and the Modern Mind"), is clearly distinguishable from the savage mind. The move from the latter to the former constitutes a copernican revolution, because it shifts the ultimate seat of legitimacy of belief(s) from "visions" to "epistemology." The difference between the two, as with Shestov, therefore, hinges essentially on the quest for knowledge – scientific knowledge – to which Gellner refers elsewhere as the "leap of science."[13] What the leap amounts to, he suggests, "is that the world is seen *within* knowledge, and not the other way around."[14] A new kind of "compulsion" with respect to thought has emerged – a "conceptual compulsion" that cannot simply be reduced to social control. "Somehow or other," Gellner writes, "men have become susceptible, in their thought, to constraints other than those of mere social consensus."[15] In managing to subject at least a part of the cognitive life to external criteria a profound change has occurred – a change which would have occurred even if this transcendence of cultural compulsion were simply an illusion. The leap of science therefore provides a structure for the adjudication of the validity of all claims to scientific knowledge, which knowledge claims alone provide an "entry permit" to our world.[16]

In summary: "The great transition between the old, as it were non-epistemic worlds, in which the principles of cognition are subject to the pervasive constitutive principles of a given vision, and thus have

---

her experience is a part (p. 307). See also the argument against reason by Grant in his *Technology and Justice*.

13. Gellner, *Legitimation of Belief*, p. 170.

14. Ibid., p. 29.

15. Gellner, *Relativism and The Social Sciences*, p. 182.

16. Gellner, *Spectacles and Predicaments*, p. 1. In *Relativism and the Social Sciences* he writes: "the really significant difference is between what may be called validation systems: the procedures and principles employed for extending and deciding the acceptance of new items. Primitive societies do not codify these, and they can only be extracted from their practice, which need not be consistent. Literacy, by creating a norm outside custom, or rather, providing the means for stabilizing such a norm, is supremely important. In the end, however, it is the establishment and institutional underpinning of the *one* outstanding cumulative cognitive style, atomistic and symmetrical which produces the really decisive parting of the ways. It is then that the practice of *some* men finally generates *one* world" (p. 95).

little to fear, and a world in which this is no longer possible, is a fundamental transition indeed."[17] In an essay on "An Ethic of Cognition" he describes the difference in the modes of thought as even more glaringly obvious: "The biggest, most conspicuous simple fact about the human world is the Big Divide between what may rightly be called the industrial-scientific society and the Rest," and the difference is one of morality and cognition, but not one of race.[18] The historical situation of that community of persons that gave birth to science may have been unique, but this basic constitution of persons in that community was not. Science, that is, is accessible to all persons.[19]

In his book *Legitimation of Belief*, from which I have already quoted, he sets out this difference of mind and cognition in terms of two epistemological models – there are, that is, two theories concerning cognitive legitimacy, namely "re-endorsement" theories and "selector" theories. The former are "mentalistic" in that their distinguishing feature is the acceptance of mental powers as self-explanatory. The latter are "empiricistic" and they deny that consciousness is an explanatory principle rather than something itself in need of explanation. In the essay on an ethic of cognition, also referred to above, he writes: "The essence of empiricism is that all, but *all*, theoretical structures are accountable; that none can claim such an awful majesty as to be exempt from the indignity of inquiry and judgement; and that substantive theoretical systems as to elude and evade this indignity are out. *Out*."[20] Selector theories and, consequently, knowledge, for Gellner, as for Shestov, thoroughly disenchant the universe and seem to stand opposed to life in the sense of a meaningful existence. This perhaps requires a little further elaboration.

Selector theories, based as they are upon empiricist principles of legitimating knowledge claims, are, according to Gellner, essentially

---

17. Gellner, *Legitimation of Belief*, p. 174.

18. Gellner, *Spectacles and Predicaments*, p. 175. See also Gellner's *Relativism and the Social Sciences*: "In my view, epistemological principles are basically normative or ethical; they are prescriptions for the conduct of cognitive life . . . . An epistemologist is a species of moralist" (p. 34).

19. On this matter see notes 4 and 36 to chapter 2. See also Gellner's *Relativism and the Social Sciences*: "Science needs one world. It does not need one kind of man within it. But one kind of man did make the single world. His historical situation may have been unique, his basic constitution was *not*. The single world seems to be gradually adopted by all of them, and appears manifestly accessible to all men" (p. 100).

20. Gellner, *Spectacles and Predicaments*, p. 182.

mechanistic: "The growth of knowledge presupposes its communicability, storage, public and independent testing, independence of anyone's status, identity, moral or ritual condition and so forth. This is what makes such knowledge powerful, and it is also what makes it 'cold' 'disenchanting,' 'mechanical.' "[21] Such a view, I have argued above, is already perceptible in the philosophy/science of the Milesians in their attempt to account for the existence and nature of the universe, not through divine agency as in mythic forms of thought, but rather in terms of substance and causal transformations of that substance.[22] It is that same scientific view that animates the radical disenchantment of the universe in the philosophy/science of Watson, Skinner, et al. Thus, subsumption of persons under impersonal explanatory principles is dehumanizing, because it seems to remove ultimate significance from purposive activity, and hence meaning from human existence. A meaningful universe is one amenable to human concerns and purposes; one that is sympathetically in tune with our human fears and anxieties. The prescientific world, therefore, is meaningful because it is still enchanted. Mechanism as in that of the selector theories of knowledge destroys all this, for "enchantment is tied to the identity and individuality of the participants, and all these are excluded by orderly regularity."[23]

The agreement here between Shestov's existentialist perspective and Gellner's empiricist stance is remarkable. The language of life becomes problematic in light of the language of knowledge.General visions of life in archaic cultures and religious systems or views of life in modern ones, provide meaning in a picture of the universe as enchanted, where agency, whether transcendent or purely immanent, is in no need of explanation. They stand opposed, however, to science and its causal understanding of that same universe. And the conflict is not merely contingent but necessary: "There is no escape: it is not the content, the *kind* of explanation which de-humanizes us; it is *any* genuine explanation, as such, that does it."[24] As he puts it elsewhere and in more detail: "the disenchantment is not a contingent consequence of this or

21. Gellner, *Legitimation of Belief*, p. 127. See also Gellner, *Relativism and the Social Sciences*, pp. 62, 90.

22. Gellner, *Relativism and the Social Sciences*: "the correct vision or cognitive style appears at a definite point in time, and thus introduces a radical discontinuity in history" (p. 92).

23. Gellner, *Legitimation of Belief*, p. 189.

24. Ibid., p. 106; see also p. 132.

that specific discovery, but inheres in the very method and procedure of rational inquiry, of impartial subsumption under geometrical generalisations, of treating all data as equal. Reductionism is not an aberration, but it is inherent in the very method of science. If we 'scientifically' establish the reality of some 'human' and seemingly reduction-resisting element in the world, we would *ipso facto* thereby also 'reduce' it, in some new way."[25]

Although Gellner's description of our present state of affairs as described here is almost identical to that of Shestov, his evaluation of that condition in which we find ourselves is radically different. There is a sense in which, like Shestov, he sees the quest for knowledge as a "fall": "All in all, mankind has already made its choice, or been propelled into it in truly Faustian manner, by a greed for wealth, power, and by mutual rivalry."[26] The style of knowing that is chosen commits one to a particular kind of society, he suggests here, and all we can do is to try, in looking back at the copernican revolution, to understand what happened.[27] But such pessimism is not characteristic of Gellner's overall view. On epistemological grounds it seems we are forced into opting out of the world – our moral world included – in order to evaluate it, because neither our "selves" nor our cultures are unproblematic or solutions to problems, but rather are problems themselves that require elucidation and explanation.[28] The only way to achieve that understanding is to break free from our ethnocentrism and anthropomorphism and to adopt a noncircular framework of reasoning, in which "human requirements are not allowed to limit or even create presuppositions, in the sphere of scientific theory."[29]

Gellner does admit that the empiricism he advises is, in the final analysis, a choice, an arbitrary decision. In this he seems to echo Shestov's *charge* of the arbitrariness of reason/rationality. However,

25. Gellner, *Spectacles and Predicaments*, pp. 7–8. See also Gellner, *Legitimation and Belief*, pp. 99, 107, 151.

26. Gellner, *Legitimation and Belief*, p. 127.

27. This seems to be the kind of counsel offered by Ellul, for example, in his analysis of modern technological society (e.g., in his *The Technological Society* and elsewhere), but the "sentiments" are radically different. Ellul "rejects" knowledge and affirms faith in a fashion not dissimilar to Shestov (see especially Ellul's *Living Faith*). A more popular response of the same kind can be found in Wheelis's persuasive *The End of the Modern Age*. See also Moreno's *Between Faith and Reason*. From a psychological point of view, similar problems are raised by Becker, especially in his *The Denial of Death*.

28. Gellner, *Spectacles and Predicaments*, p. 205.

29. Gellner, *Cause and Meaning in the Social Sciences*, p. 50.

Gellner's stance is much more positive than it might seem. There may indeed be no proof of the rightness of this empiricist knowledge, but it is nevertheless the best ideology available to us, for its prejudgments, as he puts it, are indirect and negative. And this ideology, he further maintains, is supported by the argument from illusion and the important difference between its success and that of other abortive styles of thinking.[30] In this, the scientific attitude transcends religion.[31]

Unlike other positions regarding the nature of modern science, Gellner's stance cannot be charged with naiveté. He is quite aware, for example, that the viewpoint of the "surrogate angel" – the opting out of the world in order to evaluate it – is not actually possible. He admits convergence, that is, between re-endorsement and selector theories. It is obvious that no particular explanation at any given moment is absolutely acceptable, and yet the principle of mechanism itself is not questionable. Consequently, when particular explanations are in question, it is *persons* who make judgments about them. He concludes, therefore, that "we shall never find ourselves without either ghosts or machines, or without the tension arising from their joint presence. Knowledge means explanation, and explanation means the specification of a structure that will apply generally and impersonally to all like cases. The mechanistic vision of the world is the shadow of this ideal, our ideal, of explanation. Yet at the same time, no particular explanation is ever permanent or sacred; it is judged by us ghosts."[32] But, as he points out elsewhere, this does not mean that one must, because of this, rule out altogether the possibility of a nonanthropomorphic account of persons. The fact that the "study of man" (persons) is "man" (persons) does not entail that the explanatory concepts must also be "human"; the account may quite reasonably be causal in form.[33]

---

30. For further elaboration see Gellner, *Spectacles and Predicaments*, pp. 177–78; and Gellner, *Cause and Meaning*, p. 69.

31. This does not, however, commit the scientist/rationalist to assuming that science will be, as is often stated, the "saviour" of mankind; it does not, that is, make of science a religion. It does mean, however, that there is no longer a passive dependence on some agency other than human persons (agencies), on whom the world, so to speak, rests. To survive, persons must act, and such action, it is claimed by the rationalist, is the more successful, the more accurate and complete the knowledge is on which it is based. Consequently, the "scientific response" to life is not one of offering some absolute solution to life's problems, but it does urge an active, informed reaction to the problems and, therefore, in the final analysis, it transcends religion.

32. Gellner, *Legitimation of Belief*, pp. 111–12.

33. Gellner, *Cause and Meaning*, p. 73.

It is obvious from this discussion of Gellner, that even though he provides an account of modes of thought that parallels that of Shestov, his evaluation of the situation that ensues is radically different. He affirms scientific as opposed to religious thought and its vestiges in humanism and humanistic thinking. "The requirements of life and thought," he writes, "are incompatible," and on this he is in agreement with Shestov.[34] As he points out in his most recent work, complex and cognitively progressive societies, where cognition has been separated out from other activities in the economy of the intellect, show a high level of logical coherence; but also seem to lack social coherence; "their moral and cognitive orders simply do not constitute any unity."[35] He suggests, in fact, that one might even postulate a rough law for the intellectual history of humankind, namely, that *"logical and social coherence are inversely related."*[36] A consequence of that development, as he argues later in this essay, is that a significant proportion of humankind will have to live with a permanent tension between cognition and culture: "Cognition: one strong possibility is that mankind, or a significant portion of it, will continue to live with a permanent tension between cognition and culture. Cognition will remain the domain of serious, socially neutral and disconnected exploration of nature, unpredictable in its outcomes, volatile and hence altogether unusable for the chartering or marker-provision of social life. It will remain inherently technical and discontinuous from the discourse of daily life. This means that the symbol-system used for daily social life is deprived of the kind of validation it had in the agro-literate age. The world we seriously *think* in and the world we *live* in will remain distinct."[37] The price of such a science is, Gellner recognizes, rather high, since persons in life's crises and tragedies have usually required the succour of ideas believed to be cognitively valid, whereas science has brought the age of cognitive validation of such generic salvations sought by us to an end.[38] But Gellner refuses either to give up thought and the quest for knowledge or to allow it, for nonepistemological reasons or ends, to be adulterated by the mentalism of "theological"/religious thought, or of contemporary idealistic social sciences which are but contemporary

34. Gellner, *Spectacles and Predicaments*, p. 6. See also Gellner, *Legitimation of Belief*, p. 101.
35. Gellner, *Plough, Sword and Book*, p. 61.
36. Ibid., p. 61.
37. Ibid., p. 213.
38. Ibid., p. 214.

attempts to reenchant the universe. Those modes of thought are simply mutually exclusive and incompatible.

CONCLUSION

I have attempted in this work to clarify the nature of the relation of theology to religion in the hope of coming to an understanding of the nature of religious thought – not the religious thought of any particular tradition, community, or individual, but of religious thinking in general. I have in the process of this argument established, amongst other things, (1) that the history of the development of the human mind reveals the existence of at least two mutually exclusive modes of thought in the process, one mythopoeic and the other scientific in character; (2) that the scientific or modern mind emerged from within a preexisting mythopoeic matrix and that, once free from it, it stands in tension with it – is, in fact, incompatible with it; (3) that religious thought (at least in the Greek, Hebrew, and Christian traditions) is essentially mythopoeic and theology essentially scientific; and finally (4) that theology therefore stands in the same relation to religion as philosophic/scientific thinking in general stands to the mythopoeic mind. In short, this study has corroborated Lévy-Bruhl's theory about the mythopoeic character of religious thought. And the discussion of the religious and scientific arguments of Shestov and Gellner in this chapter, with respect to the nature of religious and scientific beliefs, has added further support to that theory. Shestov and Gellner, from their very different "life-stances," are agreed that a coherent structure of thought cannot operate simultaneously, so to speak, in terms of the principles inherent in both religion ("theology") and science. Their "believings" are incompatible. They have shown that religion transcends science and science transcends religion – each providing a reductionistic account of the principles in terms of which the other operates. In each case, the transcendence of the principles of the other implies their abrogation. They are not only incommensurable systems of thought, therefore, but also incompatible systems of thought.[39]

---

39. Although I have not here analysed the work of F. Overbeck, it is a reference to his work by Kahl in *The Misery of Christianity* that pushed me into serious consideration of the plausibility of this claim. Unfortunately Overbeck's work still remains untranslated. A brief introduction to his thought can be found in Löweth's *From Hegel to Nietzsche*, pp. 377–88.

That claim may sound odd, given the fact that our modern western (i.e., European/Anglo-American) civilization is at once a religious and a scientific culture. However, the achievement of a *modus vivendi* between scientific and religious groups – and so between scientific and religious modes of thought – does not in itself justify the further claim that they must therefore be logically compatible structures of thought. It is quite obvious that what may be logically incompatible may nevertheless not be so psychologically or socially. Logically incompatible modes of thought often coexist in one and the same individual, and communities of persons can similarly harness together what on the logical level are mutually exclusive structures of thought. The assumption implicit in such acquiescence to a simultaneously scientific and religious culture that if, to put it crudely, both science and religion are necessary to that present form of cultural experience, then scientific and religious modes of thought must be logically compatible, is hardly self-evident. Moreover, the constant tension between the scientific and religious communities ever since the emergence of modern western science at the close of the Middle Ages speaks against it. Indeed, so often has that tension deteriorated into outright hostility that it is not at all inappropriate, as some have recently suggested, to describe the relationship between the two in warfare imagery. The perpetual conflict therefore, stands as a strong prima facie case against the assumption and suggests rather the possibility that a fundamental contradiction lies at the core of western civilization. And there is no reason to think that a rational explanation of "irrational" social reality is impossible. To assume that we must find a new interpretation of science or religion that entails their compatibility and complementarity is unnecessary, unless, of course, our central concern is really a "theological" one.

Bibliography of Works Cited

Abraham, Willie E. *The Mind of Africa*. London: Weidenfeld and Nicolson, 1962.

Adam, James. *The Religious Teachers of Greece*. Edinburgh: T. and T. Clarke, 1908.

Adkins, A. W. H. "Greek Religion." In *Historia Religionem: Handbook for the History of Religions*, edited by C. J. Bleeker, and G. Widengren, Vol. 1, *Religions of the Past*. Leiden: E. J. Brill, 1969.

Albright, William Foxwell. *From the Stone Age to Christianity: Monotheism and the Historical Process*. Baltimore: Johns Hopkins Press, 1940.

– "The Place of the Old Testament in the History of Thought." In his *History, Archaeology and Christian Humanism*. London: Adam and Charles Black, 1965.

– *Archaeology and the Religion of Israel*. Baltimore: Johns Hopkins Press, 1968.

Allier, Paul. *The Mind of the Savage*. Trans. Fred Rothwell. New York: Harcourt, Brace, 1927.

Altizer, Thomas J. J. *Oriental Mysticism and Biblical Eschatology*. Philadelphia: Westminster Press, 1961.

– Scharleman, R., et al. *De-construction and Theology*. New York: Crossroads Press, 1982.

Arendt, Hannah. *The Life of the Mind*, Vol. 1, *Thinking*. London: Secker and Warburg, 1971.

Arieti, Silvano. *Creativity: The Magic Synthesis*. New York: Basic Books, 1976.

Armstrong, Arthur H. *An Introduction to Ancient Philosophy*. Boston: Beacon Press, 1963 [1947].

Baker, Herschel. *The Image of Man*. New York: Harper and Row, 1961 [1947].

Banton, Michael, ed. *Anthropological Approaches to the Study of Religion*. London: Tavistock, 1966.

Barbu, Zevedei. *Problems of Historical Psychology*. New York: Grove Press, 1960.

Barden, Garrett. "The Symbolic Mentality." *Philosophical Studies* 15 (1966): 29–57.
– "Method and Meaning." In *Zande Themes*, ed. André Singer and Brian V. Street. Oxford: Blackwell, 1972.
Barnes, Barry. "The Comparison of Belief-Systems: Anomaly Versus Falsehood." In *Modes of Thought*, ed. Robin Horton and Ruth Finnegan. London: Faber and Faber, 1973.
Barnes, Jonathon. *The PreSocratic Philosophers*. London: Routledge and Kegan Paul, 1982.
Barr, James. *The Semantics of Biblical Language*. Oxford: Oxford University Press, 1961.
Beattie, John. *Other Cultures: Aims, Methods and Achievements in Social Anthropology*. London: Cohen and West, 1964.
Becker, Ernest. *The Denial of Death*. New York: Free Press, 1973.
Bellah, Robert N. *Beyond Belief: Essays in Religion in a Post-Traditional World*. New York: Harper and Row, 1970.
Ben-David, Joseph. *The Scientists' Role in Society: A Comparative Study*. Chicago: University of Chicago Press, 1984.
Berger, Peter L. "Some Second Thoughts on Substantive Versus Functional Definitions of Religion." *Journal for the Scientific Study of Religion* 13 (1974): 125-33.
Bergouinoux, F. M. "Notes on the Mentality of Primitive Man." In *Social Life of Early Man*, ed. Sherwood L. Washburn. Chicago: Aldine Publishing, 1961.
Bernal, Martin. *Black Athena: The Afroasiatic Roots of Classical Civilization*, Vol. 1, *The Fabrication of Ancient Greece 1785–1985*. London: Free Association Books, 1987.
Bernstein, Basil. "On the Classification and Framing of Educational Knowledge." In his *Class, Codes and Control*, Vol. 1. St Albans: Paladin, 1973.
Bidney, David. "The Concept of Meta-Anthropology and Its Significance for Contemporary Anthropological Science." In *Ideological Differences and World Order: Studies in the Philosophy and Science of the World's Cultures*, ed. F.S.C. Northrop. New Haven: Yale University Press, 1963.
Bleeker, C. J. and Widengren, G. eds. *Historia Religionem: Handbook for the History of Religions*. Vol. I. *Religions of the Past*. Leiden: E. J. Brill, 1969.
Boas, Franz. *The Mind of Primitive Man*. New York: Macmillan, 1919 [1911].
Boas, George. *Primitivism and Related Ideas in Antiquity*. Baltimore: Johns Hopkins Press, 1935.
– *Essays on Primitivism and Related Ideas in the Middle Ages*. Baltimore: Johns Hopkins Press, 1948.
Boman, Thorlief. *Hebrew Thought Compared With Greek*. Trans. Jules L. Moreau. London: SCM Press, 1960 [1954].

Bovet, Pierre. *Le dieu de platon d'après l'ordre chronologique des dialogues*. (thèse Genève), 1902.

Bremmer, Jan. ed. *Interpretation of Greek Mythology*. London: Croom Helm, 1987.

Bringuier, Jean-Claude. *Conversations with Jean Piaget*. Trans. Basia Miller Gulati. Chicago: University of Chicago Press, 1980.

Brown, S. C., ed. *Philosophical Disputes in the Social Sciences*. Sussex: Humanities Press, 1979.

– *Objectivity and Cultural Divergence*. Cambridge: Cambridge University Press, 1984.

Buber, Martin. *I and Thou*. Trans. Ronald Gregory Smith. New York: Scribners, 1958.

Budick, Sanford. *Poetry of Civilization: Mythopoeic Displacement in the Verse of Milton, Dryden, Pope and Johnston*. New Haven: Yale University Press, 1974.

Bultmann, Rudolph. "What Does It Mean to Speak of God." In his *Faith and Understanding*. London: SCM, 1969.

Burkert, Walter. *Structure and History in Greek Mythology and Ritual*. Los Angeles: University of California Press, 1979.

– *Greek Religion: Archaic and Classical*. Trans. J. Raffan. Oxford: Basil Blackwell, 1985.

– "Oriental and Greek Mythology: The Meeting of Parallels." In *Interpretation of Greek Mythology*. ed. Jan Bremmer. London: Croon Helm, 1987.

Burnet, John. *Greek Philosophy: Thales to Plato*. London: Macmillan, Ltd., 1961 [1914].

– *Early Greek Philosophy*. London: A. and C. Black, 1920.

Burrow, W. *Evolution and Society: A Study of Victorian Social Theory*. Cambridge: Cambridge University Press, 1970.

Caird, Edward. *The Evolution of Religion*. Vols. 1 and 2. Glasgow: James Maclehose and Sons, 1894.

– *The Evolution of Theology in the Greek Philosophers*. Vols. 1 and 2. Glasgow: James Maclehose and Sons, 1904.

Capra, F. *The Tao of Physics*. New York: Bantam Books, 1977.

Casagrande, J.B. "Comments on Richard A. Schweder's 'Likeness and Likelihood in Everyday Thought: Magical Thinking in Judgements about Personality.'" *Current Anthropology* 18 (1977): 648–49.

Cassirer, Ernst. *Language and Myth*. Trans. Susan K. Langer. New York: Dover, 1946 [1923].

– *The Philosophy of Symbolic Forms*. Trans. R. Mannheim. Vol. 2, *Mythical Thought*. New Haven: Yale University Press, 1955 [1925].

Cazeneuve, Jean. *Explorations in Interpretative Sociology: Lucien Lévy-Bruhl*. Trans. Peter Rivière. New York: Harper and Row, 1973.

Chenu, M.D. "The Masters of the Theological 'Science'." In his *Nature, Man and Society in the Twelfth Century: Essays in New Theological Perspectives in the Latin West.* Chicago: University of Chicago Press, 1968.

– *Nature, Man and Society in the Twelfth Century: Essays in New Theological Perspectives in the Latin West.* Chicago: University of Chicago Press, 1968.

Clark, Stephen R. L. *From Athens to Jerusalem: The Love of Wisdom and the Love of God.* Oxford: Clarendon Press, 1984.

Cornford, Francis M. *From Religion to Philosophy: A Study in the Origins of Western Speculation.* New York: Harper and Row, 1957 [1912].

– *Before and After Socrates.* Cambridge: Cambridge University Press, 1965 [1932].

– "Mystery Religions and Pre-Socratic Philosophy." In *The Cambridge Ancient History,* ed. J. B. Bury *et al.* Vol. 4. Cambridge: Cambridge University Press, 1939.

– *The Unwritten Philosophy and Other Essays.* Ed. W. K. C. Guthrie. Cambridge Universtiy Press, 1967 [1950]

– "Greek Natural Philosophy and Modern Science." In his *The Unwritten Philosophy and Other Essays.* Cambridge: Cambridge University Press, 1967 [1950].

– "Introduction" to his *Greek Religious Thought.* Boston: Beacon Press, 1950.

– "Silent Philosophy." In his *The Unwritten Philosophy and Other Essays.* Cambridge: Cambridge University Press, 1967 [1950].

– "Unwritten Philosophy." In his *The Unwritten Philosophy and Other Essays.* Cambridge: Cambridge University Press, 1967 [1950].

– *Principium Sapientiae: A Study of the Origins of Greek Philosophical Thought.* New York: Harper and Row, 1965 [1952].

Crick, Malcolm. *Explorations in Language and Meaning: Towards a Semantic Anthropology.* London: Malaby Press, 1976.

Daiches, David. *God and the Poets.* Oxford: Oxford University Press, 1984.

De Deugd, C. *From Religion to Criticism: Notes on the Growth of the Aesthetic Consciousness in Greece.* Utrecht: University of Utrecht Press, 1964.

De Santillana, G. *The Origins of Scientific Thought.* New York: New American Library, 1970 [1961].

Despland, Michel. *The Education of Desire: Plato and the Philosophy of Religion.* Toronto: University of Toronto Press, 1985.

Diamond, Stanley, ed. *Culture in History.* New York: Columbia University Press, 1960.

Dihle, Albrecht. *The Theory of the Will in Classical Antiquity.* Los Angeles: University of California Press, 1982.

Diop, Cheik Anta. *The African Origin of Civilization.* Trans. Mercer Cook. New York: Lawrence Hill, 1974.

Dodds, Eric R. *The Greeks and the Irrational.* Berkeley: University of California Press, 1968 [1951].

– *The Ancient Concept of Progress and Other Essays on Greek Literature and Belief.* Oxford: Clarendon Press, 1973.

– "The Religion of the Ordinary Man in Classical Athens." In his *The Ancient Concept of Progress.* Oxford: Clarendon Press, 1973.

– "The Sophistic Movement and the Failure of Greek Liberalism." In his *The Ancient Concept of Progress.* Oxford: Clarendon Press, 1973.

Douglas, Mary. *Purity and Danger: An Analysis of Concepts of Pollution and Taboo.* London: Routledge and Kegan Paul, 1966.

Dupré, Wilhelm. *Religion in Primitive Cultures: A Study in Ethnophilosophy.* The Hague: Mouton Publishers, 1975.

Durkheim, Emile. *The Evolution of Educational Thought.* Trans. Peter Collins. London: Routledge and Kegan Paul, 1977.

Easlea, Brian. *Witch-Hunting, Magic and the New Philosophy: An Introduction to Debates of the Scientific Revolution 1450–1750.* Brighton: Harvester Press, 1980.

Eastering, P.E. "Greek Poetry and Greek Religion." In *Greek Religion and Society*, ed. P.E. Easterling and J.V. Muir. Cambridge: Cambridge University Press, 1985

– and Muir, J. V. *Greek Religion and Society.* Cambridge: Cambridge University Press, 1985.

Eisenstadt, Samuel N. ed. *The Origins and Diversity of Axial Age Civilizations.* Albany: State University Press of New York, 1986.

Eliade, Mircea. *Cosmos and History: The Myth of the Eternal Return.* New York: Harper and Row, 1959 [1949].

– *Myth and Reality.* London: George Allen and Unwin, 1964.

– *Australian Religions.* Ithaca: Cornell University Press, 1973.

Elias, Julias A. *Plato's Defence of Poetry.* London: Macmillan, 1984.

Elkana, Yehuda. "The Emergence of Second-Order Thinking in Classical Greece." In *Axial Age Civilizations*, ed. S. N. Eisenstadt. 1986.

Ellul, Jacques. *The Technological Society.* Trans. John Wilkinson. New York: Vintage Books, 1964.

– *The Meaning of the City.* Trans. Dennis Pardee. Grand Rapids, Mi: Eerdmans, 1970.

– *Living Faith.* Trans. Peter Heinegg. New York: Harper and Row, 1980.

Emlyn-Jones, C. J. *The Ionians and Hellenism.* London: Routledge and Kegan Paul, 1980.

Emmet, D. and MacIntyre, A., eds. *Sociological Theory and Philosophical Analysis.* New York: Macmillan, 1970.

Evans, Donald. *The Logic of Self-Involvement.* London: SCM Press, 1963.

Evans, Gillian R. *Old Arts and New Theology: The Beginnings of Theology as an Academic Discipline.* Oxford: Clarendon Press, 1980.

– *The Mind of St. Bernard of Clairvaux.* Oxford: Clarendon Press, 1983.

– *The Language and Logic of the Bible: The Early Middle Ages*. Cambridge: Cambridge University Press, 1984.

Evans, T. M. S. "On the Social Anthropology of Religion." *The Journal of Religion* 62 (1982): 376–91.

Evans-Pritchard, Edward E. "Lévy-Bruhl's Theory of Primitive Mentality." *Journal of the Anthropological Society of Oxford* 1 (1970) [1934]: 39-60 (reprinted from *Bulletin of the Faculty of Arts*, Egyptian University, Cairo, 2 [1934]).

– *Theories of Primitive Religions*. Oxford: Oxford University Press, 1965.

– *A History of Anthropological Thought*. New York: Basic Books, 1981.

Fairservice, Walter A. *The Threshold of Civilization: An Experiment in Prehistory*. New York: Scribners, 1975.

Farnell, Lewis R. *The Evolution of Religion: An Anthropological Study*. London: Williams and Norgate, 1905.

– *Greece and Babylon: A Comparative Study of Mesopotamian, Anatolian and Hellenic Religion*. Edinburgh: T. and T. Clark, 1911.

Farrington, Benjamin. *Greek Science: Its Meaning For Us*. Vols. 1 and 2. Harmondsworth: Penguin Books, 1961.

Fay, Thomas A. *Heidegger: The Critique of Logic*. The Hague: Martinus Nijhoff, 1977.

Feuer, Lewis S. *The Scientific Intellectual: The Psychological and Sociological Origins of Modern Science*. New York: Basic Books, 1963.

Findlay, John N. *Plato: The Written and Unwritten Doctrines*. New York: Humanities Press, 1974.

Finkelbergh, Aryeh. "On the Unity of Orphic and Milesian Thought." *Harvard Theological Review* 79 (1986): 321–35.

Finley, J. H., Jr. *Four Stages of Greek Thought*. Stanford: Stanford University Press, 1966.

Finley, Moses I. *The Ancient Greeks*. Harmondsworth: Penguin Books, 1966.

– "Foreword." In *Greek Religion and Society*, ed. P.E. Easterling and J.V. Muir. Cambridge: Cambridge University Press, 1985.

Finnegan, Ruth. "Literary versus Non-Literary: The Great Divide?" In *Modes of Thought*, ed. R. Horton and R. Finnegan. London: Faberand Faber, 1973.

Foster, Michael B. "The Christian Doctrine of Creation and the Rise of Modern Natural Science." *Mind* n.s. 43 (1934): 446–69.

– "Christian Theology and Modern Science of Nature." *Mind*, n.s. 45 (1935): 1–27.

Fränkel, Hermann. *Early Greek Poetry and Philosophy*. Trans. Moses Hadas James Willis. London: Harcourt Brace Jovanovich, 1973 [1962].

Frankfort, Henri and Henriette A. eds. *Before Philosophy: The Intellectual Adventure of Ancient Man*. Harmondsworth: Penquin Books, 1944.

Furley, David. *The Greek Cosmologists*, Vol. 1, *The Formation of Atomic Theory and Its Earliest Critics*. Cambridge: Cambridge University Press, 1987.

Furley, David J. and Allen, E., eds. *Studies in Presocratic Philosophy*, Vol. I. London: Routledge and Kegan Paul, 1970.

Gadamer, Hans G. "The Religious Dimension of Heidegger." In *Transcendence and the Sacred*, ed. A. M. Oloon and L.S. Rouner. Notre Dame: University of Notre Dame Press, 1981.

Gagarin, Michael. *Aeschylean Drama*. Los Angeles: University of California Press, 1976.

Gay, Peter. *The Enlightenment: The Rise of Modern Paganism*. New York: Random House, 1968.

Geertz, Clifford. *The Interpretation of Cultures*. New York: Basic Books, 1973.

– "The Cerebral Savage: On the Work of Claude Lévi-Strauss." In his *The Interpretation of Cultures*. New York: Basic Books, 1973.

– "The Growth of Culture and the Evolution of Mind." In his *The Interpretation of Cultures*. New York: Basic Books, 1973.

– *Local Knowledge: Further Essays in Interpretative Anthropology*. New York: Basic Books, 1983.

– "The Way We Think Now: Toward an Ethnology of Modern Thought." In his *Local Knowledge: Further Essays in Interpretative Anthropology*. New York: Basic Books, 1983.

– "Notions of Primitive Thought: Dialogue with C. Geertz." In *States of Mind*, ed. J. Miller. London: Methuen, 1983.

Gellner, Ernest. "Concepts and Society." In *Sociological Theory and Philosophical Analysis*, ed. D. Emmet and A. MacIntyre. New York: Macmillan, 1970.

– *Cause and Meaning in the Social Sciences*. London: Routledge and Kegan Paul, 1973.

– "The Savage and the Modern Mind." In *Modes of Thought*, ed. R. Horton and R. Finnegan. London: Faber and Faber, 1973.

– *Legitimation of Belief*. Cambridge: Cambridge Univesity Press, 1974.

– *Spectacles and Predicaments: Essays in Social Theory*. Cambridge: Cambridge University Press, 1979.

– "An Ethic of Cognition." In his *Spectacles and Predicaments*. Cambridge: Cambridge University Press, 1979.

– "A Wittgensteinian Philosophy of (or Against) the Social Sciences." In his *Spectacles and Predicaments*. Cambridge: Cambridge University Press, 1979.

– "Tractatus Sociologico-Philosophicus." In *Objectivity and Cultural Divergence*, ed. S.C. Brown. Cambridge: Cambridge University Press, 1984.

– *Relativism and the Social Sciences*. Cambridge: Cambridge University Press, 1985.

– *Plough, Sword and Book: The Structure of Human History*. London: Collins Harvell, 1988.

Gellner, Ernest. ed. *Soviet and Western Anthropology*. London: Duckworth, 1980.

Gernet, Jacques and Vernant, Jean-Pierre. "Social History and the Evolution of Ideas in China and Greece from the Sixth to the Second Centuries BC" In *Myth and Society in Ancient Greece*, ed. J.-P. Vernant. Sussex: Harvester Press, 1980.

Gernet, Louis. "The Origins of Greek Philosophy." In his *The Anthropology of Ancient Greece*. Baltimore: Johns Hopkins University Press, 1981.

– *The Anthropology of Ancient Greece*. Trans. John Hamilton S. J. and Blais Nagy. Baltimore: Johns Hopkins University Press, 1981.

Gershenson, Daniel E. and Greenberg, Daniel A. *Anaxagoras and the Birth of Modern Physics*. New York: Blaisdell Publishing, 1964.

Gilson, Etienne. *The Spirit of Medieval Philosophy*. Trans. A. H. C. Downes. London: Sheed and Ward, 1936.

– *The Philosopher and Theology*. Trans. Cécile Gilson. New York: Random House, 1962.

Godlove, Terry. "In What Sense Are Religions Conceptual Frameworks?" *Journal of the American Academy of Religion* 52 (1984): 289–306.

– *Religion, Interpretation and Diversity of Belief: The Framework Model from Kant to Durkheim to Davidson*. Cambridge: Cambridge University Press, 1989.

Golden, Leon. *In Praise of Prometheus*. Chapel Hill: University of North Carolina Press, 1966.

Goldstein, Kurt. "Concerning the Concept of 'Primitivity'." In *Primitive Views of the World*, ed. Stanley Diamond. New York: Columbia University Press, 1960.

Goldstein, Thomas. *The Dawn of Science*. Boston: Houghton Mifflin, 1980.

Gomperz, Theodore. *The Greek Thinkers*, Vol 1. Trans. Laurie Magnus. London: John Murray, 1964 [1901].

Goody, Jack. *The Domestication of the Savage Mind*. Cambridge: Cambridge University Press, 1977.

– "Thought and Writing." In *Soviet and Western Anthropology*, ed. E. Gellner. London: Duckworth, 1980.

– *The Logic of Writing and the Organization of Society*. Cambridge: Cambridge University Press, 1986.

– *The Interface Between the Written and the Oral*. Cambridge: Cambridge University Press, 1987.

Goody, Jack, ed. *Literacy in Traditional Societies*. Cambridge: Cambridge University Press, 1968.

Goody, Jack, and Watt, Ian. "The Consequences of Literacy." In *Literacy in Traditional Societies*, ed. Jack Goody. Cambridge: Cambridge University Press, 1968.

– "Literate Culture: Some General Considerations." in Musgrave, P. W. ed. *Sociology, History and Education*. London: Methuen, 1970.

Gordon, Cyrus H. *The Common Background of Greek and Hebrew Civilizations*. New York: W. W. Norton, 1965.

Goudge, Thomas A. "Ryle's Last Thoughts on Thinking." *Dialogue* 21 (1982): 125–32.

Gould, John. "On Making Sense of Greek Religion." In *Greek Religion and Society*, ed. P. E. Easterling and J. V. Muir. Cambridge: Cambridge University Press, 1985.

Graham, A. C. "China, Europe and the Origins of Modern Science: Needham's *The Grand Titration*." In *Chinese Science: Explorations of an Ancient Tradition*, ed. Shigeru Hakayama and Nathan Sivin. Cambridge, MA: MIT Press, 1973.

Graham, William A. *Beyond the Written Word: Oral Aspects of Scripture in the History of Religion*. Cambridge: Cambridge University Press, 1987.

Grant, George. *Technology and Justice*. Toronto: Anansi, 1986.

Greenway, John L. *The Golden Horns: Mythic Imagination and the Nordic Past*. Athens: University of Georgia Press, 1977.

Gregory, Richard L. *Mind in Science: A History of Explanations in Psychology and Physics*. Cambridge: Cambridge University Press, 1981.

Grube, G. M. A. *Plato's Thought*. Indianapolis: Hackett Publishing, 1980.

Guthrie, William K. C. *The Greeks and Their Gods*. Boston: Beacon Press, 1950.

– *The Greek Philosophers*. London: Methuen, 1950.

– *The History of Greek Philosophy*, Vol. 1, *The Earlier Presocratics and the Pythagoreans*. Cambridge: Cambridge University Press, 1962.

– "Introduction." In *Principium Sapientiae: A Study of the Origins of Greek Philosophical Thought*, ed. F.M. Cornford. New York: Harper and Row, 1965.

Haas, William S. *The Destiny of the Mind, East and West*. New York: Macmillan, 1956.

Hack, Roy Kenneth. *God in Greek Philosophy to the Time of Socrates*. New York: Burt Franklin, 1970 [1931].

Hadas, Moses. *The Greek Ideal and Its Survival*. New York: Harper and Row, 1960.

– "The Supernatural." In his *The Greek Ideal and Its Survival*. New York: Harper and Row, 1966.

Hakayama, Shigeru and Sivin, Nathan, eds. *Chinese Science: Explorations of an Ancient Tradition*. Cambrdige, MA: MIT Press, 1973.

Hallen, B. and Sodipo, J. O. *Knowledge, Belief and Witchcraft: Analytic Experiments in African Philosophy*. London: Ethnographica, 1986.

Halliburton, David. *Poetic Thinking: An Approach to Heidegger*. Chicago: University of Chicago Press, 1981.

Hallpike, C. R. "Is There a Primitive Mind?" *Man: The Journal of the Royal Anthropological Institute* 11 (1976): 253–69

– *The Foundations of Primitive Thought*. Oxford: The Clarendon Press, 1979.

Hanson, Norwood R. *The Patterns of Discovery*. Cambridge: Cambridge University Press, 1958.

Hatch, Edwin. *The Influence of Greek Ideas and Usages Upon the Christian Church*. London: Williams and Norgate, 1890.

Havelock, Eric. *The Crucifixion of Intellectual Man*. Boston: Beacon Press, 1951.

– *The Liberal Temper in Greek Politics*. New Haven: Yale University Press, 1964.

– "Pre-literacy and the Pre-Socratics." *Institute of Classical Studies* 13 (1966): 44–67.

– *Preface to Plato*. New York: Grosset and Dunlap, 1967.

– *Prologue to Greek Literacy*. Cincinnati: University of Cincinnati Press, 1971.

– *The Greek Concept of Justice: From Its Shadow in Homer to Its Substance in Plato*. Cambridge, MA: Harvard University Press, 1978.

– "The Alphabetization of Homer." In *Communication Arts in the Ancient World*, ed. E. A. Havelock and J. P. Hershbell. New York: Hastings House, 1978.

– *The Literate Revolution in Greece and Its Cultural Consequences*. Princeton, NJ: Princeton University Press, 1982.

– "The Alphabetic Mind: A Gift of Greece to the Modern Mind." *Oral Tradition* 1 (1986): 134–50.

Havelock, Eric A. and Hershbell, J. P., eds. *Communication Arts in the Ancient World*. New York: Hastings House, 1978.

Heidegger, Martin. *Discourse on Thinking*. Trans. John M. Anderson and E. Hans Freund. New York: Harper and Row, 1959.

– *Introduction to Metaphysics*. Trans. Ralph Manheim. New York: Doubleday, 1961.

– *What is Called Thinking*. Trans. Fred D. Wieck and J. Glen Gray. New York: Harper and Row, 1968.

– *On Time and Being*. Trans. Joan Stambaugh. New York: Harper and Row, 1972.

– *Early Greek Thinking*. Trans. David F. Krell and Frank A. Capuzzi. New York: Harper and Row, 1975.

Heidel, William A. *The Heroic Age of Science: The Conception, Ideals and Methods of Science Among the Ancient Greeks*. New York: AMS Press, 1971 [1933].

Hollis, Martin. "The Limits of Irrationality." In *Rationality*, ed. Bryan Wilson. Oxford: Oxford University Press, 1970.

Hollis, Martin and Lukes, Steven, eds. *Rationality and Relativism*. Oxford: Basil Blackwell, 1982.

Horton, Robin "African Traditional Thought and Western Science I." *Africa* 37 (1967): 50–71.

– "African Traditional Thought and Western Science II. The 'Closed' and 'Open' Predicaments." *Africa* 37 (1967): 155–87.

– "Neo-Tylorianism: Sound Sense or Sinister Prejudice?" *Man*, n.s. 3 (1968): 625–33.

– "Lévy-Bruhl Durkheim and the Scientific Revolution." In *Modes of Thought*, ed. R. Horton and R. Finnegan. London: Faber and Faber, 1973.

– "Paradox and Explanation: A Reply to Mr. Skorupski." *Philosophy of the Social Sciences* 3/3 (part I), 3/4 (part II) (1973): 231–56; 289–314.

– "Lévy-Bruhl Among the Scientists." *Second Order* 2 (1973).

– "Material-Object Language and Theoretical Language: Toward a Strawsonian Sociology of Thought." In *Philosophical Disputes in the Social Sciences*, ed. S. C. Brown. Sussex: Humanities Press, 1979.

– "Tradition and Modernity Revisited" (with a reply to a response by M. Hollis). In *Rationality and Relativism*, ed. M. Hollis and S. Lukes. Oxford: Basil Blackwell, 1982.

– "Social Psychologies: African and Western" (a companion essay to republication of), Meyer Fortes. *Oedipus and Job in West African Religion*. Cambridge: Cambridge University Press, 1983.

Horton, R. and Finnegan, Ruth, eds. *Modes of Thought: Essays on Thinking in Western and Non-Western Societies*. London: Faber and Faber, 1973.

Horton, R. (with R. Finnegan). "Introduction." In *Modes of Thought*, ed. R. Horton and R. Finnegan. London: Faber and Faber, 1973.

Hountondji, Paulin J. *African Philosophy: Myth and Reality*. Trans. Henri Evans and Jonathan Rée. London: Hutchinson, 1983.

Huff, Toby E., ed. *On the Roads to Modernity: Conscience, Science and Civilizations*. New Jersey: Rowman and Littlefield, 1981.

Humphreys, S. C. *Anthropology and the Greeks*. London: Routledge and Kegan Paul, 1978.

– "Evolution and History: Approaches to the Study of Structural Differentiation." In his *Anthropology and the Greeks*. London: Routledge and Kegan Paul, 1978.

– " 'Transcendence' and Intellectual Roles: The Ancient Greek Case." In his *Anthropology and the Greeks*. London: Routledge and Kegan Paul, 1978.

– "Dynamics of the Greek Breakthrough: The Dialogue Between Philosophy and Religion." In *The Origin and Diversity of Axial Age Civilizations*. Albany: State University of New York, 1986.

Hussey, Edward. *The Presocratics*. New York: Charles Scribner's Sons, 1972.

Hutchins, Edwin. *Culture and Inference: A Trobriand Case Study*. Cambridge, MA: Harvard University Press, 1980.

Irele, Abiola. "Introduction." *For African Philosophy: Myth and Reality*. Paulin J. Hountondji. Trans. Henri Evans and Jonathan Ree. London: Hutchinson, 1983.

Izard, N. and Smith, P., eds. *Between Belief and Transgression: Structuralist Essays in Religion, History and Myth*. Chicago: University of Chicago Press, 1982.

Jacobson, Thorkild. *Toward the Image of Tammuz and Other Essays on Mesopotamian History and Culture*. Cambridge, MA: Harvard University Press, 1970.

– *The Treasures of Darkness: A History of Mesopotamian Religion*. New Haven: Yale University Press, 1976.

Jaeger, Werner. *Humanism and Theology*. Milwaukee: Marquette University Press, 1943.

– *Paideia: The Ideals of Greek Culture*. 3 vols. Trans. Gilbert Highet. Oxford: Oxford University Press, 1946.

– *The Theology of the Early Greek Philosophers*. Trans. Edward S. Robinson. Oxford: Oxford University Press, 1947.

– *Early Christianity and Greek Pardeia*. Oxford: Oxford University Press, 1961.

James, Edwin O. *Myth and Ritual in the Ancient Near East: An Archaeological and Documentary Study*. London: Thames and Hudson, 1958.

Jarvie, Ian C. *Rationality and Relativism: In Search of A Philosophy and History of Anthropology*. London: Routledge and Kegan Paul, 1984.

Jaynes, Julian. *The Origin of Consciousness in the Breakdown of the Bicameral Mind*. Boston: Houghton Mifflin, 1976.

Jenkins, Hilary. "Religion and Secularism: The Contemporary Significance of Newman's Thought." In *Modes of Thought*, ed. R. Horton and R. Finnegan. London: Faber and Faber, 1973.

Jones, Richard Foster. *Ancients and Moderns: A Study of the Rise of the Scientific Movement in Seventeenth-Century England*. New York: Dover Publications, 1961.

Kahl, J. *The Misery of Christianity or A Plea for a Humanity Without God*. Trans. N. D. Smith. Harmondsworth: Penguin Books, 1971.

Kahn, Charles M. *Anaximander and the Origins of Greek Cosmology*. New York: Columbia University Press, 1960.

– *The Art and Thought of Heraclitus*. Cambridge: Cambridge University Press, 1979.

Katz, Fred E., ed. *Contemporary Sociological Theory*. New York: Random House, 1971.

Keita, Lancinay. "The African Philosophical Tradition." In *African Philosophy: An Introduction*, ed. Richard A. Wright. Washington: University Press of America, 1984.

Kelber, Werner. *The Oral and the Written Gospel: The Hermeneutics of Speaking and Writing in the Synoptic Tradition; Mark, Paul, and Q*. Philadelphia: Fortress Press, 1983.

Kirk, Geoffrey S. "Popper on Science and the Presocratics." *Mind*, n.s. 69 (1960): 318–39.

– "Sense and Common-sense in the Development of Greek Philosophy." *Journal of Hellenic Studies* 81 (1961): 105–17.

– *Myth: Its Meaning and Function in Ancient Greece and Other Cultures*. Cambridge: Cambridge University Press, 1970.

– *The Nature of Greek Myths*. Harmondsworth: Penguin Books, 1974.

Kluckhohn, Clyde. "The Philosophy of the Navaho Indians." In *Ideological Differences and World Order: Studies in the Philosophy and Science of the World's Cultures*, ed. F. S. C. Northrop. New Haven: Yale University Press, 1963.

Knight, George A. F. *A Biblical Approach to the Doctrine of the Trinity*. Edinburgh: Oliver and Boyd, 1953.

Koestler, Arthur. "Is Man's Brain an Evolutionary Mistake?" *Horizon* 10 (1968): 34–43.

Kohanski, Alexander S. *The Greek Mode of Thought in Western Philosophy*. London: Associated University Press, 1984.

Kramer, Samuel N. Review of H. and H. A. Frankfurt, *et al.* "The Intellectual Adventure of Ancient Man: An Essay on Speculative Thought in the Ancient Near East, The University of Chicago Press, Chicago, 1946, VI, 401 pp." *Journal of Cuneiform Studies* 2 (1948): 39–70.

– *The Sumerians: Their History, Culture and Character*. Chicago: University of Chicago Press, 1963.

Kroner, Richard. *The Primacy of Faith*. London: Macmillan, 1943.

– *Culture and Faith*. Chicago: University of Chicago Press, 1951.

– *Speculation and Revelation in the History of Philosophy*. Vol. 1, *Speculation in Pre-Christian Philosophy*. Vol. 2, *Speculation and Revelation in the Age of Christian Philosophy*. Vol. 3, *Speculation and Revelation in Modern Philosophy*. Philadelphia: Westminster Press, 1959, 1959, 1961.

– *Between Faith and Thought: Reflections and Suggestions*. Oxford: Oxford University Press, 1966.

Kuhn, Thomas. *The Structure of Scientific Revolutions*. Chicago: University of Chicago Press, 1962.

Lancey, David F. "Comments on Richard Shweder's 'Likeness and Likelihood in Everyday Thought: Magical Thinking in Judgements about Personality'." *Current Anthropology* 18 (1977); 652.

Langer, Susan K. "Introduction." In E. Cassirer. *Language and Myth*. New York: Dover, 1946

– "On Cassirer's Theory of Language and Myth." In *The Philosophy of Ernst Cassirer*, ed. P. A. Schilpp. La Salle: Open Court, 1973.

Leclerq, Jean. *The Love of Learning and the Desire for God: A Study of Monastic Culture*. Trans. Catherine Misrahi. New York: New American Library, 1962.

Le Pan, Don. *The Cognitive Revolution in Western Culture*. Vol. I, *The Birth of Expectation*. London: Macmillan, 1989.

Leibrecht, Walter, ed. *Religion and Culture: Essays in Honour of Paul Tillich*. New York: Harper and Brothers, 1959.

Lévi-Strauss, Claude. *The Savage Mind*. Chicago: Chicago University Press, 1968.

– *Myth and Meaning*. Toronto: University of Toronto Press, 1978.

Levy, Gertrude Rachel. *The Gate of Horn: A Study of the Religious Conceptions of the Stone Age and Their Influence Upon European Thought.* London: Faber and Faber, 1953.

Lévy-Bruhl, Lucien. *How Natives Think.* Trans. Lilian A. Clare. New York: Washington Square Press, 1966 [1910].

– *Primitive Mentality.* Trans. Lilian A. Clare. Boston: Beacon Press, 1966 [1922].

– *The Soul of the Primitive.* Trans. Lilian A. Clare. London: George Allen and Unwin, 1965 [1927].

– *Primitive Mythology: The Mythic World of the Australian and Papuan Natives.* Trans. Brian Elliott. St. Lucia: University of Queensland Press, 1983 [1935].

– *Primitives and the Supernatural.* Trans. Lilian A. Clare. New York: E. P. Dutton, 1935.

– *L'Experience mystique et les Symboles chez les primitifs.* Paris: Alian, 1938.

– *The Notebooks on Primitive Mentality.* Trans. Peter Rivière. Oxford: Basil Blackwell, 1975 [1938].

– "A Letter to E. E. Evans-Pritchard." *British Journal of Sociology* 3 (1952): 117–23.

Little, Alan M. G. *Myth and Society in Attic Drama.* New York: Columbia University Press, 1942.

Littleton, C. Scott. "Introduction: Lucien Lévy-Bruhl and the Concept of Cognitive Relativity." In C. Lévy-Bruhl, *How Natives Think.* Princeton, NJ: Princeton University Press, 1985.

Lloyd, Geoffrey E. R. *Polarity and Analogy: Two Types of Argumentation in Early Greek Thought.* Cambridge: Cambridge University Press, 1966.

– "Popper Versus Kirk: A Controversy in the Interpretation of Greek Science." *British Journal for the Philosophy of Science* 18 (1967): 21–38.

– *Early Greek Science: Thales to Aristotle.* London: Chatto and Windus, 1970.

– *Magic, Reason and Experience: Studies in the Origins and Development of Greek Science.* Cambridge: Cambridge University Press, 1979.

– *Science, Folklore and Ideology: Studies in the Life Sciences of Ancient Greece.* Cambridge: Cambridge University Press, 1983.

– *Science and Morality in Greco-Roman Antiquity.* Inaugural Lecture. Cambridge: Cambridge University Press, 1985.

– *The Revolutions of Wisdom: Studies in the Claims and Practices of Ancient Greek Science.* Berkeley: University of California Press, 1987.

Lloyd, G. E. R. ed. *Hippocratic Writings.* Trans. J. Chadwick and W. N. Mann (I. M. Louie and E. T. Withington). Harmondsworth: Penguin Books, 1983.

Louth, Andrew. *Discerning the Mystery: An Essay on the Nature of Theology.* Oxford: Clarendon Press, 1983.

Löweth, Karl. "Knowledge and Faith: From the Pre-Socratics to Heidegger."

In *Religion and Culture: Essays in Honor of Paul Tillich*, ed. Walter Leibrecht. New York: Harper and Brothers, 1959.

Lovejoy, A. (and others), eds. *A Documentary History of Primitivism*. Baltimore: Johns Hopkins Press, 1935.

– *From Hegel to Nietzsche: The Revolution in Nineteenth Century Thought*. Trans. David E. Green. New York: Holt, Rinehart and Winston, 1964.

Luckmann, Thomas. *The Invisible Religion*. New York: Macmillan, 1969.

Lukes, Steven. "Some Problems About Rationality." In *Rationality*, ed. Bryan Wilson. Oxford: Basil Blackwell, 1970.

– "On the Social Determination of Truth." In *Modes of Thought*, ed. R. Horton and R. Finnegan. London: Faber and Faber, 1973.

Luria, Aleksandr R. *Cognitive Development: Its Cultural and Social Foundations*. Trans. Martin Lopez-Morillas and Lynn Solotaroff. Cambridge, MA: Harvard University Press, 1976.

Lyons, William. *Gilbert Ryle: An Introduction to His Philosophy*. Sussex: The Harvester Press, 1980.

Machinist, Peter. "On Self-Consciousness in Mesopotamia." In *The Origins and Diversity of Axial Age Civilizations*, ed. S. N. Eisenstadt. Albany: State University Press of New York, 1986.

Maclean, Paul D. *A Triune Concept of Brain and Behaviour*. Toronto: University of Toronto Press, 1973.

Macquarrie, John. *Martin Heidegger*. London: Lutterworth Press, 1968.

Marshak, Alexander. *The Roots of Civilization: The Cognitive Beginnings of Man's First Art, Symbol and Notation*. London: Weidenfeld and Nicolson, 1972.

McDonald, Duncan Black. *The Hebrew Philosophical Genius: A Vindication*. New York: Russell and Russell, 1965.

McFague, Sallie. *Speaking in Parables: A Study in Metaphor and Theology*. Philadelphia: Fortress Press, 1975.

– *Metaphorical Theology: Models of God in Religious Language*. Philadelphia: Fortress Press, 1982.

McGinty, Paul. *Interpretation and Dionysus: Method in the Study of a God*. The Hague: Mouton, 1978.

Meek, Theophile J. "Review of Frankfort." *Journal of Near Eastern Studies* 7 (1948): 123–24.

Meier, Christian. "The Emergence of Autonomous Intelligence Among the Greeks." In *the Origins and Diversity of Axial Age Civilizations*, ed. S. N. Eisenstadt. Albany State University Press of New York, 1986.

Meijer, P. A. "Philosophers, Intellectuals and Religion in Hellas." In *Faith, Hope and Worship: Aspects of Religious Mentality in the Ancient World*, ed. H. S. Versnel. Leiden: E. J. Brill, 1981.

Miller, Jonathan. "Notions of Primitive Thought: Dialogue with C. Geertz." In *States of Mind*, ed. J. Miller. London: Methuen, 1983.

Miller, Jonathan, ed. *States of Mind*. London: Methuen, 1983.

Moreno, Francisco J. *Between Faith and Reason*. New York: Harper and Row, 1977.

Moscati, Sabatino. *The Face of the Ancient Orient*. New York: Doubleday, 1968.

Muir, J. V. "Religion and the New Education: The Challenge of the Sophists." In *Greek Religion and Society*, ed. P. E. Easterling and J. V. Muir. Cambridge: Cambridge University Press, 1985.

Muller, Herbert J. *The Loom of History*. New York: Oxford University Press, 1966 [1958].

Munz, Peter. *Our Knowledge of the Growth of Knowledge: Popper or Wittgenstein?* London: Routledge and Kegan Paul, 1985.

Murray, Albert Victor. *Abelard and St. Bernard: A Study in Twelfth Century 'Modernism'*. Manchester: Manchester University Press, 1967.

Murray, Gilbert. *Five Stages of Greek Religion*. New York: Doubleday, 1955 [1912].

Musgrave, P. W., ed. *Sociology, History and Education*. London: Methuen, 1970.

Needham, Joseph. *Within the Four Seas: The Dialogue of East and West*. Toronto: University of Toronto Press, 1969.

– *The Grand Titration: Science and Society, East and West*. Toronto: University of Toronto Press, 1969.

– *The Shorter Science and Civilization in China: I*. Cambridge: Cambridge University Press, 1980.

Needham, Rodney, *Belief, Language and Experience*. Oxford: Basil Blackwell, 1972.

Nelson, Benjamin. *On the Roads to Modernity: Conscience, Science and Civilizations. Selected Writings by Benjamin Nelson*. Ed. Toby E. Huff. New Jersey: Rowman and Littlefield, 1981.

– "Civilizational Complexes and Inter-Civilizational Encounters." In his *On the Roads to Modernity*. New Jersey: Rowman and Littlefield, 1981.

– "Eros, Logos, Nomos, Polis: Shifting Balances of the Structures of Existence." In his *On the Roads to Modernity*. New Jersey: Rowman and Littlefield, 1981.

– "Sciences and Civilizations, 'East' and 'West': Joseph Needham and Max Weber." In his *On the Roads to Modernity*. New Jersey: Rowman and Littlefield, 1981.

Neville, Robert C. *Reconstruction of Thinking*. New York: State University of New York Press, 1981.

Nilsson, Martin P. *A History of Greek Religion*. Trans. F. J. Fielden. New York: W. W. Norton, 1964 [1925].

Northrop, F. S. C., ed. *Ideological Differences and World Order: Studies in the Philosophy and Science of the World's Cultures*. New Haven: Yale University Press, 1963.

Nygren, Anders. *Eros and Agape*. Trans. Philip S. Watson. Chicago: University of Chicago Press, 1982.

Okpewho, Isidore. *Myth in Africa: A Study of Its Aesthetic and Cultural Relevance*. Cambridge: Cambridge University Press, 1983.

O'Keefe, Daniel L. *Stolen Lightening: The Social Theory of Magic*. New York: Vintage Books, 1982.

Olela, Henry. "The African Foundations of Greek Philosophy." In *African Philosophy: An Introduction*, ed. Richard A. Wright. Washington: University Press of America, 1984.

Olson, A. M. and Rouner, L. S., eds. *Transcendence and the Sacred*. Notre Dame: University of Notre Dame Press, 1981.

Olson, Richard. *Science Deified and Science Defied: The Historical Significance of Science in Western Culture. From the Bronze Age to the Beginnings of the Modern Era ca. 3500 BC to ca AD 1640*. Los Angeles: University of California Press, 1982.

Ong, Walter J. *The Presence of the Word: Some Prolegomena for Cultural and Religious History*. New York: Simon and Shuster, 1970.

– *Interfaces of the Word: Studies in the Evolution of Consciousness and Culture*. Ithaca: Cornell University Press, 1977.

– *Orality and Literacy: The Technologizing of the Word*. London: Methuen, 1982.

Onians, Richard B. *The Origins of European Thought*. Cambridge: Cambridge University Press, 1951

Oppenheim, A. Leo. "The Interpretation of Dreams in the Ancient Near East." *Transactions of the American Philosophical Society* n.s. 46 (1956): 179–354.

– *Ancient Mesopotamia: Portrait of a Dead Civilization*. Chicago: University of Chicago Press, 1977 [1964].

– "Position of the Intellectual in Mesopotamian Society." *Daedalus* 104 (1975): 37–46.

Otto, Walter F. *The Homeric Gods*. Trans. Moses Hadas. New York: Pantheon, 1954.

Overbeck, Franz C. *Christentum und Kultur. Gedanken und Anmerkungen zur modernen Theologie*. Ed. C. A. Bernoulli. Darmstadt: Wissenschaftliche Buchgesellschaft, 1963.

– *Über die Christlichkeit unserer heutigen Theologie*. 2nd edition. Leipzig: Wissenschaftliche Buchgesellschaft, 1963 [1903].

– *Selbstbekenntnisse*. Frankfurt: Peter Lang, 1966 [1909].

Piaget, Jean. *Biology and Knowledge: An Essay on the Relations Between Organic Regulations and Cognitive Processes*. Trans. Beatrix Walsh. Chicago: University of Chicago Press, 1971.

Pietsch, Paul. *Shuffle Brain: The Quest for the Holographic Mind*. Boston: Houghton Mifflin, 1981.

Polanyi, Michael. *Personal Knowledge: Towards a Post-Critical Philosophy*. New York: Harper and Row, 1958.

Popper, Karl R. "Back to the Presocratics." In his *Conjectures and Refutations*. New York: Harper and Row, 1963.

– "Historical Conjectures and Heraclitus on Change." In his *Conjecture and Refutations*. New York: Harper and Row, 1963.

– *Conjectures and Refutations*. New York: Harper and Row, 1963.

– *The Open Society and Its Enemies*. Vol. 1, *The Spell of Plato*, Vol. 2, *The High Tide of Prophecy: Hegel, Marx and the Aftermath*. New York: Harper and Row, 1967.

Pribram, Karl. *Languages of the Brain*. Englewood Cliffs, NJ: Prentice Hall, 1971.

Price, Henry H. *Thinking and Experience*. London: Hutchinson University Press, 1969.

Radding, Charles M. *A World Made by Men: Cognition and Society, 400–1200*. Chapel Hill: University of North Carolina Press, 1985.

Radin, Paul. *Primitive Man as Philosopher*. New York: Dover, 1957.

– *The World of Primitive Man*. New York: E. P. Dutton, 1979.

– "Psychological Types, the Man of Action and the Thinker." In his *The World of Primitive Man*. New York: E. P. Dutton, 1979.

Redfield, R. "Thinker and Intellectual in Primitive Society." In *Culture in History*, ed. Stanley Diamond. New York: Columbia University Press, 1960.

Reiss, Timothy J. *The Discourse of Modernism*. Ithaca: Cornell University Press, 1982.

Reumann, John, ed. *Understanding the Sacred Text: Essays in Honor of Morton S. Enslin on the Hebrew Bible and Christian Beginnings*. Valley Forge: Judson Press, 1972.

Ricoeur, Paul. *Symbolism of Evil*. Trans. Emerson Buchanan. Boston: Beacon Press, 1969.

– *Freud and Philosophy: An Essay on Interpretation*. Trans. Denis Savage. New Haven: Yale University Press, 1970.

Rieser, Max. *An Analysis of Poetic Thinking*. Trans. Herbert M. Schueller. Detroit: Wayne State University Press, 1969.

Robb, Kevin. *Language and Thought in Early Greek Philosophy*. Vol. I. La Salle, IL: Monist Library of Philosophy, 1983.

Robin, Leon. *Greek Thought and the Origin of the Scientific Spirit*. Trans. M. R. Dobie. New York: Alfred A. Knopf, 1928.

Rogerson, John W. *Myth in Old Testament Interpretation*. Berlin: Walter de Gruyter, 1974.

– *Anthropology and the Old Testament*. Oxford: Basil Blackwell, 1978.

Runciman, W. G. *Sociology In Its Place and Other Essays*. Cambridge: Cambridge University Press, 1970.

– "The Sociological Explanation of 'Religious' Beliefs." In his *Sociology In Its Place and Other Essays*. Cambridge: Cambridge University Press, 1970.

Sagan, Carl. *The Dragons of Eden: Speculations on the Evolution of Human Intelligence*. New York: Random House, 1977.

Sambursky, Samuel. *The Physical World of the Greeks*. London: Routledge and Kegan Paul, 1960.

Sandmel, Samuel. "The Ancient Mind and Ours." In *Understanding the Sacred Text: Essays in Honor of Morton S. Enslin on the Hebrew Bible and Christian Beginnings*, ed. John Reumann. Valley Forge: Judson Press, 1972.

Schilpp, P. A. *The Philosophy of Ernst Cassirer*. La Salle: Open Court, 1973.

Schlagel, Richard H. *From Myth to the Modern Mind: A Study of the Origins and Growth of Scientific Thought*. Vol. 1, *Animism to Archimedes*. Bern: Peter Lang, 1985.

Schneidau, Herbert N. *Sacred Discontent: The Bible and Western Tradition*. Los Angeles: University of California Press, 1976.

Seidel, George Joseph. *Martin Heidegger and the Presocratics: An Introduction to His Thought*. Lincoln: University of Nebraska Press, 1964.

Sewell, Elizabeth. *The Orphic Voice: Poetry and Natural History*. New York: Harper and Row, 1971.

Shestov, Lev. *Potestas Clavium*. Trans. Bernard Martin. New York: Henry Regnery, 1970 [1926].

– *Kierkegaard and the Existentialist Philosophy*. Trans. Elinor Hewitt. Athens, OH: Ohio University Press, 1969 [1936].

– *Athens and Jerusalem*. Trans. Bernard Martin. New York: Simon and Shuster, 1966 [1938].

Shiel, J. *Greek Thought and the Rise of Christianity*. London: Longmans, Green, 1968.

Shils, Edward. "Some Observations on the Place of Intellectuals in Max Weber's Sociology, with Special Reference to Hinduism." In *The Origins and Diversity of Axial Age Civilization*, ed. S. N. Eisenstadt. 1986.

Shweder, Richard A. "Likeness and Likelihood in Everyday Thought: Magical Thinking in Judgements About Personality." *Current Anthropology* 18 (1977): 637–58.

Sieber, Tobin. *The Mirror of Medusa*. Los Angeles: University of California Press, 1983.

Singer, André and Street, Brian V. eds. *Zande Themes*. Oxford: Basil Blackwell, 1972.

Skorupski, John. "Science and Traditional Religious Thought." *Philosophy of the Social Sciences* 3/2 (parts I & II), 3/3 (parts III & IV) (1973): 97–115; 204–330.

– *Symbol and Theory: A Philosophical Study of Theories of Religion in Social Anthropology*. Cambridge: Cambridge University Press, 1976.

Slater, Peter. *The Dynamics of Religion*. New York: Harper and Row, 1978.

Slochower, H. *Mythopoesis: Mythic Patterns in the Literary Classics*. Detroit: Wayne State University Press, 1970.

Smart, Ninian. *The Phenomenon of Religion.* London: Macmillan, 1973.

– *The Science of Religion and the Sociology of Knowledge.* Princeton, NJ: Princeton University Press, 1973.

Smith, Huston. "Western Philosophy as a Great Religion." In *Transcendence and the Sacred*, ed. A. M. Olson and L. S. Rouner. Notre Dame: University of Notre Dame Press, 1981.

Smith, Jonathan Z. "I Am a Parrot (Red)." In his *Map is Not Territory: Studies in the History of Religions.* Leiden: E. J. Brill, 1978.

– "Map is Not Territory." In his *Map is Not Territory: Stuides in the History of Religions.* Leiden: E. J. Brill, 1978.

Smith, W. C. *Belief and History.* Charlottesville: Virginia University Press, 1978.

– "*Philosophia*, as One of the Religious Traditions of Humankind." In *Différences, valeurs, hiérarchie: textes offerts à Louis Dumont*, ed. Jean-Claude Godey. Paris. Éditions de l'École des Hautes Études en Sociales, 1984.

Snaith, Norman H. *The Distinctive Ideas of the Old Testament.* London: Epworth Press, 1944.

Snell, Bruno. *The Discovery of the Mind.* Trans. T. G. Rosenmeyer. New York: Harper and Row, 1960 [1953].

Solmsen, Friederich, *Plato's Theology.* Ithaca: Cornell University Press, 1942.

– *Intellectual Experiments of the Greek Enlightenment.* New Jersey: Princeton University Press, 1975.

Sperber, Daniel. "Apparently Irrational Beliefs." In *Rationality and Relativism*, ed. M. Hollis and S. Lukes. Oxford: Basil Blackwell, 1982.

– "Is Symbolic Thought Prerational?" In *Between Belief and Transgression: Structuralist Essays in Religion, History and Myth*, ed. N. Izard and P. Smith. Chicago: University of Chicago Press, 1982.

Spiro, M. "Religion: Problems of Definition and Explanation." In *Anthropological Approaches to Religion*, ed. M. Banton. London: Tavistock, 1966.

Stark, R. and Bainbridge, W. S. *A Theory of Religion.* Bern: Peter Lang, 1987.

Stock, Brian. *The Implications of Literacy: Written Language and Models of Interpretation in the Eleventh and Twelfth Centuries.* Princeton, NJ: Princeton University Press, 1983.

Stocking, George W. *Victorian Anthropologists.* New York: The Free Press, 1987.

Stokes, Michael C. *One and Many in Presocratic Philosophy.* Cambridge, Ma: Harvard University Press, 1971.

Stone, M. E. "Eschatology, Remythologization and Cosmic *Aporia*." In *Origins and Diversity of Axial Age Civilizations*, ed. S. N. Eisenstadt. Albany: State University Press of New York, 1986.

Strawson, P. F. *Individuals, An Essay in Descriptive Metaphysics.* London: Methuen, 1959.

– *The Bounds of Sense: An Essay on Kant's Critique of Pure Reason*. London: Methuen, 1966.

Street, Brian. V. *Literacy in Theory and Practice*. Cambridge: Cambridge University Press, 1984.

Strenski, Ivan. "Ernst Cassirer's *Mythical Thought* in Weimar Culture." *History of European Ideas* 5 (1984): 363–83.

Tambiah, Stanley J. "Form and Meaning of Magical Acts: A Point of View." *Modes of Thought*, ed. R. Horton and R. Finnegan. London: Faber and Faber, 1973.

– "The Reflexive and Institutional Achievements of Early Buddhism." In *Origins and Diversity of Axial Age Civilizations*, ed. S. N. Eisenstadt. Albany: State University Press of New York, 1986.

Taylor, Marc C. *Deconstructing Theology*. New York: Crossroads Press, 1982.

Temple, William. *Nature, Man and God*. London: Macmillan, 1935.

Thomson, George. *Aeschylus and Athens*. London: Lawrence and Wishart, 1943.

– *Studies in Greek Society*. Vol. 2, *The First Philosophers*. London: Lawrence and Wishart, 1955.

Torrance, Thomas F. *Theological Science*. Oxford: Oxford University Press, 1969.

Toulmin, Stephen and Goodfield, June. *The Fabric of the Heavens*. Harmondsworth: Penguin Books, 1963.

Tresmontant, Claude. *A Study of Hebrew Thought*. Trans. Michael F. Gibson. New York: Desclee, 1963.

– *The Origins of Christian Thought*. Trans. Dom Mark Pontifex. New York: Hawthorn Books, 1963.

– *Christian Metaphysics.*, Trans. Gerard Slevin. Dublin: Gill and Son, 1965.

Turner, David. "Review of Lévy-Bruhl's *Primitive Mythology*." *The Canadian Review of Sociology and Anthropology* 22 (1985) 119–20.

– *Life Before Genesis: A Conclusion*. Bern: Peter Lang, 1985.

Uffenheimer, Benjamin. "Myth and Reality in Ancient Israel." In *Origins and Diversity of Axial Age Civilizations*, ed. S. N. Eisenstadt. Albany: State University Press of New York, 1986.

Vernant, Jean-Pierre. *Myth and Thought Among the Greeks*. London: Routledge and Kegan Paul, 1983 [1965].

– "The Formation of Positivist Thought in Archaic Greece." In his *Myth And Thought Among the Greeks*. London: Routledge and Kegan Paul, 1983 [1965].

– *Myth and Society in Ancient Greece*. Trans. Janet Lloyd. Sussex: Harvester Press, 1980.

– "The Reason of Myth." In his *Myth and Society in Ancient Greece*. Sussex: Harvester Press, 1980.

– *The Origins of Greek Thought*. Ithaca: Cornell University Press, 1982.

Vernant, Jean-Pierre and Detienne, Marcel. *Cunning Intelligence in Greek Culture and Society*. Trans. Janet Lloyd. Sussex: Harvester Press, 1978.

Versnel, H. S. *Faith, Hope and Worship: Aspects of Religious Mentality in the Ancient World*. Leiden: E. J. Brill, 1981.

Veyne, Paul. *Did the Greeks Believe in Their Myths? An Essay on the Constitutive Imagination*. Trans. Paula Wissing. Chicago: University of Chicago Press, 1988.

Vlastos, G. "Review of *Principium Sapientiae*," In *Stuides in Presocratic Philosophy*, ed. D. J. Furley and R. E. Allen. Vol. 1. London: Routledge and Kegan Paul, 1970.

– "Theology and Philosophy in Early Greek Thought." In *Studies in Presocratic Philosophy*, ed. D. J. Furley and R. E. Allen. Vol. I. London: Routledge and Kegan Paul, 1970.

Voegelin, Eric. *Order and History*. Vol. 1, *Israel and Revolution*. Vol. 2, *The World of the Polis*. Vol. 3, *Plato and Aristotle*. Vol. 4, *The Ecumenic Age*. Louisiana State University Press, 1956, 1957, 1957, 1974.

Vygotsky, L. S. *Mind in Society: The Development of Higher Psychological Processes*. Trans. A. R. Luria, M. Lopez-Morillas, M. Cole, and J. Wertsch. Cambridge, MA: Harvard University Press, 1978.

Wallace, Edwin R. *Freud and Anthropology: A History and Appraisal*. New York: International University Press, 1983.

Washburn, Sherwood L., ed. *Social Life of Early Man*. Chicago: Aldine Publishing, 1961.

Waterhouse, Roger, *Heidegger Critique*. Sussex: Harvester Press, 1981.

Watson, John. *The Interpretation of Religious Experience*. Glasgow: James Maclehose and Sons, 1912.

Weil, Simone. *Intimations of Christianity Among the Ancient Greeks*. London: Ark Paperbacks, 1987 [1957].

Werblowsky, R. J. Z. "In *Nostro Tempore*: On Mircea Eliade." *Religion* 19 (1989): 129–36.

Wernham, J. C. S. *Two Russian Thinkers: An Essay on Berdyaev and Shestov*. Toronto: University of Toronto Press, 1968.

Wheelis, Alan. *The End of the Modern Age*. New York: Harper and Row, 1971.

Wiebe, Donald. " 'Comprehensively Critical Rationalism' and Commitment." *Philosophical Studies* 21 (1973): 186–201.

– "Review Article on R. Needham's *Belief, Language and Experience*." *Philosophical Studies* 22 (1974): 239–49.

– "Science, Religion and Rationality: Problems of Method in Science and Religion." Ph.D Dissertation: University of Lancaster, 1974.

– "Science and Religion: Is Compatibility Possible?" *Christian Scholars Review* 30 (1978): 169–76.

– "The Role of Belief in the Study of Religion." *Numen* 26 (1979): 234–49.

– *Religion and Truth: Towards an Alternative Paradigm for the Study of Religion.* The Hague: Mouton, 1981.

– "Theory in the Study of Religion." *Religion* 13 (1983): 283–309.

– "Being Faithful and Being Reasonable as Mutually Exclusive. A Comment on Shein's and Grean's Interpretation of Shestov." *Ultimate Reality and Meaning* 7 (1984): 166–69.

– "The Centripetal Theology of *The Great Code.*" *Toronto Journal of Theology* 1 (1985): 122–27.

– "Religion Transcending Science Transcending Religion . . . " *The Dalhousie Review* 65 (1985): 196–202.

– "Is Science Really an Implicit Religion?" *Studies in Religion* 18 (1989): 171–83.

Wilbur, Ken ed. *The Holographic Paradigm and Other Paradoxes.* Boulder: Shambhala, 1982.

Wilder, Amos Niven. *Theopoetic: Theology and the Religious Imagination.* Philadelphia: Fortress Press, 1976.

Williams, John R. *Martin Heidegger's Philosophy of Religion.* Waterloo: Wilfred Laurier University Press, 1977.

Wilson, Bryan. *Rationality.* Oxford: Basil Blackwell, 1970.

Wind, Edgar. *Pagan Mysteries in the Renaissance: An Exploration of Philosophical and Mystical Sources of Iconography in Renaissance Art.* New York: W. W. Norton, 1958.

Wiredu, Kwasi. *Philosophy and an African Culture.* Cambridge: Cambridge University Press, 1980.

Wolfram, Sybil. "Basic Differences of Thought." In *Modes of Thought*, ed. R. Horton and R. Finnegan. London: Faber and Faber, 1973.

Wright, Richard A. *African Philosophy: An Introduction.* Washington: University Press of America, 1984.

Zaehner, Robert C. *Our Savage God.* London: Collins, 1974.

Zeller, Eduard. *Outlines of the History of Greek Philosophy.* Trans. L. R. Palmer. New York: Meridian Books, 1950 [1931].

Zimmer, Heinrich. *Philosophies of India.* Princeton, NJ: Princeton University Press, 1969.

Zimmerman, Robert L. "Lévi-Strauss and the Primitive." In *Contemporary Sociological Theory*, ed. Fred E. Katz. New York: Random House, 1971.

Zukav, Gary. *The Dancing Wu Li Masters: An Overview of the New Physics.* New York: Bantam Books, 1980.

Zuurdeeg, William. *Man Before Chaos: Philosophy is Born in a Cry.* Nashville: Abingdon, 1968.

Index